The O'Leary Series

Microsoft® Office PowerPoint 2007

Brief Edition

The O'Leary Series

Computing Concepts

- *Computing Essentials 2007* Introductory & Complete Editions
- *Computing Essentials 2008* Introductory & Complete Editions

Microsoft® Office Applications

- *Microsoft® Office Word 2007* Brief & Introductory Editions
- *Microsoft® Office Excel 2007* Brief & Introductory Editions
- *Microsoft® Office Access 2007* Brief & Introductory Editions
- *Microsoft® Office PowerPoint 2007* Brief Edition

The O'Leary Series

Microsoft® Office PowerPoint 2007

Brief Edition

Timothy J. O'Leary
Arizona State University

Linda I. O'Leary

McGraw-Hill
Higher Education

Boston   Burr Ridge, IL   Dubuque, IA   New York   San Francisco   St. Louis
Bangkok   Bogotá   Caracas   Kuala Lumpur   Lisbon   London   Madrid   Mexico City
Milan   Montreal   New Delhi   Santiago   Seoul   Singapore   Sydney   Taipei   Toronto

**McGraw-Hill
Higher Education**

THE O'LEARY SERIES MICROSOFT® OFFICE POWERPOINT 2007 BRIEF
Published by McGraw-Hill, a business unit of The McGraw-Hill Companies, Inc., 1221 Avenue of the Americas, New York, NY, 10020.

Some ancillaries, including electronic and print components, may not be available to customers outside the United States.

This book is printed on acid-free paper.

1 2 3 4 5 6 7 8 9 0 QPD/QPD 0 9 8 7

ISBN 978-0-07-329456-8
MHID 0-07-329456-X

Vice President/Editor in Chief: *Elizabeth Haefele*
Vice President/Director of Marketing: *John Biernat*
Associate sponsoring editor: *Janna Martin*
Developmental editor: *Kelly L. Delso*
Marketing manager: *Sarah Wood*
Media producer: *Benjamin Curless*
Project manager: *Marlena Pechan*
Production supervisor: *Jason Huls*
Designer: *Srdjan Savanovic*
Senior photo research coordinator: *Jeremy Cheshareck*
Media project manager: *Mark Dierker*
Typeface: *10.5/13 New Aster*
Compositor: *Laserwords Private Limited*
Printer: *Quebecor World Dubuque Inc.*

Library of Congress Cataloging-in-Publication Data

O'Leary, Timothy J.
    Microsoft Office PowerPoint 2007 / Timothy J. O'Leary, Linda I. O'Leary.—Brief ed.
  p. cm.—(The O'Leary series)
      Includes index.
      ISBN-13: 978-0-07-329456-8 (alk. paper)
      ISBN-10: 0-07-329456-X (alk. paper)
      1. Presentation graphics software. 2. Microsoft PowerPoint (Computer file) I. O'Leary, Linda I. II. Title.
  T385.O335345 2008
  005.5'8—dc22
                                                                    2007008917

www.mhhe.com

DEDICATION

We dedicate this edition to Nicole and Katie who have brought love and joy to our lives.

Brief Contents

Detailed Contents

Lab 2

Modifying and Refining a Presentation

Lab 3

Using Advanced Presentation Features   PP3.1

Acknowledgments

We would like to extend our thanks to the professors who took time out of their busy schedules to provide us with the feedback necessary to develop the 2007 Edition of this text. The following professors offered valuable suggestions on revising the text:

Adida Awan, Savannah State University

Jacqueline Bakal, Felician College

Chet Barney, Southern Utah University

Bruce W. Bryant, University of Arkansas Community College Morrilton

Kelly D. Carter, Mercer University

Cesar Augusto Casas, St. Thomas Aquinas College

Sally Clements, St. Thomas Aquinas College

Donna N. Dunn, Beaufort County Community College

Donna Ehrhart, Genesee Community College

Saiid Ganjalizadeh, The Catholic University of America

Dr. Jayanta Ghosh, Florida Community College

Carol Grazette, Medgar Evers College/CUNY

Susan Gundy, University of Illinois at Springfield

Greg R. Hodge, Northwestern Michigan College

Christopher M. J. Hopper, Bellevue Community College

Ginny Kansas, Southwestern College

Robert Kemmerer, Los Angeles Mission College

Diana I. Kline, University of Louisville

Linda Klisto, Broward Community College North Campus

Nanette Lareau, University of Arkansas Community College Morrilton

Deborah Layton, Eastern Oklahoma State College

Keming Liu, Medgar Evers College/CUNY

J. Gay Mills, Amarillo College

Kim Moorning, Medgar Evers College/CUNY

Dr. Belinda J. Moses, University of Phoenix/Baker College/Wayne County Community College

Lois Ann O'Neal, Rogers State University

Andrew Perry, Springfield College

Michael Philipp, Greenville Technical College

Julie Piper, Bucks County Community College

Brenda Price, Bucks County Community College

Thali N. Rajashekhara, Camden County College

Dr. Marcel Marie Robles, Eastern Kentucky University

Jose (Joe) Sainz, Naugatuck Valley Community College

Pamela J. Silvers, Asheville-Buncombe Technical Community College

Glenna Stites, Johnson County Community College

Joyce Thompson, Lehigh Carbon Community College

Michelle G. Vlaich-Lee, Greenville Technical College

Mary A. Walthall, St. Petersburg College

We would like to thank those who took the time to help us develop the manuscript and ensure accuracy through pain-staking edits: Brenda Nielsen of Mesa Community College–Red Mountain, Rajiv Narayana of SunTech Info-Labs, and Craig Leonard.

Our thanks also go to Linda Mehlinger of Morgan State University for all her work on creating the PowerPoint presentations to accompany the text. We are grateful to Carol Grazette of Medgar Evers College, the author of the Instructor's Manual, for her revision of this valuable resource, and to Harry Knight of Franklin University for his careful revision of the test bank materials and creation of online quizzing materials.

Finally, we would like to thank team members from McGraw-Hill, whose renewed commitment, direction, and support have infused the team with the excitement of a new project. Leading the team from McGraw-Hill are Janna Martin, Associate Editor; Sarah Wood, Marketing Manager; and Developmental Editors Kelly Delso and Alaina Grayson.

The production staff is headed by Marlena Pechan, Project Manager, whose planning and attention to detail have made it possible for us to successfully meet a very challenging schedule; Srdjan Savanovic, Designer; Jason Huls, Production Supervisor; Ben Curless, Media Producer; Jeremy Cheshareck, Photo Researcher; and Betsy Blumenthal, copyeditor—team members whom we can depend on to do a great job.

Preface

The 20th century brought us the dawn of the digital information age and unprecedented changes in information technology. There is no indication that this rapid rate of change will be slowing—it may even be increasing. As we begin the 21st century, computer literacy is undoubtedly becoming a prerequisite in whatever career you choose.

The goal of the O'Leary Series is to provide you with the necessary skills to efficiently use these applications. Equally important is the goal to provide a foundation for students to readily and easily learn to use future versions of this software. This series does this by providing detailed step-by-step instructions combined with careful selection and presentation of essential concepts.

Times are changing, technology is changing, and this text is changing too. As students of today, you are different from those of yesterday. You put much effort toward the things that interest you and the things that are relevant to you. Your efforts directed at learning application programs and exploring the Web seem, at times, limitless.

On the other hand, students often can be shortsighted, thinking that learning the skills to use the application is the only objective. The mission of the series is to build upon and extend this interest by not only teaching the specific application skills but by introducing the concepts that are common to all applications, providing students with the confidence, knowledge, and ability to easily learn the next generation of applications.

Instructor's Resource CD-ROM

The **Instructor's Resource CD-ROM** contains a computerized Test Bank, an Instructor's Manual, and PowerPoint Presentation Slides. Features of the Instructor's Resource are described below.

- **Instructor's Manual CD-ROM**   The Instructor's Manual, authored by Carol Grazette of Medgar Evers College, contains lab objectives, concepts, outlines, lecture notes, and command summaries. Also included are answers to all end-of-chapter material, tips for covering difficult materials, additional exercises, and a schedule showing how much time is required to cover text material.

- **Computerized Test Bank**   The test bank, authored by Harry Knight, contains over 1,300 multiple choice, true/false, and discussion questions. Each question will be accompanied by the correct answer, the level of learning difficulty, and corresponding page references. Our flexible Diploma software allows you to easily generate custom exams.

- **PowerPoint Presentation Slides**   The presentation slides, authored by Linda Mehlinger of Morgan State University, include lab objectives, concepts, outlines, text figures, and speaker's notes. Also included are bullets to illustrate key terms and FAQs.

Online Learning Center/Web Site

Found at **www.mhhe.com/oleary,** this site provides additional learning and instructional tools to enhance the comprehension of the text. The OLC/Web Site is divided into these three areas:

- **Information Center**   Contains core information about the text, supplements, and the authors.

- **Instructor Center**   Offers instructional materials, downloads, and other relevant links for professors.

- **Student Center**   Contains data files, chapter competencies, chapter concepts, self-quizzes, flashcards, additional Web links, and more.

Simnet Assessment for Office Applications

Simnet Assessment for Office Applications provides a way for you to test students' software skills in a simulated environment. Simnet is available for Microsoft Office 2007 and provides flexbility for you in your applications course by offering:

Pre-testing options

Post-testing options

Course placement testing

Diagnostic capabilities to reinforce skills

Web delivery of test

MCAS preparation exams

Learning verification reports

For more information on skills assessment software, please contact your local sales representative, or visit us at **www.mhhe.com**.

O'Leary Series

The O'Leary Application Series for Microsoft Office is available separately or packaged with *Computing Essentials*. The O'Leary Application Series offers a step-by-step approach to learning computer applications and is available in both brief and introductory versions. The introductory books are MCAS Certified and prepare students for the Microsoft Certified Applications Specialist exam.

Computing Concepts

Computing Essentials 2007 offers a unique, visual orientation that gives students a basic understanding of computing concepts. *Computing Essentials* encourages "active" learning with exercises, explorations, visual illustrations, and inclusion of screen shots and numbered steps. While combining the "active" learning style with current topics and technology, this text provides an accurate snapshot of computing trends. When bundled with software application lab manuals, students are given a complete representation of the fundamental issues surrounding the personal computing environment.

GUIDE TO THE O'LEARY SERIES

The O'Leary Series is full of features designed to make learning productive and hassle free. On the following pages you will see the kind of engaging, helpful pedagogical features that have helped countless students master Microsoft Office Applications.

EASY-TO-FOLLOW INTRODUCTORY MATERIALS

INTRODUCTION TO MICROSOFT OFFICE 2007

Each text in the O'Leary Series opens with an Introduction to Office 2007, providing a complete overview of this version of the Microsoft Office Suite.

What Is the 2007 Microsoft Office System?

Microsoft's 2007 Microsoft Office System is a comprehensive, integrated system of programs, servers, and services designed to solve a wide array of business needs. Although the programs can be used individually, they are designed to work together seamlessly, making it easy to connect people and organizations to information, business processes, and each other. The applications include tools used to create, discuss, communicate, and manage projects. If you share a lot of documents with other people, these features facilitate access to common documents. This version has an entirely new user interface that is designed to make it easier to perform tasks and help users more quickly take advantage of all the features in the applications. In addition, the communication and collaboration features and integration with the World Wide Web have been expanded and refined.

The 2007 Microsoft Office System is packaged in several different combinations of programs or suites. The major programs and a brief description are provided in the following table.

Program	Description
Word 2007	Word Processor program used to create text-based documents
Excel 2007	Spreadsheet program used to analyze numerical data
Access 2007	Database manager used to organize, manage, and display a database
PowerPoint 2007	Graphics presentation program used to create presentation materials
Outlook 2007	Desktop information manager and messaging client
InfoPath 2007	Used to create XML forms and documents
OneNote 2007	Note-taking and information organization tools
Publisher 2007	Tools to create and distribute publications for print, Web, and e-mail
Visio 2007	Diagramming and data visualization tools
SharePoint Designer 2007	Web site development and management for SharePoint servers
Project 2007	Project management tools
Groove 2007	Collaboration program that enables teams to work together

The four main components of Microsoft Office 2007—Word, Excel, Access, and PowerPoint—are the applications you will learn about in this series of labs. They are described in more detail in the following sections.

Overview of Microsoft Office Word 20[07]

What Is Word Processing?

Office Word 2007 is a word processing software application whose p[urpose] is to help you create any type of written communication. A word pro[cessor] can be used to manipulate text data to produce a letter, a report, a [memo,] an e-mail message, or any other type of correspondence. Text data [is any] letter, number, or symbol that you can type on a keyboard. The group[ing of] the text data to form words, sentences, paragraphs, and pages [of text] results in the creation of a document. Through a word processor, y[ou can] create, modify, store, retrieve, and print part or all of a document.

Word processors are one of the most widely used application software programs. Putting your thoughts in writing, from the simplest note to the most complex book, is a time-consuming process. Even more time-consuming is the task of editing and retyping the document to make it better. Word processors make errors nearly nonexistent—not because they are not made, but because they are easy to correct. Word processors let you throw away the correction fluid, scissors, paste, and erasers. Now, with a few keystrokes, you can easily correct errors, move paragraphs, and reprint your document.

Word 2007 Features

Word 2007 excels in its ability to change or edit a document. Editing involves correcting spelling, grammar, and sentence-structure errors. In addition, you can easily revise or update existing text by inserting or deleting text. For example, a document that lists prices can easily be updated to reflect new prices. A document that details procedures can be revised by deleting old procedures and inserting new ones. This is especially helpful when a document is used repeatedly. Rather than recreating the whole document, you change only the parts that need to be revised.

Revision also includes the rearrangement of selected areas of text. For example, while writing a report, you may decide to change the location of a single word or several paragraphs or pages of text. You can do it easily by cutting or removing selected text from one location, then pasting or placing the selected text in another location. The selection also can be copied from one document to another.

To help you produce a perfect document, Word 2007 includes many additional support features. The AutoCorrect feature checks the spelling and grammar in a document as text is entered. Many common errors are corrected automatically for you. Others are identified and a correction suggested. A thesaurus can be used to display alternative words that have a meaning similar or opposite to a word you entered. A Find and Replace feature can be used to quickly locate specified text and replace it with other text throughout a document. In addition, Word 2007 includes a

WD0.1

INTRODUCTION TO WORD 2007

Each text in the O'Leary Series also provides an overview of the specific application features.

ENGAGING LAB INTRODUCTIONS

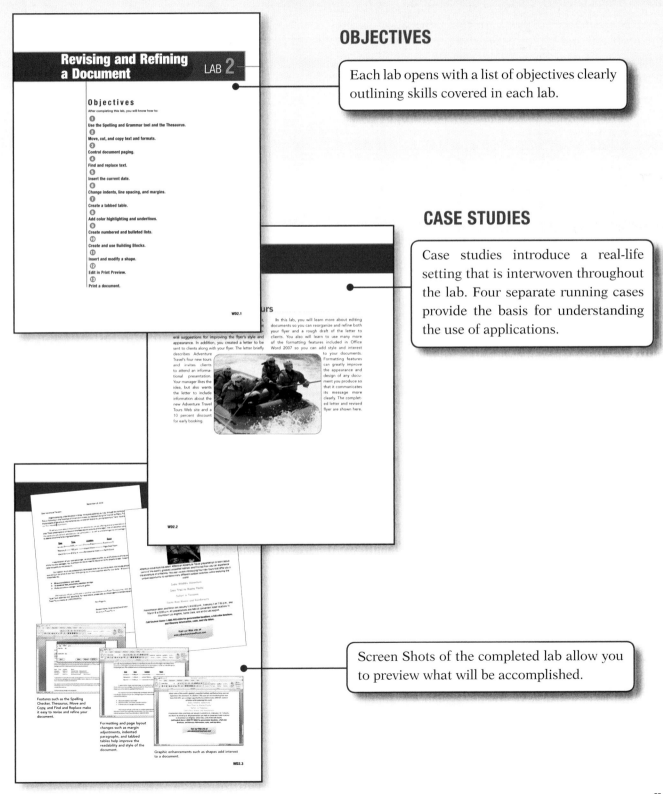

OBJECTIVES

Each lab opens with a list of objectives clearly outlining skills covered in each lab.

CASE STUDIES

Case studies introduce a real-life setting that is interwoven throughout the lab. Four separate running cases provide the basis for understanding the use of applications.

Screen Shots of the completed lab allow you to preview what will be accomplished.

STEP-BY-STEP INSTRUCTION

NUMBERED AND BULLETED STEPS

Numbered and bulleted steps provide clear step-by-step instructions on how to complete a task, or series of tasks.

All steps and bullets appear in the left-hand margin, making it easy not to miss a step.

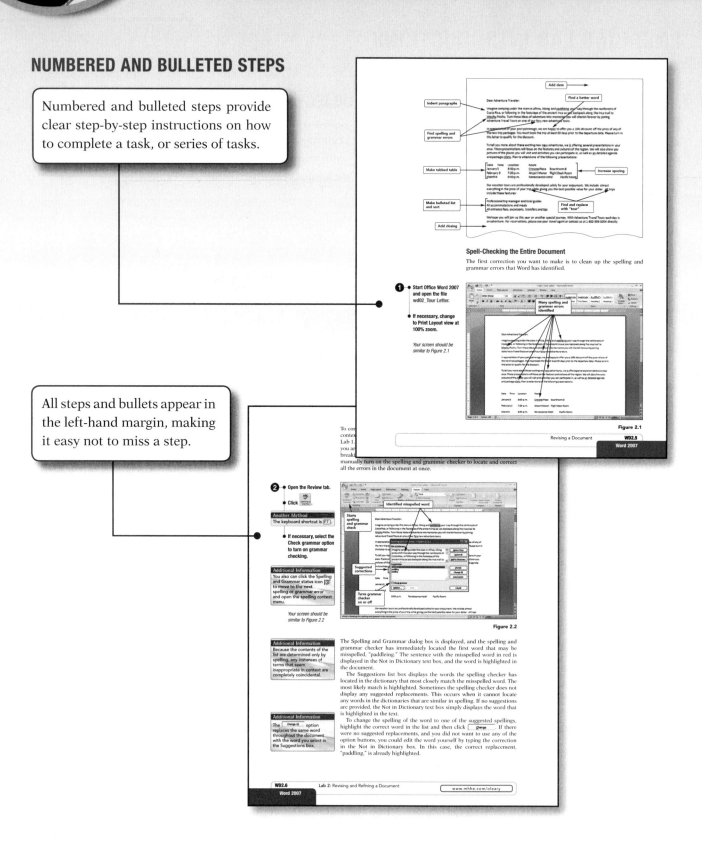

AND EASY-TO-FOLLOW DESIGN

TABLES

Tables provide quick summaries of concepts and procedures for specific tasks.

FIGURES

Large screen figures make it easy to identify elements and read screen content.

SCREEN CALLOUTS

Meaningful screen callouts identify the results of the steps as well as reinforce the associated concept.

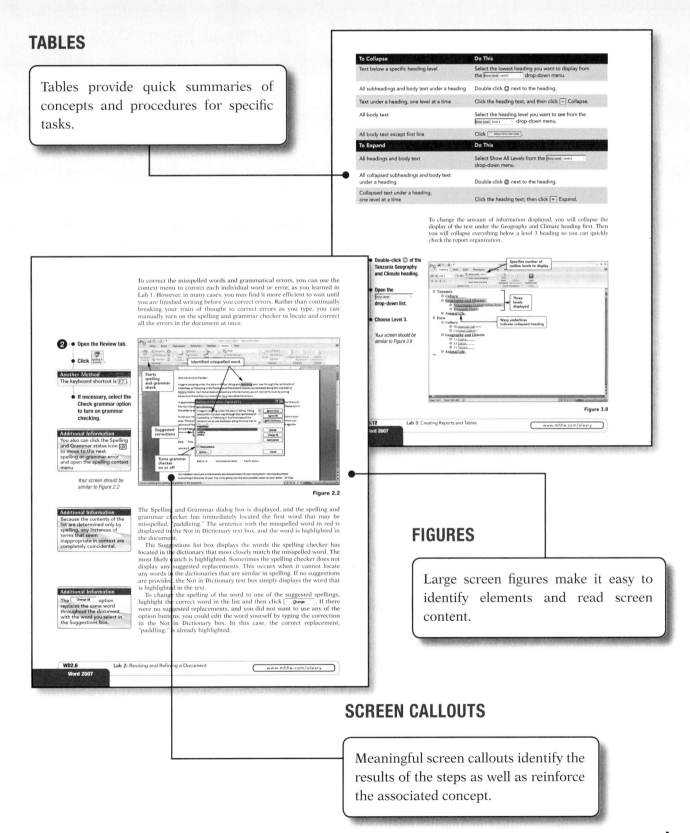

SUPPORTIVE MARGIN NOTES

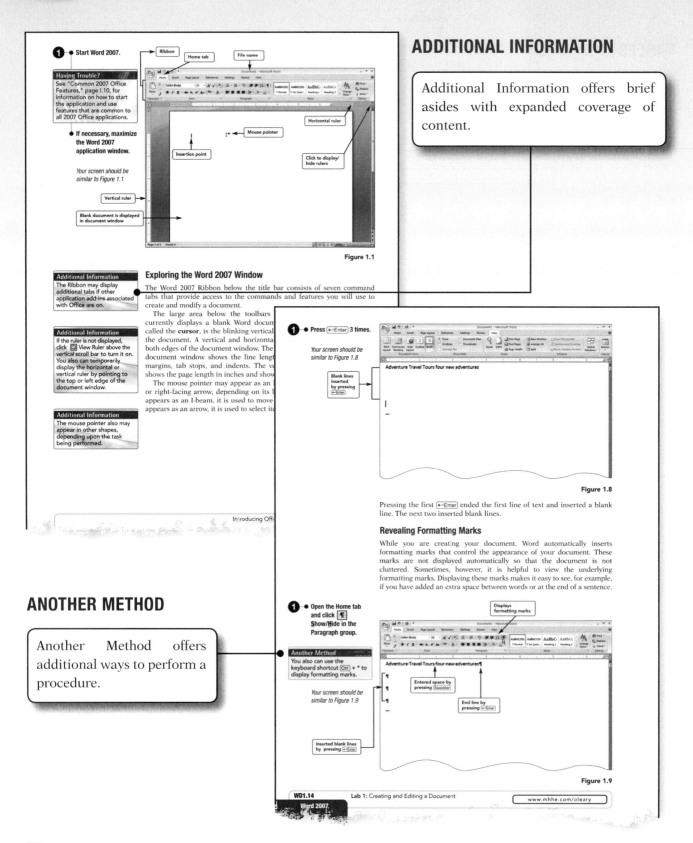

ADDITIONAL INFORMATION

Additional Information offers brief asides with expanded coverage of content.

ANOTHER METHOD

Another Method offers additional ways to perform a procedure.

The document now displays the formatting marks. The ¶ character on the line above the insertion point represents the pressing of ←Enter that created the blank line. The ¶ character at the end of the text represents the pressing of ←Enter that ended the line and moved the insertion point to the beginning of the next line. Between each word, a dot shows where the Spacebar was pressed. Formatting marks do not appear when the document is printed. You can continue to work on the document while the formatting marks are displayed, just as you did when they were hidden.

You have decided you want the flyer heading to be on two lines, with the words "four new adventures" on the second line. To do this, you will insert a blank line after the word Tours. You will move the insertion point to the location in the text where you want to insert the blank line.

② ● Click on the right side of the "s" in "Tours" before the dot for a space.

● Press ←Enter 2 times.

● Press Delete to remove the space at the beginning of the line.

● Press ↓.

Your screen should be similar to Figure 1.10

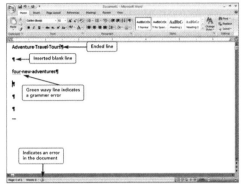

Figure 1.10

As you continue to create a document, the formatting marks are automatically adjusted.

Identifying and Correcting Errors Automatically

Notice that a green wavy underline appears under the word "four." This indicates an error has been detected.

As you enter text, Word is constantly checking the document for spelling and grammar errors. The Spelling and Grammar Status icon in the status bar displays an animated pencil icon 🖉 while you are typing, indicating Word is checking for errors as you type. When you stop typing, it displays either a blue checkmark ✅, indicating the program does not detect any errors, or a red X ❌, indicating the document contains an error.

Having Trouble?
If the green underline is not displayed, click 🖽 Office Button, click ▣ Word Options , Proofing, and select the "Check spelling as you type", "Mark grammar errors as you type", and "Check grammar with spelling" options.

Identifying and Correcting Errors Automatically **WD1.15**
Word 2007

HAVING TROUBLE

Having Trouble helps resolve potential problems as you work through each lab.

---

② ● Click OK .

● Delete the closing in the letter.

● Click 📋 Quick Parts ▾ .

● Click on the Best Regards building block.

● Save the document again.

Your screen should be similar to Figure 2.57

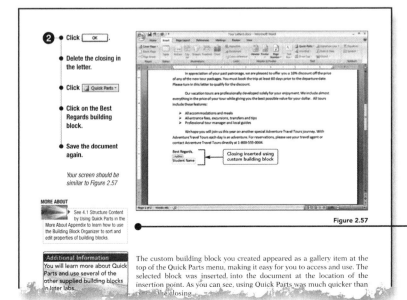

Figure 2.57

MORE ABOUT
See 4.1 Structure Content by Using Quick Parts in the More About Appendix to learn how to use the Building Block Organizer to sort and edit properties of building blocks.

Additional Information
You will learn more about Quick Parts and use several of the other supplied building blocks in later labs.

The custom building block you created appeared as a gallery item at the top of the Quick Parts menu, making it easy for you to access and use. The selected block was inserted into the document at the location of the insertion point. As you can see, using Quick Parts was much quicker than retyping the closing.

MORE ABOUT

New to this edition, the More About icon directs students to the More About appendix found at the end of the book. Without interrupting the flow of the text, this appendix provides additional coverage required to meet MCAS certification.

The default range setting, All, is the correct setting. In the Copies section, the default setting of one copy of the document is acceptable. You will print using the default print settings.

2 ● If you need to change the selected printer to another printer, open the Name drop-down list box and select the appropriate printer (your instructor will tell you which printer to select).

● Click [OK]

Your printer should be printing the document. The printed copy of the flyer should be similar to the document shown in the Case Study at the beginning of the lab.

Exiting Word

You are finished working on the flyer for now and want to save the last few changes you have made to the document and close the Word application. The [X Exit Word] command in the File menu is used to quit the Word program. Alternatively, you can click the [X] Close button in the application window title bar. If you attempt to close the application without first saving your document, Word displays a warning asking if you want to save your work. If you do not save your work and you exit the application, any changes you made since last saving it are lost.

Another Method
The keyboard shortcut for the Exit command is
[Alt] + [F4].

1 ● Click [X] Close.

● Click [Yes] to save the changes you made to the file.

The Windows desktop is visible again.
If multiple Word documents are open, clicking [X] closes the application window containing the document you are viewing only.

Focus on Careers

EXPLORE YOUR CAREER OPTIONS

Food Service Manager
Have you noticed flyers around your campus advertising job positions? Many of these jobs are in the food service industry. Food service managers are traditionally responsible for overseeing the kitchen and dining room. However, these positions increasingly involve administrative tasks, including recruiting new employees. As a food service manager, your position would likely include creating newspaper notices and flyers to attract new staff. These flyers should be eye-catching and error-free. The typical salary range of a food service manager is $34,000 to $41,700. Demand for skilled food service managers is expected to increase through 2010.

Exiting Word   **WD1.71**
Word 2007

FOCUS ON CAREERS

Focus on Careers provides an example of how the material covered may be applied in the "real world."

Each lab highlights a specific career, ranging from forensic science technician to food services manager, and presents job responsibilities and salary ranges for each.

CONTINUING CASE STUDIES

Within each series application, the same Case Study is used to illustrate concepts and procedures.

Case Study

Adventure Travel Tours

Adventure Travel Tours provides information on their tours in a variety of forms. Travel brochures, for instance, contain basic tour information in a promotional format and are designed to entice potential clients to sign up for a tour. More detailed regional information packets are given to people who have already signed up for a tour, so they can prepare for their vacation. These packets include facts about each region's climate, geography, and culture. Additional informational formats include pages on Adventure Travel's Web site and scheduled group presentations.

Part of your responsibility as advertising coordinator is to gather the information that Adventure Travel will publicize about each regional tour. Specifically, you have been asked to provide background information for two of the new tours: the Tanzania Safari and the Machu Picchu trail. Because this information is used in a variety of formats, your research needs to be easily adapted. You will therefore present your facts in the form of a general report on Tanzania and Peru.

In this lab, you will learn to use many of the features of Office Word 2007 that make it easy to create an attractive and well-organized report. A portion of the completed report is shown here.

WD3.2

AND INTEGRATION

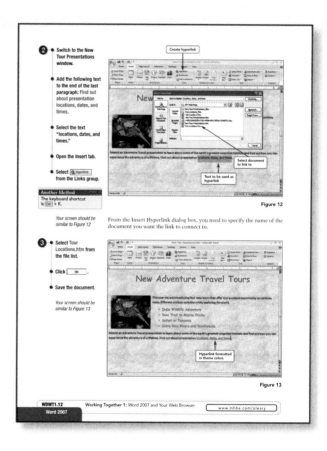

WORKING TOGETHER LABS

At the completion of the brief and introductory texts, a final lab demonstrates the integration of MS office applications. Each Working Together lab contains a complete set of end-of-chapter materials.

REINFORCED CONCEPTS

CONCEPT PREVIEW

Concept Previews provide an overview to the concepts that will be presented throughout the lab.

Concept Preview

The following concepts will be introduced in this lab:

1. **Grammar Checker** The grammar checker advises you of incorrect grammar as you create and edit a document, and proposes possible corrections.
2. **Spelling Checker** The spelling checker advises you of misspelled words as you create and edit a document, and proposes possible corrections.
3. **AutoCorrect** The AutoCorrect feature makes some basic assumptions about the text you are typing and, based on these assumptions, automatically corrects the entry.
4. **Word Wrap** The word wrap feature automatically decides where to end a line and wrap text to the next line based on the margin settings.
5. **Font and Font Size** Font, also commonly referred to as a typeface, is a set of characters with a specific design that has one or more font sizes.
6. **Alignment** Alignment is the positioning of text on a line between the margins or indents. There are four types of paragraph alignment: left, centered, right, and justified.
7. **Graphics** A graphic is a nontext element or object such as a drawing or picture that can be added to a document.

Introducing Office Word 2007

Adventure Travel Tours has recently upgraded their computer systems at all locations across the country. As part of the upgrade, they have installed the latest version of the Microsoft Office 2007 suite of applications. You are very excited to see how this new and powerful application can help you create professional letters and reports as well as eye-catching flyers and newsletters.

Starting Office Word 2007

...tion Microsoft Office Word 2007 ...and presentations.

CONCEPT BOXES

Concept boxes appear throughout the lab providing clear, concise explanations and serving as a valuable study aid.

3 ● Click outside the menu to close it.

● Open the spelling context menu for "lern" and choose "learn".

The spelling is corrected, and the spelling indicator in the status bar indicates that the document is free of errors.

Using Word Wrap

Now you will continue entering more of the paragraph. As you type, when the text gets close to the right margin, do not press ←Enter to move to the next line. Word will automatically wrap words to the next line as needed.

Concept 4

Word Wrap

4 The word wrap feature automatically decides where to end a line and wrap text to the next line based on the margin settings. This feature saves time when entering text because you do not need to press ←Enter at the end of a full line to begin a new line. The only time you need to press ←Enter is to end a paragraph, to insert blank lines, or to create a short line such as a salutation. In addition, if you change the margins or insert or delete text on a line, the program automatically readjusts the text on the line to fit within the new margin settings. Word wrap is common to all word processors.

Enter the following text to complete the sentence.

1 ● Press End to move to the end of the line.

www.mhhe.com/oleary

CONCEPT SUMMARIES

The Concept Summary offers a visual summary of the concepts presented throughout the lab.

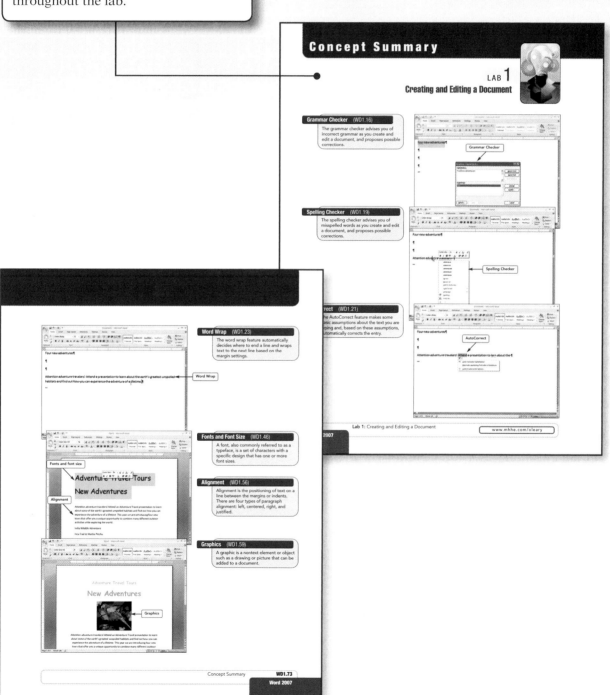

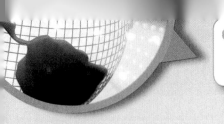

LAB REVIEW

KEY TERMS

Includes a list of all bolded terms with page references.

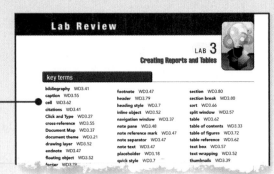

COMMAND SUMMARY

Command Summaries provide a table of commands and keyboard and toolbar shortcuts for all commands used in the lab.

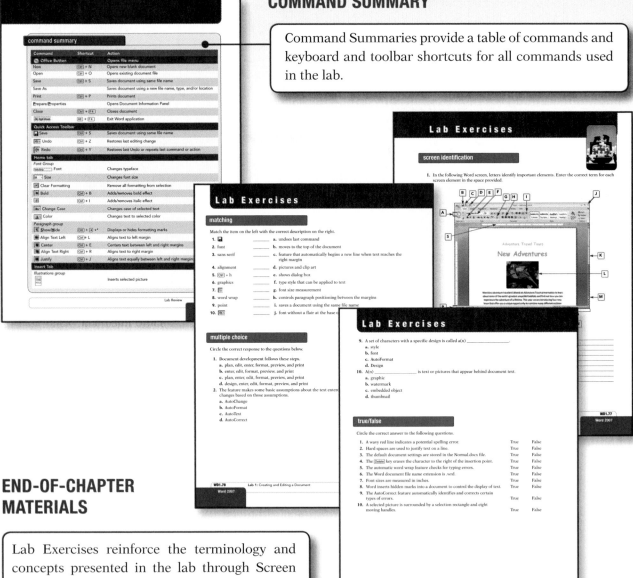

END-OF-CHAPTER MATERIALS

Lab Exercises reinforce the terminology and concepts presented in the lab through Screen Identification, Matching, Multiple Choice, True/False, and Fill-In questions.

AND SKILL DEVELOPMENT

LAB EXERCISES

Lab Exercises provide hands-on practice and develop critical-thinking skills through step-by-step and on-your-own practice exercises. Many cases in the practice exercises tie to a running case used in another application lab. This helps demonstrate the use of the four applications across a common case setting. For example, the Adventure Tours case used in Word is continued in practice exercises in Excel, Access, and PowerPoint.

ON YOUR OWN

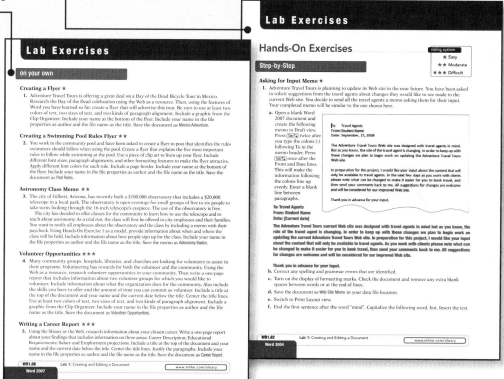

These exercises have a rating system from easy to difficult and test your ability to apply the knowledge you have gained in each lab. Exercises that build off of previous exercises are noted with a Continuing Exercises icon.

END-OF-BOOK RESOURCES

2007 Word Brief Command Summary

Command	Shortcut	Action
Office Button		Opens File menu
New	Ctrl + N	Opens new document
Open	Ctrl + O	Opens existing document file
Save	Ctrl + S, 💾	Saves document using same file name
Save As	F12	Saves document using a new file name, type, and/or location
Save as/Save As type/ Web Page		Saves file as a Web page document
Print	Ctrl + P	Specify print settings before printing document
Print/Print Preview		Displays document as it will appear when printed
Print/Quick Print		Prints document using default printer settings
Prepare/Properties		Opens Document Information Panel
Close	Ctrl + F4	Closes document
Word Options /Proofing		Changes settings associated with Spelling and Grammar checking
Word Options /Advanced/ Mark formatting inconsistencies		Checks for formatting inconsistencies
Exit Word	Alt + F4, X	Closes the Word application
Quick Access Toolbar		
Save		Saves document using same file name
Undo	Ctrl + Z	Restores last editing change
Redo	Ctrl + Y	Restores last Undo or repeats last command or action
Home tab		
Clipboard Group		
Cut	Ctrl + X	Cuts selection to Clipboard
Copy	Ctrl + C	Copies selection to Clipboard
	Ctrl + V	Pastes item from Clipboard
Format Painter		Copies format to selection

COMPREHENSIVE COMMAND SUMMARY

Provides a table of commands and keyboard and toolbar shortcuts for all commands used throughout each text in the O'Leary Series.

Command	Shortcut	Action
Font Group		
Calibri (Body) - Font		Changes typeface
11 - Size		Changes font size
Grow Font		Increases font size
Clear Formatting		Clears all formatting from selected text, leaving plain text
Bold	Ctrl + B	Makes selected text bold
Italic	Ctrl + I	Applies italic effect to selected text
Underline	Ctrl + U	Adds underline below selected text
Change Case		Changes case of selected text
Text Highlight Color		Applies highlight color to selection
Font Color		Changes selected text to selected color
Paragraph group		
Bullets		Creates a bulleted list
Numbering		Creates a numbered list
Indents and Spacing		Indents paragraph from left margin
Sort		Rearranges items in a selection into ascending alphabetical/numerical order
Show/Hide	Ctrl + → + *	Displays or hides formatting marks
Align Text Left	Ctrl + L	Aligns text to left margin
Center	Ctrl + E	Centers text between left and right margins
Align Text Right	Ctrl + R	Aligns text to right margin
Justify	Ctrl + J	Aligns text equally between left and right margins
Line Spacing	Ctrl + #	Changes amount of white space between lines
Styles Group		
More		Opens Quick Styles gallery
Editing Group		
Find	Ctrl + F	Locates specified text
Replace	Ctrl + H	Locates and replaces specified text
Insert tab		
Pages group		
Cover Page		Inserts a preformatted cover page
Blank Page		Inserts a blank page
Page Break	Ctrl + ←Enter	Inserts a hard page break
Tables group		
		Inserts a table

Glossary of Key Terms

active window The window containing the insertion point and that will be affected by any changes you make.

alignment How text is positioned on a line between the margins or indents. There are four types of paragraph alignment: left, centered, right, and justified.

antonym A word with the opposite meaning.

author The process of creating a Web page.

AutoCorrect A feature that makes basic assumptions about the text you are typing and automatically corrects the entry.

bibliography A listing of source references that appears at the end of the document.

browser A program that connects you to remote computers and displays the Web pages you request.

building blocks Document fragments that include text and formatting and that can be easily inserted into a document.

bulleted list Displays items that logically fall out from a paragraph into a list, with items preceded by bullets.

caption A title or explanation for a table, picture, or graph.

case sensitive The capability to distinguish between uppercase and lowercase characters.

cell The intersection of a column and row where data are entered in a table.

character formatting Formatting features such as bold and color that affect the selected characters only.

citations Parenthetical source references that give credit for specific information included in a document.

Click and Type A feature available in Print Layout and Web Layout views that is used to quickly insert text, graphics, and other items in

a blank area of a document, avoiding the need to enter blank lines.

clip art Professionally drawn graphics.

control A graphic element that is a container for information or objects.

cross-reference A reference in one part of a document related to information in another part.

cursor The blinking vertical bar that shows you where the next character you type will appear. Also called the insertion point.

custom dictionary A dictionary of terms you have entered that are not in the main dictionary of the spelling checker.

default The initial Word document settings that can be changed to customize documents.

destination The location to which text is moved or copied.

Document Map A feature that displays the headings in the document in the navigation window.

document properties Details about a document that describe or identify it and are saved with the document content.

document theme A predefined set of formatting choices that can be applied to an entire document in one simple step.

document window The area of the application window that displays the contents of the open document.

drag and drop A mouse procedure that moves or copies a selection to a new location.

drawing layer The layer above or below the text layer where floating objects are inserted.

drawing object A simple object consisting of shapes such as lines and boxes.

edit The process of changing and correcting existing text in a document.

GLOSSARY

Bolded terms found throughout each text in the O'Leary Series are defined in the glossary.

MORE ABOUT APPENDICES

A More About appendix appears at the end of the brief and introductory texts. This appendix offers students additional coverage needed to meet MCAS requirements. Skills pertaining to additional MCAS coverage are denoted by a More About icon in the margins of the text.

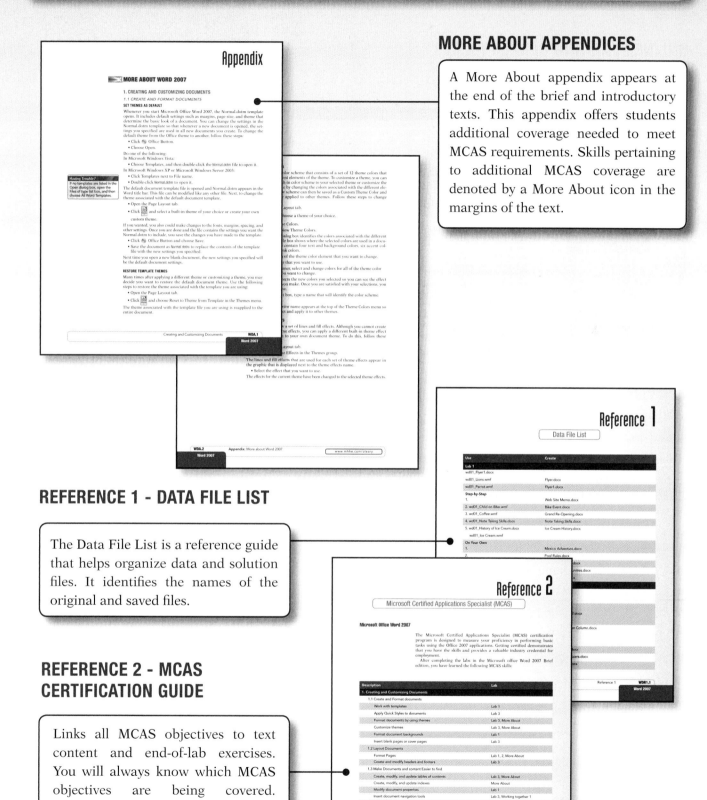

REFERENCE 1 - DATA FILE LIST

The Data File List is a reference guide that helps organize data and solution files. It identifies the names of the original and saved files.

REFERENCE 2 - MCAS CERTIFICATION GUIDE

Links all MCAS objectives to text content and end-of-lab exercises. You will always know which MCAS objectives are being covered. Introductory texts are MCAS certified.

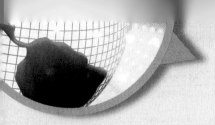

ONLINE LEARNING CENTER (OLC)

www.mhhe.com/oleary

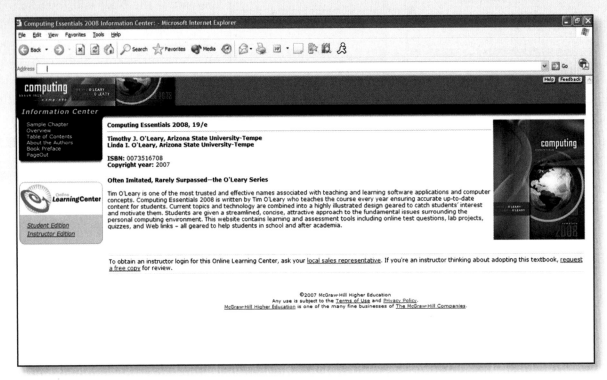

The Online Learning Center follows The O'Leary Series lab by lab, offering all kinds of supplementary help for you. OLC features include:

- Learning Objectives
- Student Data Files
- Chapter Competencies
- Chapter Concepts
- Self-Grading Quizzes
- Additional Web Links

Tim and Linda O'Leary live in the American Southwest and spend much of their time engaging instructors and students in conversation about learning. In fact, they have been talking about learning for over 25 years. Something in those early conversations convinced them to write a book, to bring their interest in the learning process to the printed page. Today, they are as concerned as ever about learning, about technology, and about the challenges of presenting material in new ways, in terms of both content and method of delivery.

A powerful and creative team, Tim combines his 25 years of classroom teaching experience with Linda's background as a consultant and corporate trainer. Tim has taught courses at Stark Technical College in Canton, Ohio, and at Rochester Institute of Technology in upstate New York, and is currently a professor at Arizona State University in Tempe, Arizona. Linda offered her expertise at ASU for several years as an academic advisor. She also presented and developed materials for major corporations such as Motorola, Intel, Honeywell, and AT&T, as well as various community colleges in the Phoenix area.

Tim and Linda have talked to and taught numerous students, all of them with a desire to learn something about computers and applications that make their lives easier, more interesting, and more productive.

Each new edition of an O'Leary text, supplement, or learning aid has benefited from these students and their instructors who daily stand in front of them (or over their shoulders). The O'Leary Series is no exception.

Introduction to Microsoft Office 2007

Objectives

After completing the Introduction to Microsoft Office 2007, you should be able to:

 Describe the 2007 Microsoft Office System.

 Describe the Office 2007 applications.

 Start an Office 2007 application.

 Recognize the basic application features.

 Use menus, context menus, and shortcut keys.

 Use the Ribbon, dialog boxes, and task panes.

7 Use Office Help.

8 Exit an Office 2007 application.

What Is the 2007 Microsoft Office System?

Microsoft's 2007 Microsoft Office System is a comprehensive, integrated system of programs, servers, and services designed to solve a wide array of business needs. Although the programs can be used individually, they are designed to work together seamlessly, making it easy to connect people and organizations to information, business processes, and each other. The applications include tools used to create, discuss, communicate, and manage projects. If you share a lot of documents with other people, these features facilitate access to common documents. This version has an entirely new user interface that is designed to make it easier to perform tasks and help users more quickly take advantage of all the features in the applications. In addition, the communication and collaboration features and integration with the World Wide Web have been expanded and refined.

The 2007 Microsoft Office System is packaged in several different combinations of programs or suites. The major programs and a brief description are provided in the following table.

Program	Description
Word 2007	Word Processor program used to create text-based documents
Excel 2007	Spreadsheet program used to analyze numerical data
Access 2007	Database manager used to organize, manage, and display a database
PowerPoint 2007	Graphics presentation program used to create presentation materials
Outlook 2007	Desktop information manager and messaging client
InfoPath 2007	Used to create XML forms and documents
OneNote 2007	Note-taking and information organization tools
Publisher 2007	Tools to create and distribute publications for print, Web, and e-mail
Visio 2007	Diagramming and data visualization tools
SharePoint Designer 2007	Web site development and management for SharePoint servers
Project 2007	Project management tools
Groove 2007	Collaboration program that enables teams to work together

The four main components of Microsoft Office 2007—Word, Excel, Access, and PowerPoint—are the applications you will learn about in this series of labs. They are described in more detail in the following sections.

Word 2007

Word 2007 is a word processing software application whose purpose is to help you create text-based documents. Word processors are one of the most flexible and widely used application software programs. A word processor can be used to manipulate text data to produce a letter, a report, a memo, an e-mail message, or any other type of correspondence.

Two documents you will produce in the first two Word 2007 labs, a letter and flyer, are shown here.

A letter containing a tabbed table, indented paragraphs, and text enhancements is quickly created using basic Word features.

September 15, 2008

Dear Adventure Traveler:

Imagine camping under the stars in Africa, hiking and paddling your way through the rainforests of Costa Rica, or following in the footsteps of the ancient Inca as you backpack along the Inca trail to Machu Picchu. Turn these dreams of adventure into memories you will cherish forever by joining Adventure Travel Tours on one of our four new adventure tours.

To tell you more about these exciting new adventures, we are offering several presentations in your area. These presentations will focus on the features and cultures of the region. We will also show you pictures of the places you will visit and activities you can partici... to attend one of the following presentations:

Date   **Time**

January 5 -------- 8:00 p.m. --------- Cro...

February 3 ------ 7:30 p.m. --------- Air...

March 8 --------- 8:00 p.m. --------- Res...

In appreciation of your past patronage, we ... of the new tour packages. You must book the trip at... letter to qualify for the discount.

Our vacation tours are professionally devel... everything in the price of your tour while giving you ... these features:

➤ All accommodations and meals
➤ All entrance fees, excursions, transfers and ...
➤ Professional tour manager and local guides

We hope you will join us this year on anothe... Travel Tours each day is an adventure. For reservati... Travel Tours directly at 1-800-555-0004.

A flyer incorporating many visual enhancements such as colored text, varied text styles, and graphic elements is both eye-catching and informative.

Adventure Travel Tours
New Adventures

Attention adventure travelers! Attend an Adventure Travel presentation to learn about some of the earth's greatest unspoiled habitats and find out how you can experience the adventure of a lifetime. This year we are introducing four new tours that offer you a unique opportunity to combine many different outdoor activities while exploring the world.

India Wildlife Adventure

Inca Trail to Machu Picchu

Safari in Tanzania

Costa Rica Rivers and Rainforests

Presentation dates and times are January 5 at 8:00 p.m., February 3 at 7:30 p.m., and March 8 at 8:00 p.m. All presentations are held at convenient hotel locations in downtown Los Angeles, Santa Clara, and at the LAX airport.

Call Student Name 1-800-555-0004 for presentation locations, a full color brochure, and itinerary information, costs, and trip dates.

Visit our Web site at
www.adventuretraveltours.com

PowerPoint 2007

The beauty of a word processor is that you can make changes or corrections as you are typing. Want to change a report from single spacing to double spacing? Alter the width of the margins? Delete some paragraphs and add others from yet another document? A word processor allows you to do all these things with ease.

Word 2007 includes many group collaboration features to help streamline how documents are developed and changed by group members. You also can create and send e-mail messages directly from within Word using all its features to create and edit the message. In addition, you can send an entire document as your e-mail message, allowing the recipient to edit the document directly without having to open or save an attachment.

Word 2007 is closely integrated with the World Wide Web, detecting when you type a Web address and automatically converting it to a hyperlink. You also can create your own hyperlinks to locations within documents, or to other documents, including those at external locations such as a Web site or file server. It also includes features that help you quickly create Web pages and blog entries.

Excel 2007

Excel 2007 is an electronic worksheet that is used to organize, manipulate, and graph numeric data. Once used almost exclusively by accountants, worksheets are now widely used by nearly every profession. Marketing professionals record and evaluate sales trends. Teachers record grades and calculate final grades. Personal trainers record the progress of their clients.

Excel 2007 includes many features that not only help you create a well-designed worksheet, but one that produces accurate results. Formatting features include visual enhancements such as varied text styles, colors, and graphics. Other features help you enter complex formulas and identify and correct formula errors. You also can produce a visual display of data in the form of graphs or charts. As the values in the worksheet change, charts referencing those values automatically adjust to reflect the changes.

Excel 2007 also includes many advanced features and tools that help you perform what-if analysis and create different scenarios. And like all Office 2007 applications, it is easy to incorporate data created in one application into another. Two worksheets you will produce in Labs 2 and 3 of Excel 2007 are shown on the next page.

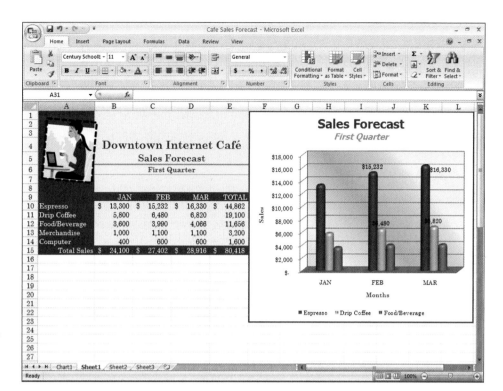

A worksheet showing the quarterly sales forecast containing a graphic, text enhancements, and a chart of the data is quickly created using basic Excel 2007 features.

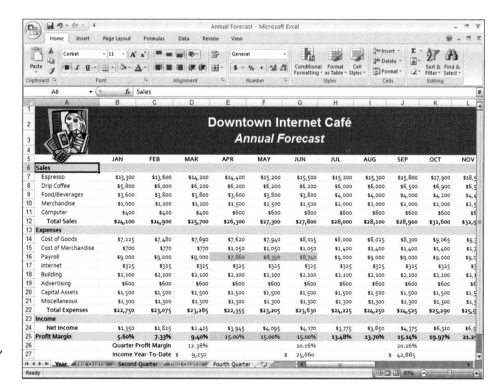

A large worksheet incorporating more complex formulas, visual enhancements such as colored text, varied text styles, and graphic elements is both informative and attractive.

What Is the 2007 Microsoft Office System?   I.5

PowerPoint 2007

You will see how easy it is to analyze data and make projections using what-if analysis and what-if graphing in Lab 3 and to incorporate Excel data in a Word document as shown in the following figures.

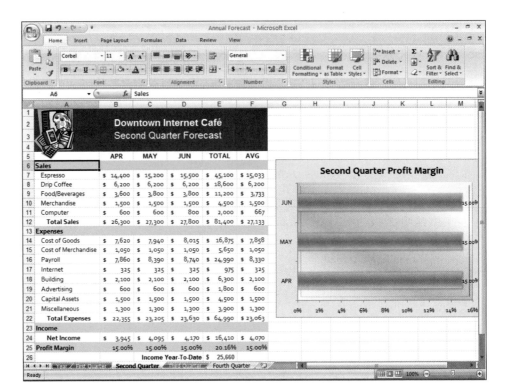

Changes you make in worksheet data while performing what-if analysis are automatically reflected in charts that reference that data.

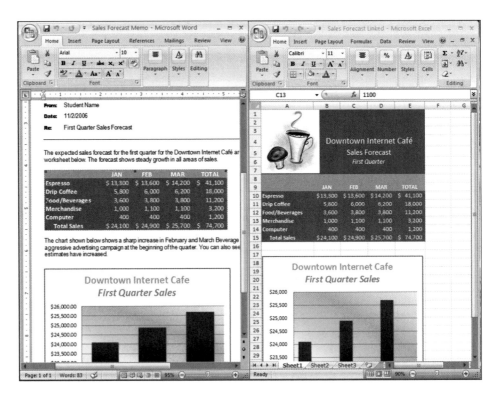

Worksheet data and charts can be copied and linked to other Office documents such as a Word document.

Access 2007

Access 2007 is a relational database management application that is used to create and analyze a database. A database is a collection of related data. In a relational database, the most widely used database structure, data is organized in linked tables. Tables consist of columns (called *fields*) and rows (called *records*). The tables are related or linked to one another by a common field. Relational databases allow you to create smaller and more manageable database tables, since you can combine and extract data between tables.

The program provides tools to enter, edit, and retrieve data from the database as well as to analyze the database and produce reports of the output. One of the main advantages of a computerized database is the ability to quickly add, delete, and locate specific records. Records also can be easily rearranged or sorted according to different fields of data, resulting in multiple table arrangements that provide more meaningful information for different purposes. Creation of forms makes it easier to enter and edit data as well. In the Access labs, you will create and organize the database table shown below.

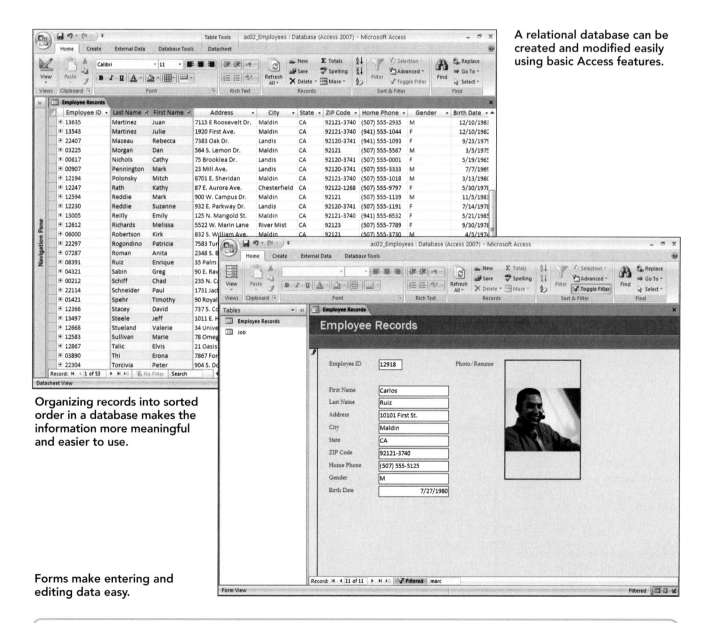

A relational database can be created and modified easily using basic Access features.

Organizing records into sorted order in a database makes the information more meaningful and easier to use.

Forms make entering and editing data easy.

What Is the 2007 Microsoft Office System?　I.7

PowerPoint 2007

Another feature is the ability to analyze the data in a table and perform calculations on different fields of data. Additionally, you can ask questions or query the table to find only certain records that meet specific conditions to be used in the analysis. Information that was once costly and time-consuming to get is now quickly and readily available. This information can then be quickly printed out in the form of reports ranging from simple listings to complex, professional-looking reports in different layout styles, or with titles, headings, subtotals, or totals.

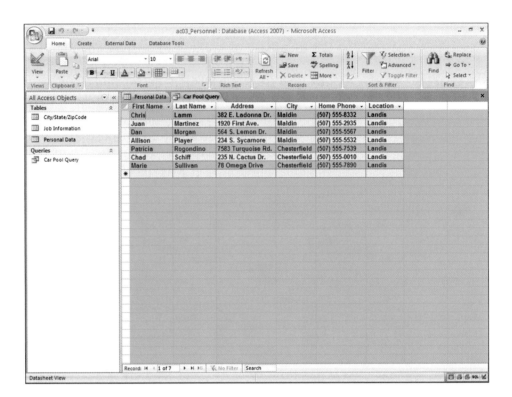

A database can be queried to locate and display only specified information.

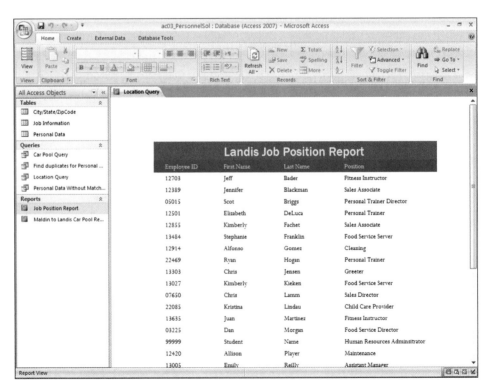

A professional-looking report can be quickly generated from information contained in a database.

PowerPoint 2007

PowerPoint 2007 is a graphics presentation program designed to help you produce a high-quality presentation that is both interesting to the audience and effective in its ability to convey your message. A presentation can be as simple as overhead transparencies or as sophisticated as an on-screen electronic display. In the first two PowerPoint labs, you will create and organize the presentation shown below.

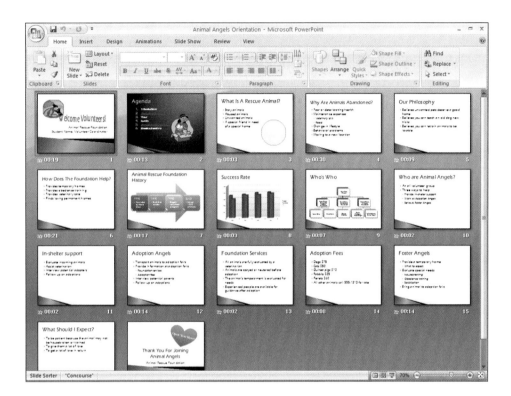

A presentation consists of a series of pages or "slides" presenting the information you want to convey in an organized and attractive manner.

When running an on-screen presentation, each slide of the presentation is displayed full-screen on your computer monitor or projected onto a screen.

Common Office 2007 Interface Features

Additional Information

Please read the Before You Begin and Instructional Conventions sections in the Overview of Microsoft Office PowerPoint 2007 (PPO.3) before starting this section.

Now that you know a little about each of the applications in Microsoft Office 2007, we will take a look at some of the interface features that are common to all Office 2007 applications. This is a hands-on section that will introduce you to the features and allow you to get a feel for how Office 2007 works. Although Word 2007 will be used to demonstrate how the features work, only common **user interface** features, a set of graphical images that represent various features, will be addressed. These features include using the File menu, Ribbon, Quick Access Toolbar, task panes, and Office Help, and starting and exiting an application. The features that are specific to each application will be introduced individually in each application text.

Starting an Office 2007 Application

There are several ways to start an Office 2007 application. The two most common methods are by using the Start menu or by clicking a desktop shortcut for the program if it is available. If you use the Start menu, the steps will vary slightly depending on the version of Windows you are using.

1 ● Click **start** to display the Start menu.

Having Trouble?

In Windows Vista, click

● Choose Microsoft Office Word 2007.

Having Trouble?

If you do not see the program name on the Start menu, select All Programs, select Microsoft Office, and then choose Microsoft Office Word 2007.

OR

1 ● Double-click the shortcut on the desktop.

2 ● If necessary, click Maximize in the title bar to maximize the window.

Your screen should be similar to Figure 1

Having Trouble?

Your screen may look slightly different based on your Windows operating system settings.

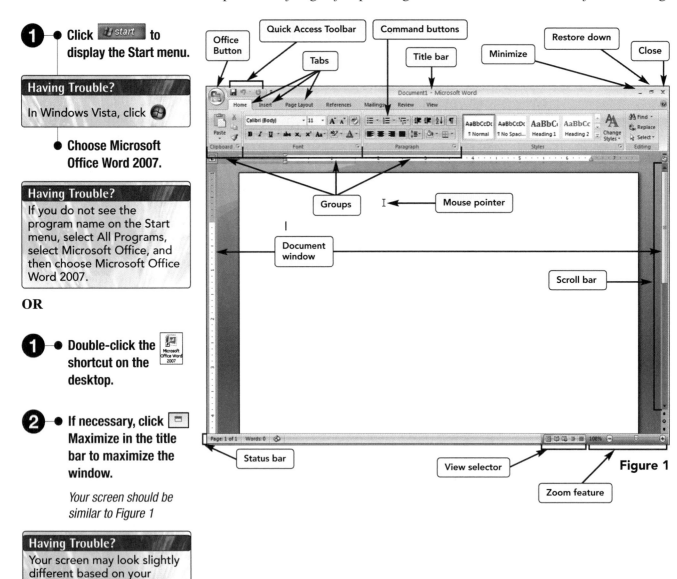

Figure 1

The Word 2007 program is started and displayed in a window on the desktop. The application window title bar displays the file name followed by the program name, Microsoft Word. The right end of the title bar displays the [-] Minimize, [◽] Restore Down, and [x] Close buttons. They perform the same functions and operate in the same way as all Windows versions.

Below the title bar is the **Ribbon**, which provides a centralized area that makes it easy to find ways to work in your document. The Ribbon has three basic parts: tabs, groups, and commands. **Tabs** are used to divide the Ribbon into major activity areas. Each tab is then organized into **groups** that contain related items. The related items are commands that consist of command buttons, a box to enter information, or a menu. As you use the Office applications, you will see that the Ribbon contains many of the same groups and commands across the applications. You also will see that many of the groups and commands are specific to an application.

The upper left area of the window's title bar displays the Office Button and the Quick Access Toolbar. Clicking Office Button opens the File menu of commands that allows you to work *with* your document, unlike the Ribbon that allows you to work *in* your document. For example, it includes commands to open, save, and print files. The **Quick Access Toolbar** (QAT) provides quick access to frequently used commands. By default, it includes the Save, Undo, and Redo buttons, commands that Microsoft considers to be crucial. It is always available and is a customizable toolbar to which you can add your own favorite buttons.

The large center area of the program window is the **document window** where open application files are displayed. Currently, there is a blank Word document open. In Word, the mouse pointer appears as I when positioned in the document window and as a ⏳ when it can be used to select items.

On the right of the document window is a vertical scroll bar. A **scroll bar** is used with a mouse to bring additional lines of information into view in a window. The vertical scroll bar is used to move up or down. A horizontal scroll bar is also displayed when needed and moves side to side in the window. At the bottom of the window is the **status bar**, a view selector, and a document zoom feature. Similar information and features are displayed in this area for different Office applications. You will learn how these features work in each individual application.

Using the File Menu

Clicking the Office Button opens the File menu of commands that are used to work with files.

① ● Click 🔘 **Office Button**
to open the File menu.

*Your screen should be
similar to Figure 2*

File menu of nine
commands

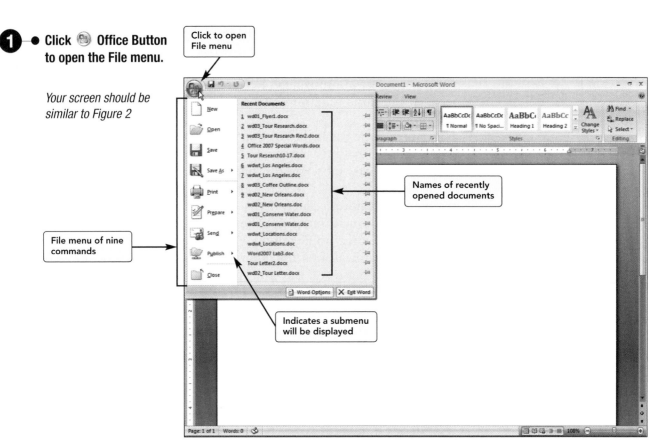

Click to open
File menu

Names of recently
opened documents

Indicates a submenu
will be displayed

Figure 2

Additional Information

Clicking the 📌 next to a
file name pins the file and
permanently keeps the file
name in the recently used list
until it is unpinned.

The menu lists nine commands that are used to perform tasks associated
with files. Notice that each command displays an underlined letter. This
identifies the letter you can type to choose the command. Five commands
display a ▶, which indicates the command includes a submenu of
options. The right side of the command list currently displays the names
of recently opened files (your list will display different file names). The
default program setting displays a maximum of 17 file names. Once the
maximum number of files is listed, when a new file is opened, the oldest is
dropped from the list.

Once the File menu is open, you can select a command from the menu
by pointing to it. A colored highlight bar, called the **selection cursor**,
appears over the selected command.

② ● **Point to the Open command.**

Your screen should be similar to Figure 3

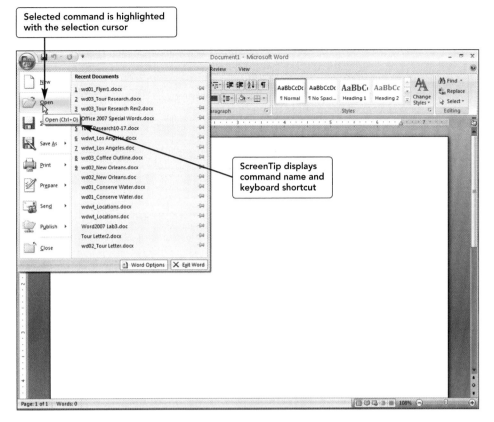

Selected command is highlighted with the selection cursor

ScreenTip displays command name and keyboard shortcut

Figure 3

A **ScreenTip**, also called a **tooltip**, briefly appears displaying the command name and the keyboard shortcut, Ctrl + O. The keyboard shortcut can be used to execute this command without opening the menu. In this case, if you hold down the Ctrl key while typing the letter O, you will access the Open command without having to open the File menu first. ScreenTips also often include a brief description of the action a command performs.

Next you will select a command that will display a submenu of options.

3 • **Point to the Prepare command.**

• **Point to the Mark as Final submenu option.**

Your screen should be similar to Figure 4

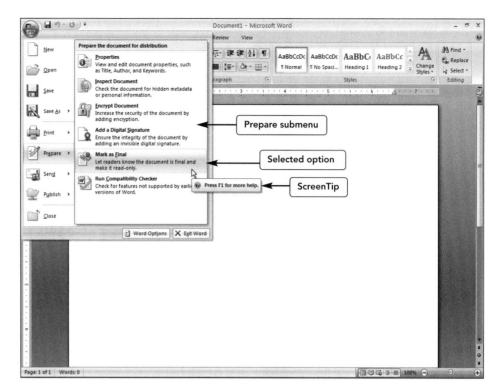

Figure 4

The submenu lists the six Prepare command submenu options and the Mark as Final option is selected. A ScreenTip provides information about how to get help on this feature. You will learn about using Help shortly.

4 • **Point to the Print command.**

• **Point to the ⊳ of the Print command.**

Your screen should be similar to Figure 5

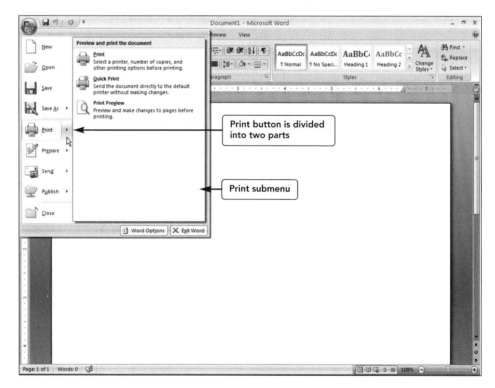

Figure 5

 **Click the Print command.**

Your screen should be similar to Figure 6

So far you have only selected commands; you have not chosen them. To choose a command, you click on it. When the command is chosen, the associated action is performed. Notice the Print command is divided into two parts. Clicking the Print section on the left will choose the command and open the Print dialog box. Clicking · in the right section has no effect.

Print dialog box is used to specify print settings →

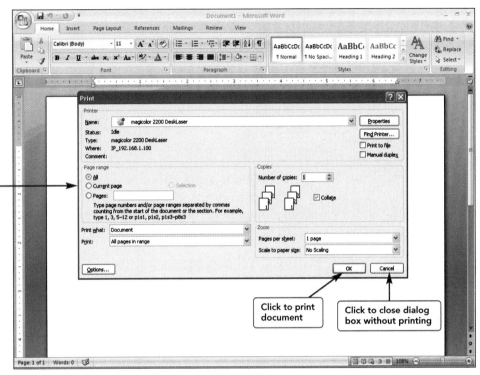

Click to print document

Click to close dialog box without printing

Figure 6

In the Print dialog box, you would specify the print settings and click ⬚OK⬚ to actually print a document. In this case, you will cancel the action and continue to explore other features of the Office 2007 application.

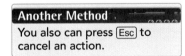 **Click** ⬚Cancel⬚.

Using Context Menus

Another way to access some commands is to use a context menu. A **context menu** is opened by right-clicking on an item on the screen. This menu is context sensitive, meaning it displays only those commands relevant to the item. For example, right-clicking on the Quick Access Toolbar will display the commands associated with using the Quick Access Toolbar only. You will use this method to move the Quick Access Toolbar.

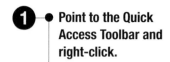

1 Point to the Quick Access Toolbar and right-click.

Another Method

You also can click 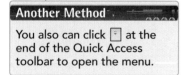 at the end of the Quick Access toolbar to open the menu.

● Click the Show Quick Access Toolbar below the Ribbon option.

Your screen should be similar to Figure 7

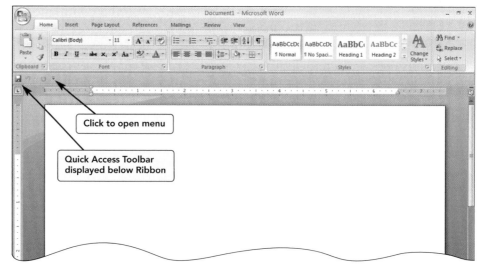

Click to open menu

Quick Access Toolbar displayed below Ribbon

Figure 7

The Quick Access Toolbar is now displayed full size below the Ribbon. This is useful if you have many buttons on the toolbar; however, it takes up document viewing space. You will return it to its compact size using the toolbar's drop-down menu.

2 ● Click  on the right end of the Quick Access Toolbar.

● Choose Show Above the Ribbon.

Your screen should be similar to Figure 8

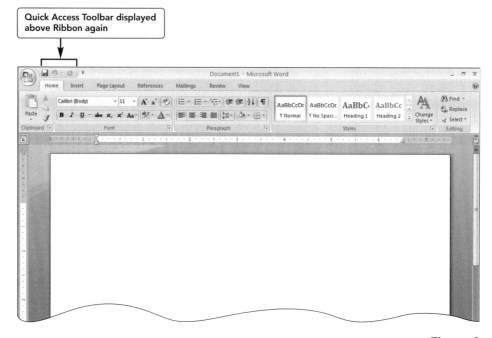

Quick Access Toolbar displayed above Ribbon again

Figure 8

MORE ABOUT

▶ See the More About appendix to learn how to customize the Quick Access Toolbar.

The Quick Access Toolbar is displayed above the Ribbon again. The toolbar's drop-down menu contains a list of commands that are often added to the toolbar. Clicking on the command selects it and adds it to the toolbar.

Using the Ribbon

The Ribbon displays tabs that organize similar features into groups. In Word, there are seven tabs displayed. To save space, some tabs, called **contextual** or **on-demand tabs**, are displayed only as needed. For example, when you are working with a picture, the Picture Tools tab appears. The contextual nature of this feature keeps the work area uncluttered when the feature is not needed and provides ready access to it when it is needed.

Opening Tabs

The Home tab is open when you first start the application or open a file. It consists of five groups: Clipboard, Font, Paragraph, Styles, and Editing. Each group contains command buttons that when clicked on perform their associated action or display a list of additional commands. The commands in the Home tab help you perform actions related to creating the content of your document.

1 ● **Click on the Insert tab.**

Your screen should be similar to Figure 9

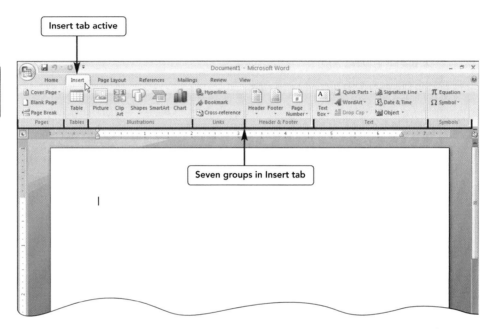

Figure 9

This Insert tab is now the active tab. It contains seven groups whose commands have to do with inserting items into a document.

2 ● **Click on each of the other tabs, ending with the View tab, to see their groups and commands.**

Your screen should be similar to Figure 10

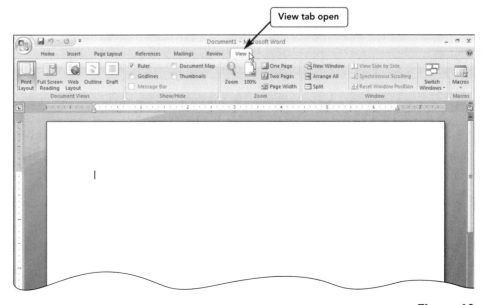

Figure 10

Each tab relates to a type of activity; for example, the View tab commands perform activities related to viewing the document. Within each tab, similar commands are grouped together to make finding the commands you want to use much easier.

Displaying Super Tooltips

Many command buttons immediately perform the associated action when you click on them. The buttons are graphic representations of the action they perform. To help you find out what a button does, you can display the button's ScreenTip.

1 ● Open the Home tab.

● Point to the upper part of the 🗐 **Paste** button in the Clipboard group.

● Point to the lower part of the Paste button in the Clipboard group.

● Point to 🖌 Format Painter in the Clipboard group.

Your screen should be similar to Figure 11

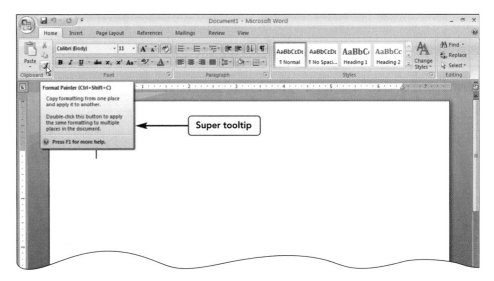

Figure 11

Additional Information
Not all commands have shortcut keys.

Additional Information
You will learn about using Help shortly.

Both parts of the Paste button display tooltips containing the button name, the shortcut key combination, Ctrl + V, and a brief description of what the button does. Pointing to 🖌 Format Painter displays a **super tooltip** that provides more detailed information about the command. Super tooltips may even display information such as procedures or illustrations. You can find out what the feature does without having to look it up in Help. If a feature has a Help article, you can automatically access it by pressing F1 while the super tooltip is displayed.

Using Galleries and Lists

Many commands in the groups appear as a **gallery** that displays small graphics that represent the result of applying a command. For example, in the Styles group, the command buttons to apply different formatting styles to text display examples of how the text would look if formatted using that command. These are called **in-Ribbon galleries** because they appear directly in the Ribbon. Other commands include multiple options that appear in **drop-down galleries** or drop-down lists that are accessed by clicking the ⬝ button on the right side of the command button. To see an example of a drop-down gallery, you will open the ⬝ Bullets drop-down gallery.

1 • Click ⊡ in the ☰⊡ Bullets button.

Your screen should be similar to Figure 12

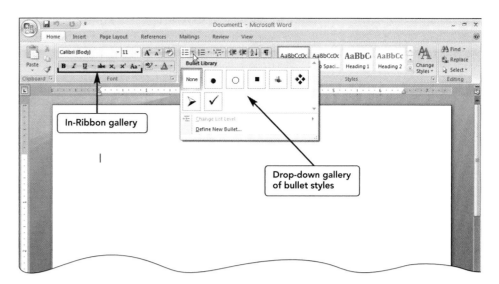

In-Ribbon gallery

Drop-down gallery of bullet styles

Figure 12

A drop-down gallery of different bullets is displayed. The drop-down gallery will disappear when you make a selection or click on any other area of the window. To see an example of a drop-down list, you will open the ⊞ 11 ⊡ Font Size drop-down list.

2 • Click outside the Bullet gallery to clear it.

• Click ⊡ in the ⊞ 11 ⊡ Font Size button.

Your screen should be similar to Figure 13

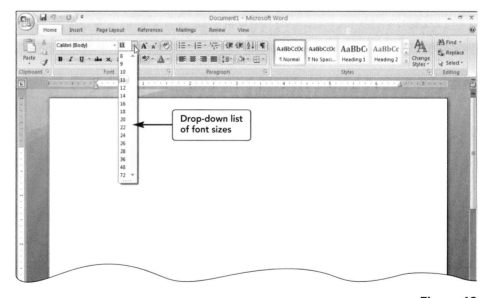

Drop-down list of font sizes

Figure 13

If you click on the button itself, not the ⊡ section of the button, the associated command is performed.

Using the Dialog Box Launcher

Because there is not enough space, only the most used commands are displayed in the Ribbon. If there are more commands available, a ⊡ button, called the **dialog box launcher**, is displayed in the lower-right corner of the group. Clicking ⊡ opens a dialog box or **task pane** of additional options.

1 • **Click outside the Font size list to clear it.**

• **Point to the** ▣ **of the Paragraph group to see the tooltip.**

• **Click** ▣ **of the Paragraph group.**

Your screen should be similar to Figure 14

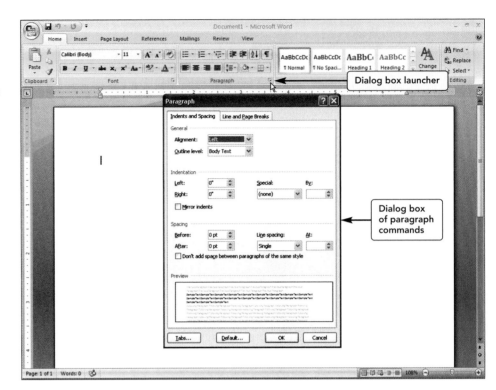

Figure 14

The Paragraph dialog box appears. It provides access to the more advanced paragraph settings features. Selecting options from the dialog box and clicking ⟨ OK ⟩ will close the dialog box and apply the settings as specified. To cancel the dialog box, you can click ⟨ Cancel ⟩ or ✕ in the dialog box title bar.

2 • **Click** ⟨ Cancel ⟩ **to close the dialog box.**

• **Click** ▣ **in the Clipboard group.**

Your screen should be similar to Figure 15

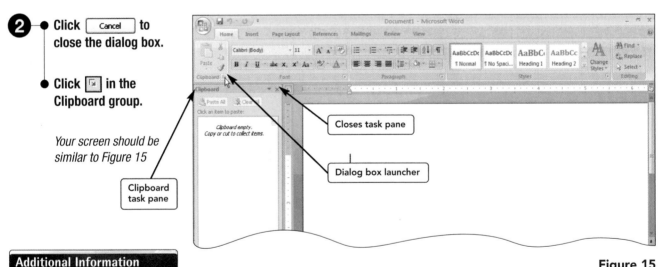

Figure 15

Additional Information
You will learn about using dialog boxes, task panes, and the Clipboard as they are used in the labs.

A task pane is open that contains features associated with the Clipboard. Unlike dialog boxes, task panes remain open until you close them. This allows you to make multiple selections from the task pane while continuing to work on other areas of your document.

3 • **Click** ✕ **in the upper-right corner of the task pane to close it.**

Using Access Key Shortcuts

Another way to use commands on the Ribbon is to display the access key shortcuts by pressing the [Alt] key and then typing the letter for the feature you want to use. Every Ribbon tab, group, and command has an access key.

● Press [Alt].

Your screen should be similar to Figure 16

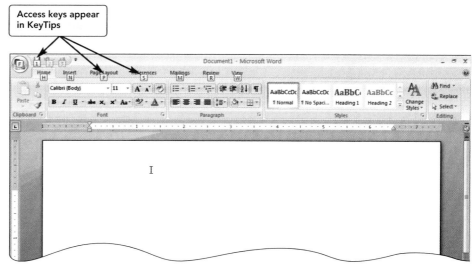

Figure 16

The letters are displayed in **KeyTips** over each available feature. Now typing a letter will access that feature. Then, depending on which letter you pressed, additional KeyTips may appear. To use a Ribbon command, press the key of the tab first, then the group, and then continue pressing letters until you press the letter of the specific command you want to use. You will use KeyTips to display the Paragraph dialog box again.

● Type the letter **H** to access the Home tab.

● Type the letters **PG** to access the Paragraph group and open the dialog box.

Your screen should be similar to Figure 17

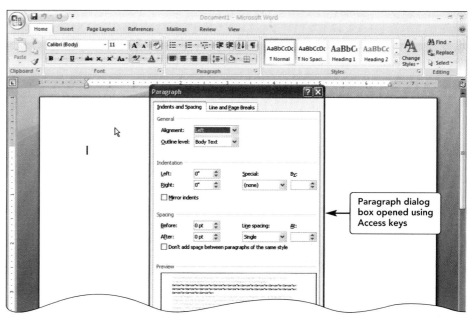

Figure 17

Three keystrokes opened the Paragraph dialog box.

Once the Access key feature is on, you can also use the ← or → directional key to move from one tab to another, and the ↓ key to move from a tab to a group and the ↑ key to move from a group to a tab. You can use all four directional keys to move among the commands in a Ribbon. [Tab⇆] and [⇧Shift] + [Tab⇆] also can be used to move right or left. Once a command is selected, you can press [Spacebar] or [←Enter] to activate it.

Minimizing the Ribbon

Sometimes you may not want to see the entire Ribbon so that more space is available in the document area. You can minimize the Ribbon by double-clicking the active tab.

> **Another Method**
> You also can press [F6] to change the focus from the Ribbon to the document area to the View Toolbar.

> **Another Method**
> You also can use the keyboard shortcut [Ctrl] + [F1] to minimize and redisplay the Ribbon.

1 ● Click ☒ to close the Paragraph dialog box.

● Double-click the Home tab.

> **Another Method**
> You also can choose Minimize the Ribbon from the Quick Access Toolbar menu.

Your screen should be similar to Figure 18

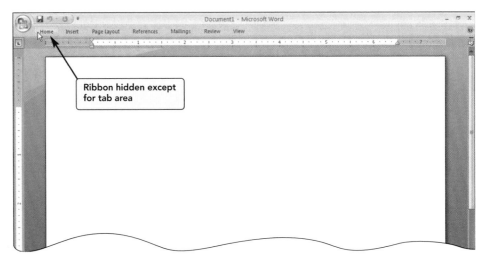

Ribbon hidden except for tab area

Figure 18

Now, the only part of the Ribbon that is visible is the tab area. This allows you to quickly reopen the Ribbon and, at the same time, open the selected tab.

2 ● Double-click the Insert tab.

Your screen should be similar to Figure 19

Ribbon redisplayed

> **Additional Information**
> If you single-click a tab, the Ribbon reappears temporarily, but minimizes again as you continue to work.

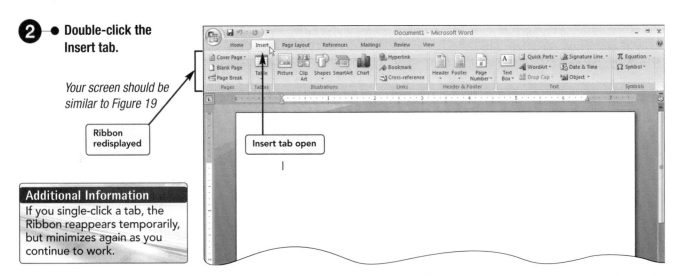

Insert tab open

Figure 19

The full Ribbon reappears and the Insert tab is open and ready for use.

Using the Mini Toolbar

Another method of accessing commands is through the Mini toolbar. The **Mini toolbar** appears automatically when you select text in a document and provides commands that are used to format (enhance) text. It also appears along with the context menu when you right-click an item in a document. Both the Mini toolbar and context menus are designed to make it more efficient to execute commands.

You can see what these features look like by right-clicking in a blank area of the document window.

1 ● **Right-click the blank document window space.**

Your screen should be similar to Figure 20

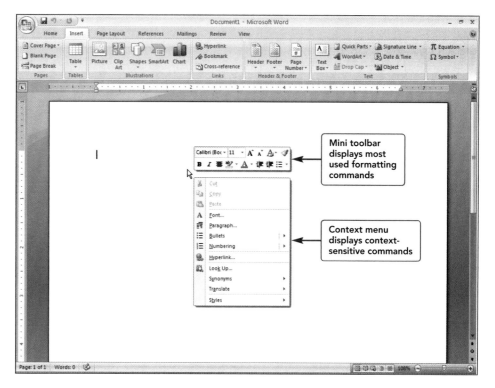

Figure 20

The Mini toolbar displays the most frequently used formatting commands. For example, when the Home tab is closed, you can use the commands in the Mini toolbar to quickly change selected text without having to reopen the Home tab to access the command. When the Mini toolbar appears automatically, it is faded so that it does not interfere with what you are doing, but changes to solid (as it is here) when you point at it.

The context menu below the Mini toolbar displays a variety of commands that are quicker to access than locating the command on the Ribbon. The commands that appear on this menu change depending on what you are doing at the time.

Using Office Help

Notice the 🔘 in the upper-right corner of the Ribbon. This button is used to access the Microsoft Help system. The Help button is always visible even when the Ribbon is hidden. Because you are using the Office Word 2007 application, Office Word Help will be accessed.

Another Method
You also can press `F1` to access Help.

1
● Click ⊙ Microsoft
   Office Word Help.

● If a Table of Contents
   list is displayed along
   the left side of the
   Help window, click ▢
   in the Help window
   toolbar to close it.

Additional Information
You will learn about using the
Table of Contents shortly.

*Your screen should be
similar to Figure 21*

Additional Information
Clicking the scroll arrows
scrolls the text in the window
line by line, and dragging the
scroll bar up or down moves
to a general location within
the window area.

Additional Information
Because Help is an online
feature, the information is
frequently updated. Your
screens may display slightly
different information than
those shown in the figures in
this lab.

Having Trouble?
In addition to being
connected to the Internet,
the feature to show content
from the Internet must be
selected. If necessary, click
the ⊙Offline button at the
bottom of the Help window
and choose Show content
from Office Online.

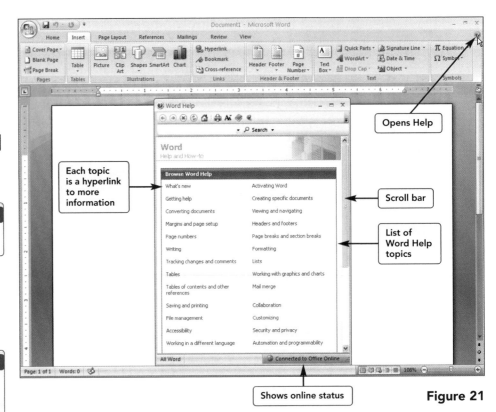

Figure 21

The Microsoft Word Help feature is opened and displayed in a separate
window. The Help window on your screen will probably be a different size
and arrangement than in Figure 21. Depending on the size of your Help
window, you may need to scroll the window to see all the Help
information provided.

It displays a listing of Help topics. If you are connected to the Internet,
the Microsoft Office Online Web site is accessed and help information
from this site is displayed in the window. If you are not connected, the
offline help information that is provided with the application and stored
on your computer is located and displayed. Generally, the listing of topics
is similar but fewer in number.

Selecting Help Topics

There are several ways you can get help. The first is to select a topic from
the listing displayed in the Help window. Each topic is a **hyperlink** or
connection to the information located on the Online site or in Help on
your computer. When you point to the hyperlink, it appears underlined
and the mouse pointer appears as 🖑. Clicking the hyperlink accesses and
displays the information associated with the hyperlink.

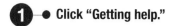

1 **Click "Getting help."**

Your screen should be similar to Figure 22

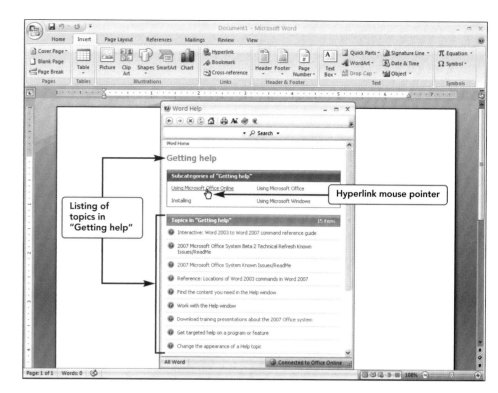

Figure 22

A listing of topics about getting help is displayed. You will get help on using Microsoft Office and the Ribbon.

2 **Click "Using Microsoft Office."**

Click "Use the Ribbon."

Your screen should be similar to Figure 23

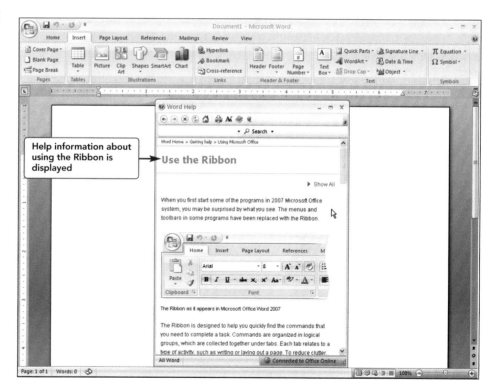

Figure 23

The information on the selected topic is displayed in the window.

3 • Use the scroll bar to scroll the Help window to read the information about the Ribbon.

• Display the "In this article" section of the window.

Your screen should be similar to Figure 24

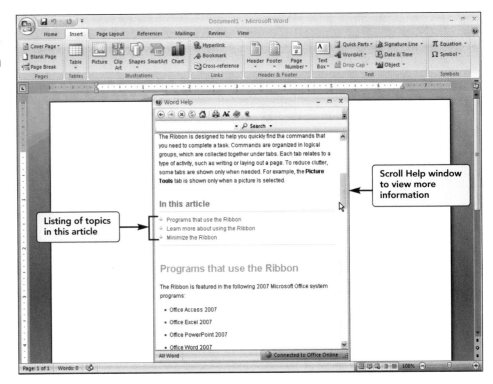

Figure 24

This area of the Help window provides a table of contents listing of the information in this window. Clicking on a link will take you directly to that location in the Help window. As you are reading the information in the window, you will see many topics preceded with ▶. This indicates the information in the topic is not displayed. Clicking on the topic heading displays the information about the topic.

4 • Click "Learn more about using the Ribbon."

• Click "Microsoft Office Word 2007."

• If necessary, scroll the window to see all the information on this topic.

Your screen should be similar to Figure 25

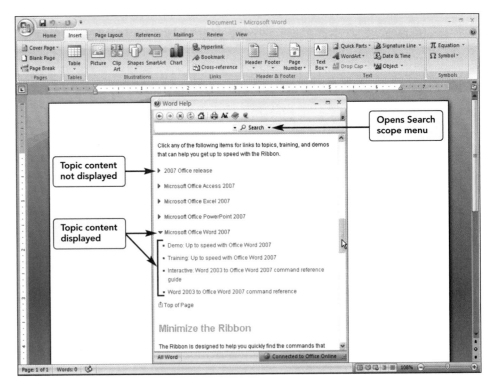

Figure 25

The information on the selected subtopic is displayed. Clicking the table of contents link jumped directly to this section of the window, saving you time by not having to scroll. The ▶ preceding the subtopic has changed to ▼, indicating the subtopic content is displayed.

You can continue to click on the subtopic headings to display the information about each topic individually. Likewise, clicking on an expanded topic hides the information. Additionally you can click ▶ Show All located at the top of the window to display all the available topic information and ▼ Hide All to hide all expanded information.

Searching Help Topics

Another method to find Help information is to conduct a search by entering a sentence or question you want help on in the Search text box of the Help window. Although you also can simply enter a word in the Search box, the best results occur when you type a phrase, complete sentence, or question. A very specific search with 2–7 words will return the most accurate results.

When searching, you can specify the scope of the search by selecting from the Search scope drop-down menu. The broadest scope for a search, All Word, is preselected. You will narrow the scope to search Word Help only.

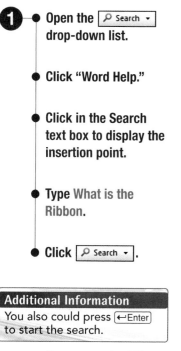

1 ● Open the 🔎 Search ▾ drop-down list.

● Click "Word Help."

● Click in the Search text box to display the insertion point.

● Type What is the Ribbon.

● Click 🔎 Search ▾ .

Additional Information

You also could press ←Enter to start the search.

Your screen should be similar to Figure 26

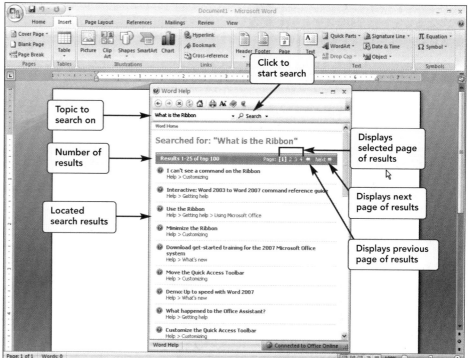

Figure 26

The first 25 located results of the top 100 are displayed in a window. There are four pages of results. The results are shown in order of relevance, with the most likely matches at the top of the list. Now you can continue to locate the information you need by selecting from the topic links provided. To see the next page of results, you can click **Next** or ➡ or click the specific page number you want to see from the Page count area. To see the previous page of results, click ⬅ .

Topics preceded with 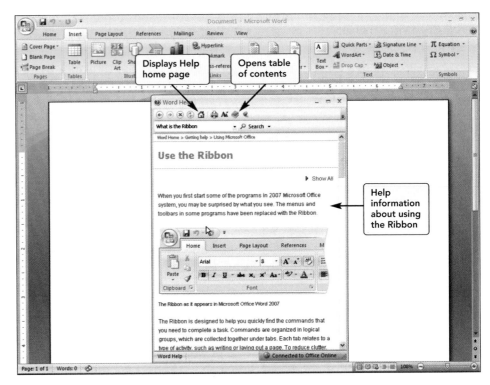 indicate the window will display the related Help topic. Those preceded with a indicate a tutorial about the topic is available from the Microsoft Training Web site.

2 ● **Click "Use the Ribbon."**

Your screen should be similar to Figure 27

Figure 27

The same Help information you saw previously is displayed.

Using the Help Table of Contents

A third source of help is to use the Help table of contents. Using this method allows you to browse the entire list of Help topics to locate topics of interest to you.

1 ● Click ⌂ Home in the Help window toolbar to return to the opening Help window.

● Click 📖 Show Table of Contents from the Help window toolbar.

Additional Information

You also could click ⬅ Back in the Help window toolbar to return to the previous page, page by page.

Your screen should be similar to Figure 28

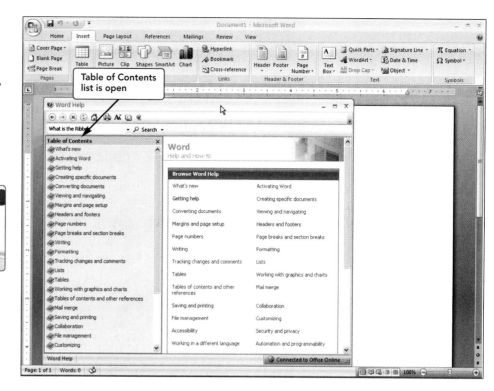

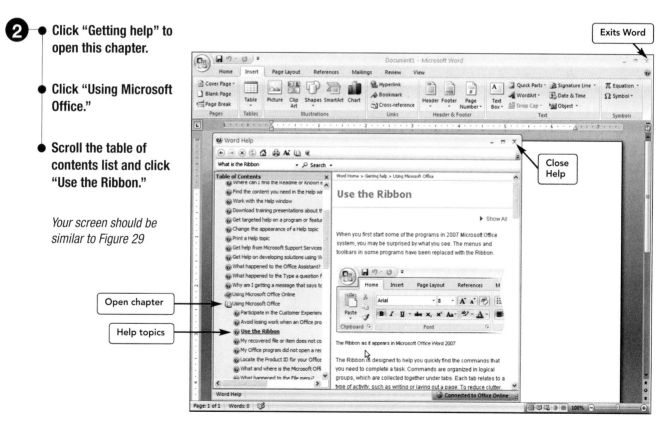

Figure 28

Additional Information

Pointing to an item in the Table of Contents displays a ScreenTip of the entire topic heading.

The entire Word Help Table of Contents is displayed in a pane on the left side of the Help window. Clicking on an item preceded with a 📖 Closed Book icon opens a chapter, which expands to display additional chapters or topics. The 📖 Open Book icon identifies those chapters that are open.

Clicking on an item preceded with ? displays the specific Help information.

2 ● Click "Getting help" to open this chapter.

● Click "Using Microsoft Office."

● Scroll the table of contents list and click "Use the Ribbon."

Your screen should be similar to Figure 29

Figure 29

The right side of the Help window displays the same Help information about the Ribbon. To close a chapter, click the ⊡ icon.

3 ● Click ⊡ to close the Using Microsoft Office chapter.

● Click ⊡ Hide Table of Contents in the Help window toolbar to hide the table of contents list again.

Exiting an Office 2007 Application

Now you are ready to close the Help window and exit the Word program. The ⊠ Close button located on the right end of the window title bar can be used to exit most application windows.

1 ● Click ⊠ Close in the Help window title bar to close the Help window.

● Click ⊠ Close in the Word window title bar to exit Word.

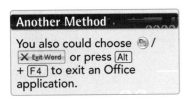

The program window is closed and the desktop is visible again.

key terms

context menu I.15

contextual tabs I.16

dialog box launcher I.19

document window I.11

drop-down gallery I.18

gallery I.18

group I.11

hyperlink I.24

in-Ribbon gallery I.18

KeyTips I.21

Mini toolbar I.23

on-demand tab I.16

Quick Access Toolbar I.11

Ribbon I.11

ScreenTip I.13

scroll bar I.11

selection cursor I.12

status bar I.11

super tooltip I.18

tab I.11

task pane I.19

tooltip I.13

user interface I.10

command summary

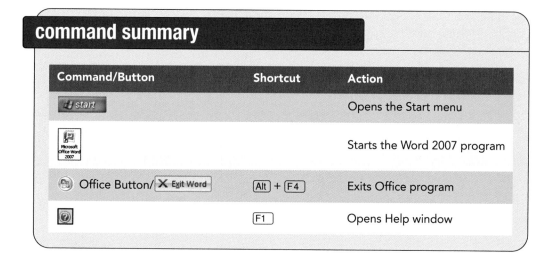

Command/Button	Shortcut	Action
start		Opens the Start menu
Microsoft Office Word 2007		Starts the Word 2007 program
Office Button/ ✕ Exit Word	Alt + F4	Exits Office program
?	F1	Opens Help window

step-by-step

rating system
★ Easy
★★ Moderate
★★★ Difficult

Using an Office Application ★

1. All Office 2007 applications have a common user interface. You will explore the Excel 2007 application and use many of the same features you learned about while using Word 2007 in this lab.

   a. Use the Start menu or a shortcut icon on your desktop to start Office Excel 2007.

   b. What shape is the mouse pointer when positioned in the document window area? _____

   c. Excel has _____ tabs. Which tabs are not the same as in Word?

   _____

   d. Open the Formulas tab. How many groups are in the Formulas tab? _____

   e. Which tab contains the group to work with charts? _____

   f. From the Home tab, click the Number group dialog box launcher. What is the name of the dialog box that opens? How many number categories are there? _____ Close the dialog box.

   g. Display ToolTips for the following buttons located in the Alignment group of the Home tab and identify what action they perform.

   ▤ _____

   ▤ _____

   ▤ _____

   h. Open the Excel Help window. Open the table of contents and locate the topic "What's new in Microsoft Office Excel 2007?" Open this topic and find information on the number of rows and columns in a worksheet. Answer the following questions:

   How many rows are in a worksheet? _____

   How many columns are in a worksheet? _____

   What are the letters of the last column? _____

   i. Close the table of contents. Close the Help window. Exit Excel.

on your own

Exploring Microsoft Help ★

1. In addition to the Help information you used in this lab, Office 2007 Online Help also includes many interactive tutorials. Selecting a Help topic that starts a tutorial will open the browser program on your computer. Both audio and written instructions are provided. You will use one of these tutorials to learn more about using Word 2007.

   Start Word 2007. Open Help and open the topic "What's New?" Click on the topic "Up to speed with Word 2007." Follow the directions in your browser to run the tutorial. When you are done, close the browser window, close Help, and exit Word 2007.

Overview of Microsoft Office PowerPoint 2007

What Is a Presentation Program?

You are in a panic! Tomorrow you are to make a presentation to an audience and you want it to be good. To the rescue comes a powerful tool: graphics presentation programs. These programs are designed to help you create an effective presentation, whether to the board of directors of your company or to your fellow classmates. An effective presentation gets your point across clearly and in an interesting manner.

Graphics presentation programs are designed to help you produce a high-quality presentation that is both interesting to the audience and effective in its ability to convey your message. A presentation can be as simple as overhead transparencies or as sophisticated as an onscreen electronic display. Graphics presentation programs can produce black-and-white or color overhead transparencies, 35 mm slides, onscreen electronic presentations called screen shows, Web pages for Web use, and support materials for both the speaker and the audience.

The graphics presentation program includes features such as text handling, outlining, graphing, drawing, animations, clip art, and multimedia support. With a few keystrokes, the user can quickly change, correct, and update the presentation. In addition, graphics presentation programs suggest layouts for different types of presentations and offer professionally designed templates to help you produce a presentation that is sure to keep your audience's attention.

Office PowerPoint 2007 Features

Creating an effective presentation is a complicated process. Graphics presentation programs help simplify this process by providing assistance in the content development phase, as well as in the layout and design phase. In addition, these programs produce the support materials you can use when making a presentation to an audience.

The content development phase includes deciding on the topic of your presentation, the organization of the content, and the ultimate message you want to convey to the audience. As an aid in this phase, PowerPoint 2007 helps you organize your thoughts based on the type of presentation you are making. Several common types of presentations sell a product or idea, suggest a strategy, or report on the progress of a program. Based on the type of presentation, the program suggests ideas and organization tips. For example, if you are making a presentation on the progress of a sales campaign, the program would suggest that you enter text on the background of the sales campaign as the first page, called a slide; the current status of the campaign as the next slide; and accomplishments, schedule, issues and problems, and where you are heading on subsequent slides.

The layout for each slide is the next important decision. Again, PowerPoint 2007 helps you by suggesting text layout features such as title placement, bullets, and columns. You also can incorporate graphs of data, tables, organizational charts, clip art, and other special text effects in the slides.

PowerPoint 2007 also includes professionally designed themes to further enhance the appearance of your slides. These themes include features that standardize the appearance of all the slides in your presentation. Professionally selected combinations of text and background colors, common typefaces and sizes, borders, and other art designs take the worry out of much of the design layout.

After you have written and designed the slides, you can use the slides in an onscreen electronic presentation or a Web page for use on the Web. An onscreen presentation uses the computer to display the slides on an overhead projection screen. When you use this type of presentation, you can use the rehearsal feature that allows you to practice and time your presentation. The length of time to display each slide can be set and your entire presentation can be completed within the allotted time. A presentation also can be modified to display on a Web site and run using a Web browser. Finally, you can package the presentation to a CD for distribution.

Using PowerPoint 2007, you also can print out the materials you have created. You can print an outline of the text showing the titles of the slides and main text but not the art. The outline allows you to check the organizational logic of your presentation. You also can print speaker notes to which you can refer while making your presentation. These notes generally consist of a small printout of each slide with any notes on topics you want to discuss while the slides are displayed. Finally, you can create printed handouts of the slides for the audience. The audience can refer to the slide and make notes on the handout page as you speak.

Case Study for Office PowerPoint 2007 Labs

You have volunteered at the Animal Rescue Foundation, a nonprofit organization that rescues unwanted animals from local animal shelters and finds foster homes for them until a suitable adoptive family can be found. With your computer skills, you have been asked to create a powerful and persuasive presentation to entice the community to volunteer.

The organization has recently purchased the 2007 Microsoft Office Suite. You will use the graphics presentation program Microsoft Office PowerPoint 2007 to create two new presentations. The first will be used to promote the volunteer group, Animal Angels, and the second will be used during the orientation program for new volunteers.

Lab 1: You use PowerPoint to enter and edit the text for the volunteer presentation. You also learn how to reorganize the presentation and enhance it with different text attributes and by adding a picture. Finally, you learn how to run a slide show and print handouts.

Lab 2: You learn about many more features to enhance the appearance of your slides. These include changing the slide theme and color scheme and adding clip art, animation, and sound. You also learn how to add transition effects to make the presentation more interesting. Finally, you create speaker notes to help you keep your cool during the presentation.

Lab 3: You create a new presentation for the volunteer orientation by modifying and expanding an existing presentation, using text from a Word outline, and inserting slides from another presentation. You will use several specialized tools to create a column chart of data and an organization chart of the management structure of the Foundation. You also learn how to save the new presentation as a Web page.

Working Together: Demonstrates the sharing of information between users by sending the presentation out for review. First you learn how to enter, edit, and respond to comments. Then you will copy a graphic created in Word into a slide. Finally, you will embed a copy of the presentation in a letter that you plan to send by e-mail.

Before You Begin

To the Student

The following assumptions have been made:

- The Microsoft Office PowerPoint 2007 program has been installed on your computer system.

- You have the data files needed to complete the series of PowerPoint 2007 Labs and practice exercises. These may be supplied by your instructor and are also available at the online learning center Web site found at www.mhhe.com/oleary.

- You have completed the McGraw-Hill Windows Labs or you are already familiar with how to use Windows and a mouse.

To the Instructor

A complete installation of Microsoft Office 2007 is required in which all components are available to students while completing the labs. In several labs, an online connection to the Web is needed to fully access a feature.

   Please be aware that the following settings are assumed to be in effect for the Office PowerPoint 2007 program. These assumptions are necessary so that the screens and directions in the labs are accurate. These settings are made using ⊞ Office Button/ PowerPoint Options in the categories shown below.

Popular

- The Mini Toolbar feature is active.
- The Live Preview feature is enabled.
- Show feature descriptions in ScreenTips is selected.
- ClearType is on.
- Language is set to English (US).

Proofing

- All AutoCorrect options are on.
- All AutoFormat options are on.
- SmartTags is off.
- Ignore words in Uppercase is on.
- Ignore words that contain numbers is on.
- Ignore Internet and file addresses is on.
- Flag repeated words is on.
- Check spelling as you type is on.

Advanced/Editing options

- Both editing options are on.
- Maximum number of undos is 20.

Advanced/Cut, Copy, and Paste

- Both options are on.

Advanced/Display

- All options are on with the following settings:
  - Show 17 Recent Documents.
  - Open documents using this view is set to The view saved in the file.

Advanced/Slide Show

- All options are on.

Advanced/Print

- Print in background is on.

Advanced/When printing this document

- Use the most recently used print settings is on.

Advanced/Save

- Link sounds with file size greater than 100 KB.

Advanced/General/Web Options

- General tab
  - Add slide navigation controls is on.
    - Colors: White text on black.
  - Resize graphics to fit browser window is on.
- Browsers tab
  - Target browsers is set to Internet Explorer 4.0 or later.
  - Save new Web pages as Single File Web Pages is on.
- Files tab
  - All options are on.

- Pictures tab
  - Screen size is set to 800 × 600.
- Encoding
  - Save this document as Western European (Windows).
- Fonts
  - Default font is set to English/Western European/Other Latin script.
  - Proportional font is Times New Roman 12 pt.
  - Fixed-width font is Courier New 10 pt.

Customize

- The Quick Access Toolbar displays the Save, Undo, and Redo buttons.

Finally, the feature to access Online Help is on. (From the Help window, open the Connection Status menu and choose Show Content from Office Online.)

All figures in the manual reflect the use of a display monitor set at 1024 by 768 and the Windows XP operating system. If other monitor display settings are used, there may be more or fewer lines of information displayed in the windows than in the figures. If the Windows Vista operating system is used, some features may look slightly different.

Instructional Conventions

Hands-on instructions you are to perform appear as a sequence of numbered steps. Within each step, a series of bullets identifies the specific actions that must be performed. Step numbering begins over within each topic heading throughout the lab.

Commands

Commands that are initiated using a command button and the mouse appear following the word "Click." The icon (and the icon name if the icon does not include text) is displayed following "Click." If there is another way to perform the same action, it appears in an Another Method margin note when the action is first introduced as shown in Example A.

As you become more familiar with the application, commands will appear as shown in Example B.

Example A

1 ● Select the text "Join Animal Angels".

● Open the Home tab.

Another Method
The keyboard shortcut is
Ctrl + B.

● Click **B** Bold in the Font group.

Example B

1 ● **Select the text "Join Animal Angels".**

● **Click B Bold.**

OR

1 ● **Bold the text "Join Animal Angels".**

File Names and Information to Type

Plain blue text identifies file names you need to select or enter. Information you are asked to type appears in blue and bold. (See Example C.)

Example C

1 ● **Open the presentation file** pp01_Volunteers.

● **Select slide 2 in the Slides pane.**

● **Type** Topics of Discussion **in the title placeholder.**

Office Button

Office Button commands that you are to perform appear following the word "Choose." The Office Button icon will precede the instructions. Items that need to be selected will follow the word "Select" and will appear in black text. You can select items with the mouse or directional keys. Initially these commands will appears as in Example A. As you become more familiar with the application, commands will appear as shown in Example B.

Example A

● Click  Office Button.

● Choose Open.

● Select My Documents from the Look In drop-down menu.

● **Select** pp01.Volunteers.

● Click  .

Example B

● Choose  Office Button/Open.

● **Choose** pp01.Volunteers.

OR

● **Open the file** pp01.Volunteers.

Creating a Presentation

Objectives

After completing this lab, you will know how to:

1 Use a template to create a presentation.

2 View and edit a presentation.

3 Save, close, and open a presentation.

4 Check spelling.

5 Delete, move, and insert slides.

6 Size and move placeholders.

7 Run a slide show.

8 Change fonts and formatting.

9 Insert pictures and clip art.

10 Preview and print a presentation.

Animal Rescue Foundation

You are the Volunteer Coordinator at the local Animal Rescue Foundation. This nonprofit organization rescues unwanted pets from local animal shelters and finds foster homes for them until a suitable adoptive family can be found. The agency has a large volunteer group called the Animal Angels that provides much-needed support for the foundation.

The agency director has decided to launch a campaign to increase community awareness about the foundation. As part of the promotion, you have been asked to create a powerful and persuasive presentation to entice more members of the community to join Animal Angels.

The agency director has asked you to preview the presentation at the weekly staff meeting tomorrow and has asked you to present a draft of the presentation by noon today.

To help you create the presentation, you will use Microsoft Office PowerPoint 2007, a graphics presentation application that is designed to create presentation materials such as slides, overheads, and handouts. Using Office PowerPoint 2007, you can create a high-quality and interesting onscreen presentation with pizzazz that will dazzle your audience.

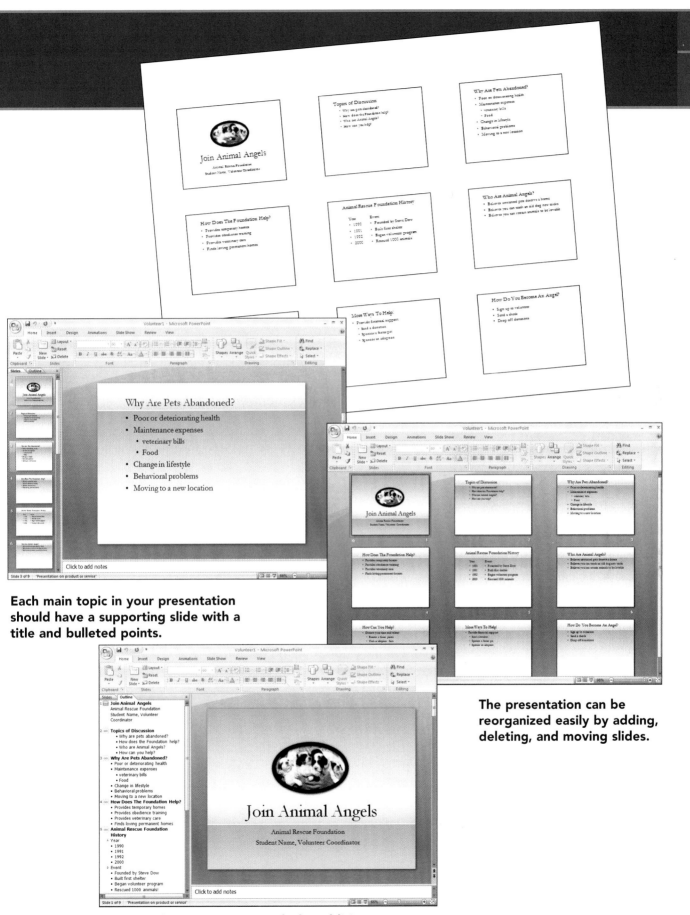

Each main topic in your presentation should have a supporting slide with a title and bulleted points.

The presentation can be reorganized easily by adding, deleting, and moving slides.

Enhance the presentation with the addition of graphics and text colors.

Introducing Office PowerPoint 2007

The Animal Rescue Foundation has just installed the latest version of the Microsoft Office Suite of applications, Office 2007, on their computers. You will use the graphics presentation program Microsoft Office PowerPoint 2007, included in the office suite, to create your presentation. Using this program, you should have no problem creating the presentation in time for tomorrow's staff meeting.

Starting Office PowerPoint 2007

1 • Start the Office PowerPoint 2007 application.

• If necessary, maximize the window.

Having Trouble?
See "Common Office 2007 Interface Features," page I.10, for information on how to start the application and use features that are common to all 2007 Office applications.

Your screen should be similar to Figure 1.1

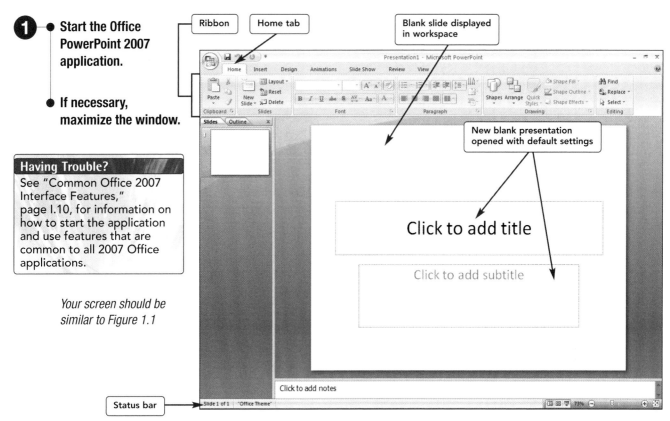

Figure 1.1

Additional Information
Because the Office 2007 applications remember settings that were on when the program was last exited, your screen may look slightly different.

The PowerPoint application window includes the Ribbon located below the title bar that consists of seven tabs. These tabs contain the commands and features you will use to create and modify a presentation.

The large area below the Ribbon is the **workspace** where your presentations are displayed as you create and edit them. The workspace currently displays a blank slide.

Concept 1

Slide

1 A **slide** is an individual "page" of your presentation. The first slide of a presentation is the title slide, which is used to introduce your presentation. Additional slides are used to support each main point in your presentation. The slides give the audience a visual summary of the words you speak, which helps them understand the content and keeps them entertained. The slides also help you, the speaker, organize your thoughts and prompt you during the presentation.

The status bar at the bottom of the window displays the slide indicator, messages and information about various PowerPoint settings, buttons to change the document view, and a window zoom feature. The slide indicator identifies the number of the slide that is displayed in the workspace of the total number of slides in the presentation. You will learn about the other features of the status bar shortly.

Developing New Presentations

During your presentation, you will present information about the Animal Rescue Foundation and why someone should want to join the Animal Angels volunteer group. As you prepare to create a new presentation, you should follow several basic steps: plan, create, edit, enhance, and rehearse.

Step	Description
Plan	The first step in planning a presentation is to understand its purpose. You also need to find out the length of time you have to speak, who the audience is, what type of room you will be in, and what kind of audiovisual equipment is available. These factors help to determine the type of presentation you will create.
Create	To begin creating your presentation, develop the content by typing your thoughts or notes into an outline. Each main idea in your presentation should have a supporting slide with a title and bulleted points.
Edit	While typing, you will probably make typing and spelling errors that need to be corrected. This is one type of editing. Another type is to revise the content of what you have entered to make it clearer, or to add or delete information. To do this, you might insert a slide, add or delete bulleted items, or move text to another location.
Enhance	You want to develop a presentation that grabs and holds the audience's attention. Choose a design that gives your presentation some dazzle. Wherever possible, add graphics to replace or enhance text. Add effects that control how a slide appears and disappears, and that reveal text in a bulleted list one bullet at a time.
Rehearse	Finally, you should rehearse the delivery of your presentation. For a professional presentation, your delivery should be as polished as your materials. Use the same equipment that you will use when you give the presentation. Practice advancing from slide to slide and then back in case someone asks a question. If you have a mouse available, practice pointing or drawing on the slide to call attention to key points.

After rehearsing your presentation, you may find that you want to go back to the editing phase. You may change text, move bullets, or insert a new slide. Periodically, as you make changes, rehearse the presentation again to see how the changes affect your presentation. By the day of the presentation, you will be confident about your message and at ease with the materials.

During the planning phase, you have spoken with the foundation director regarding the purpose of the presentation and the content in general. The purpose of your presentation is to educate members of the community about the organization and to persuade many to volunteer. In addition, you want to impress the director by creating a professional presentation.

Creating a Presentation

When you first start PowerPoint, a new blank presentation is opened. It is like a blank piece of paper that already has many predefined settings. These settings, called **default settings,** are generally the most commonly used settings and are stored as a presentation template.

Concept 2

Template

2   A **template** is a file containing predefined settings that can be used as a pattern to create many common types of presentations. Templates include features that control the slide color scheme, the type and size of bullets and fonts, placeholder sizes and positions, background designs and fills, and other layout and design elements. Every PowerPoint presentation is based on a template. The default settings for a basic blank presentation are stored in the default design template file. Whenever you create a new presentation using this template, the same default settings are used.

Many other templates that are designed to help you create professional-looking presentations are also available within PowerPoint and in the Microsoft Office Template Gallery on the Microsoft Office Web site. They include design templates, which provide a design concept, fonts, and color scheme; and content templates, which suggest content for your presentation based on the type of presentation you are making. You also can design and save your own presentation templates.

Several methods can be used to create a presentation. The first method is to start with a blank presentation that has minimal design elements and add your own content and design changes. Another is to use one of the many supplied design templates as the basis for your new presentation. A third is to save the design elements of an existing presentation as a custom template and then use it as the basis for your new presentation. Finally, you can open an existing presentation and modify the design and content as needed for the new presentation.

Using a Template

Because this is your first presentation created using PowerPoint, you decide to use one of the supplied templates.

1 ● Click 🏢 **Office Button.**

     ● Choose **New.**

Your screen should be similar to Figure 1.2

Template categories

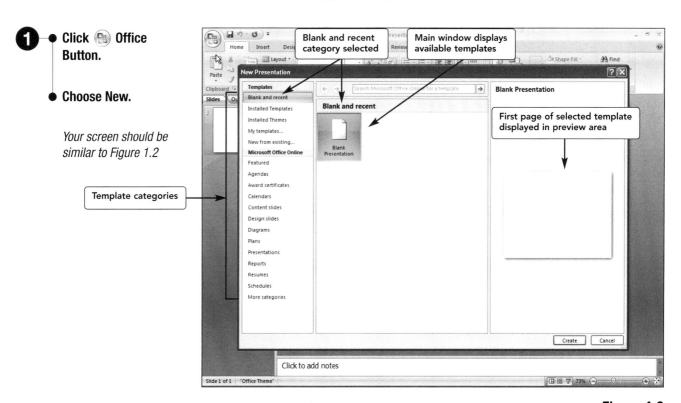

Figure 1.2

The left side of the New Presentation dialog box displays the template categories. Currently, the Blank and recent category is selected. The middle area, or main window, displays templates available from the selected category. Your screen might display a single option as in Figure 1.2, or it might show additional options. The right side of the dialog box displays a preview area presenting the first page of the selected template.

When you change categories, the main window displays the content associated with that category. For example, the Installed templates category accesses templates that are already installed on your computer. The Microsoft Office Online group lists categories of template types that are available from Microsoft online. You want to look at the online templates.

Having Trouble?

If you do not have an Internet connection or are unable to locate the "Presentation on product or service" template, choose New from existing and select the file pp01_Products from your data file location. Then skip to the next section, Viewing the Presentation.

2 • Choose Presentations from the Microsoft Office Online category.

• Scroll the list in the main window and select "Business"

• Scroll the Business options in the main window and select "Presentation on product or service."

Your screen should be similar to Figure 1.3

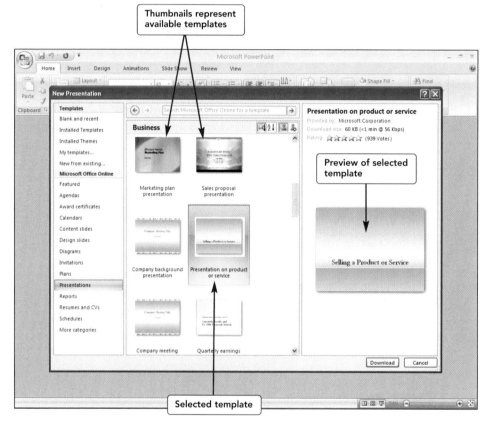

Figure 1.3

Small images, called **thumbnails,** representing the first slide in each design template are displayed in alphabetical order by name. When a template is selected, the preview area displays a larger image of the thumbnail and information about the template.

You think this design looks good and decide to begin your presentation for the volunteers using the template.

3 • Click [Download].

• If the Microsoft Office Genuine Advantage dialog box appears, click [Continue].

• If necessary, close the Help window.

Your screen should be similar to Figure 1.4

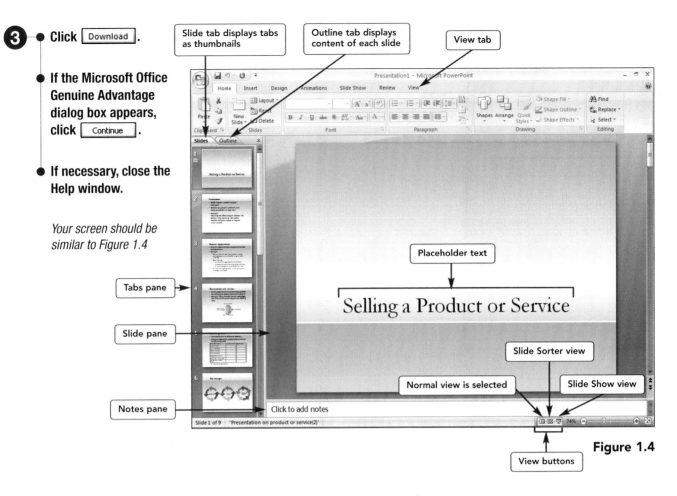

Figure 1.4

The template file is downloaded and opened in PowerPoint.

Viewing the Presentation

The first slide in the presentation is displayed in the workspace. The colors and design displayed in the new presentation are part of the template. It also contains sample text, called **placeholder text,** which suggests the content for the slide. This text will be replaced by the information you want to appear in the slide.

The presentation is initially displayed in Normal view. A **view** is a way of looking at a presentation. PowerPoint provides several views you can use to look at and modify your presentation. Depending on what you are doing, one view may be preferable to another. The commands to change views are located on the View tab. In addition, the three view buttons in the status bar can be used to switch quickly from one view to another. The three main views are described in the following table.

View	Button	Description
Normal		Provides three working areas of the window that allow you to work on all aspects of your presentation in one place.
Slide Sorter		Displays a miniature of each slide to make it easy to reorder slides, add special effects such as transitions, and set timing between slides.
Slide Show		Displays each slide in final form using the full screen space so you can practice or present the presentation.

Using Normal View

Normal view is displayed by default because it is the main view you use while creating a presentation. Normal view has four working areas: Outline tab, Slides tab, Slide pane, and Notes pane. These areas allow you to work on all components of your presentation in one convenient location. The **Outline tab** displays the text content of each slide in outline format and the **Slides tab** displays each slide as a thumbnail. You can switch between the Slides and Outline tabs by clicking on the tab. The **Slide pane** displays the selected slide. The **Notes pane** includes space for you to enter notes that apply to the current slide.

Additional Information

You can adjust the size of each pane by dragging the splitter bar that borders each pane. You can make the thumbnails larger or smaller by changing the width of the tabs pane. If it gets too small, the tab names are replaced by icons.

1
- If necessary, click on the Slides tab to open it.

- Scroll the Slides tab to view the rest of the slides.

- Click on the last slide in the Slides tab.

Your screen should be similar to Figure 1.5

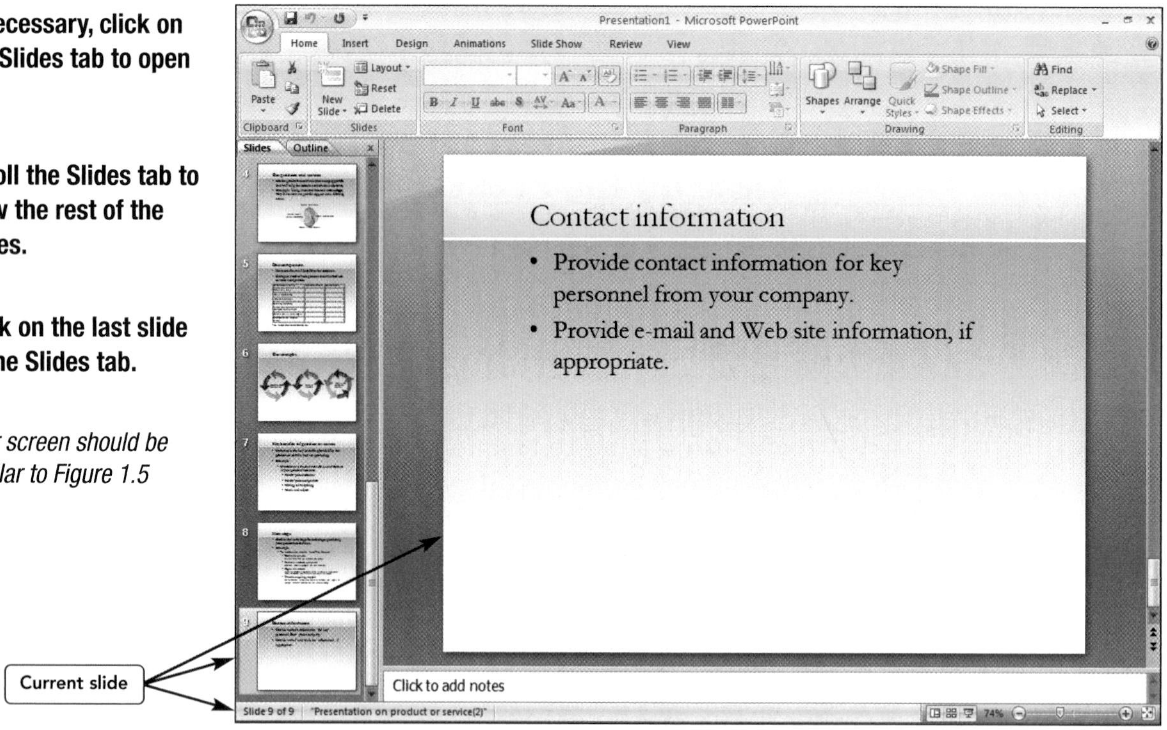

Current slide

Figure 1.5

Clicking on the thumbnail selects the slide, making it the current slide, and displays it in the Slide pane. The **current slide** is the slide that will be affected by any changes you make. The presentation has a total of nine slides. The status bar displays the number of the current slide, the total number of slides, and the name of the design template used.

② ● Click on the Outline tab to open it.

Another Method
You also can press Ctrl + ⇧Shift + Tab⇆ to switch between the Slide and Outline tabs.

Additional Information
The size of the Outline tab increases automatically to display the text.

Your screen should be similar to Figure 1.6

Placeholder text for selected slide

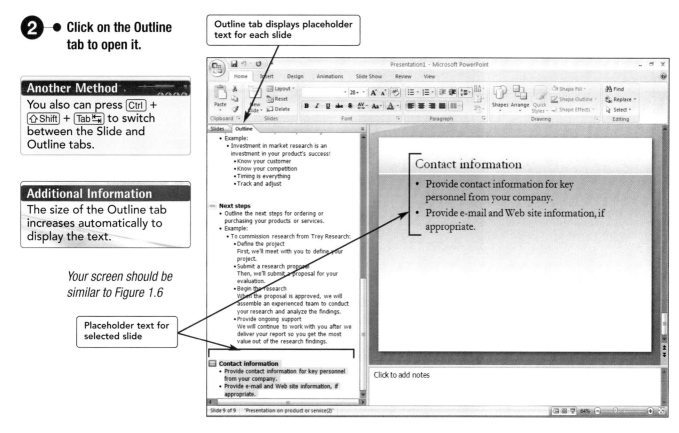

Figure 1.6

The Outline tab displays the placeholder text for each slide in the presentation. The sample text suggests the content for each slide to help you organize your presentation's content. To the left of each slide title is a number that identifies each slide.

Using Slide Sorter View

The second main view that is used while creating a presentation is Slide Sorter view. This view also displays thumbnails of the slides.

1 • Click ⊞ Slide Sorter.

Having Trouble?
Pointing to a view button displays its name in a ScreenTip.

• Click on slide 1.

Another Method
You also could Switch to Slide Sorter view by clicking ⊞ in the Presentation Views group of the View tab.

Your screen should be similar to Figure 1.7

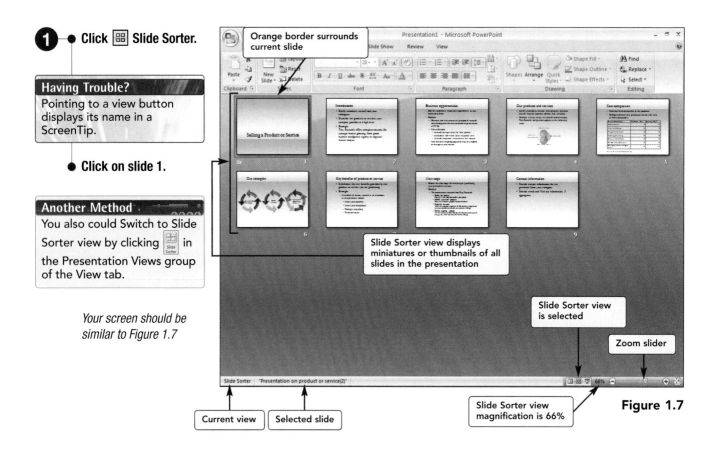

Figure 1.7

This view displays a miniature of each slide in the window. Clicking on a thumbnail selects the slide and makes it the current slide. The currently selected slide, slide 1, appears with an orange border around it.

Because the thumbnails of each slide are small, it is difficult to see the content. You will increase the magnification of the window to make it easier to read each slide. To do this, the zoom feature is used to change the amount of information displayed in the window by "zooming in" to get a close-up view or "zooming out" to see more of the document at a reduced view. Initially the Slide Sorter view magnification is 66%. In this view, you can increase the onscreen magnification to 100% or decrease it to as little as 20%. The zoom setting for each view is set independently and remains in effect until changed to another zoom setting.

You will "zoom in" on the slides so you can read the content.

Another Method
You also can click 🔍 Zoom on the View tab to specify the zoom settings.

② • **Drag the zoom slider all the way to the right to increase the zoom to 100%.**

Your screen should be similar to Figure 1.8

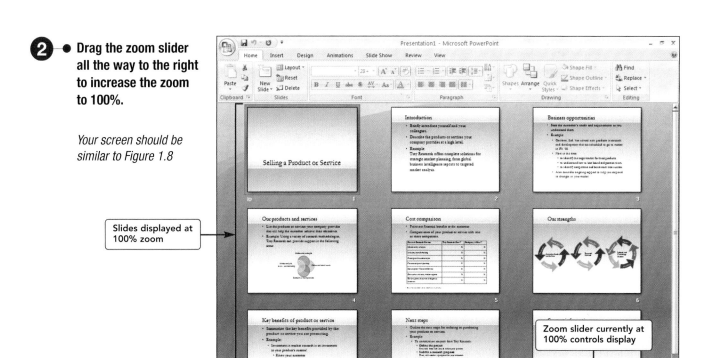

Slides displayed at 100% zoom

Zoom slider currently at 100% controls display

Figure 1.8

Additional Information

You also can click the ⊕ or ⊖ on the zoom slider to increase or decrease the zoom percentage by 10 percent increments.

At this zoom percentage, the slides are much larger and easier to read. This view is particularly useful for rearranging slides to improve the flow and organization of the presentation.

Editing a Presentation

After beginning your presentation using the template, you need to replace the sample content with the appropriate information for your presentation. Editing involves making text changes and additions to the content of your presentation. It also includes making changes to the organization of content. This can be accomplished quickly by rearranging the order of bulleted items on slides as well as the order of slides.

Navigating and Selecting Text

While editing, you will need to move to specific locations in the text. You can use the mouse to move to selected locations simply by clicking on the location. An insertion point $\rm I$ appears to show your location in the text. You also can use the arrow keys located on the numeric keypad or the directional keypad to move the insertion point. The keyboard directional keys used to move within text are described in the following table.

Key	Movement
→	One character to right
←	One character to left
↑	One line up
↓	One line down
Ctrl + →	One word to right
Ctrl + ←	One word to left
Home	Left end of line
End	Right end of line

Holding down a directional key or key combination moves the insertion point quickly in the direction indicated, saving multiple presses of the key. Many of the insertion point movement keys can be held down to execute multiple moves.

While editing, you also may need to select text. To select text using the mouse, first move the insertion point to the beginning or end of the text to be selected, and then drag when the mouse pointer is an I-beam to highlight the text you want selected. You can select as little as a single letter or as much as the entire document. To remove highlighting and deselect text, simply click anywhere in the document.

You also can quickly select a block of text, such as a word or line. The following table summarizes the mouse techniques used to select standard blocks.

To Select	Procedure
Word	Double-click in the word.
Sentence	Press Ctrl and click within the sentence.
All text in a bullet	Triple-click in the bulleted text.
Multiple lines and bullets	Drag up or down across the lines.

You also can select text with the keyboard keys shown in the following table.

Keyboard	Action
⇧ Shift + →	Selects the next space or character.
⇧ Shift + ←	Selects the previous space or character.
Ctrl + ⇧ Shift + →	Selects the next word.
Ctrl + ⇧ Shift + ←	Selects the last word.
Ctrl + ⇧ Shift + ↑	Selects text going backward.
Ctrl + ⇧ Shift + ↓	Selects text going forward.
Ctrl + A	Selects the entire document.

Using the Outline Tab

One way to make text-editing changes is to use the Outline tab in Normal view. The first change you want to make is to enter a title for the presentation on slide 1. First, you will select the sample title text on the slide and delete it.

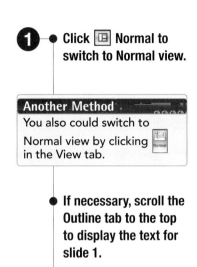

1 ● Click **Normal** to switch to Normal view.

Another Method
You also could switch to Normal view by clicking 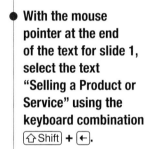 in the View tab.

● **If necessary, scroll the Outline tab to the top to display the text for slide 1.**

● **With the mouse pointer at the end of the text for slide 1, select the text "Selling a Product or Service" using the keyboard combination** ⇧Shift **+** ←**.**

● **Press** Delete**.**

Your screen should be similar to Figure 1.9

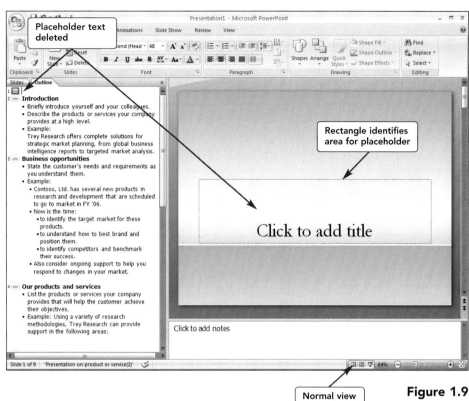

Figure 1.9

The sample text is deleted. Notice, however, that the slide still displays an outline rectangle and the default placeholder text, "Click to add title." The rectangle identifies the location of a **placeholder,** an element that is designed to contain specific types of items or **objects** such as the slide title text, bulleted item text, charts, tables, and pictures. Each slide can have several different types of placeholders. This slide has only one placeholder for the presentation title.

To enter the title, you can type it in the outline or on the slide. Since the insertion point is already in the Outline tab, you will enter the text in this area.

2 ● **Type** Join Animal
      Angels.

Having Trouble?

If you make a typing error,
press [Backspace] to delete the
characters back to the error
and retype the entry.

● **Press** [Ctrl] + [←Enter]
  to add a subtitle line.

● **Type** Animal Rescue
  Foundation.

*Your screen should be
similar to Figure 1.10*

Additional Information

If you click the slide icon to
the right of the slide number,
all text on the slide is
selected.

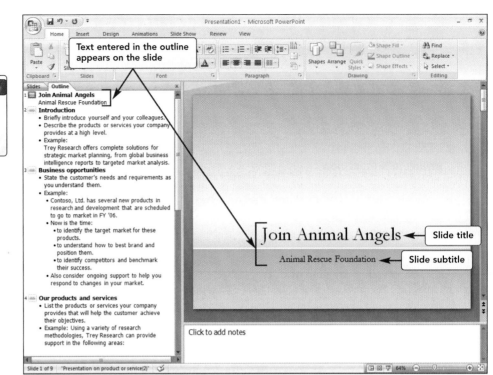

Figure 1.10

As you enter the new text in the Outline tab, it also appears in the slide
displayed in the Slide pane. When entering the title for a slide, it is a
common practice to use title case, in which the first letter of most words is
capitalized.

The next change you want to make is in the Introduction slide. The
sample text recommends that you introduce yourself and describe the
company products and services. You will replace the sample text next to
the first bullet with the text for your slide. In the Outline tab, you can
select an entire paragraph and all subparagraphs by pointing to the left of
the line and clicking when the mouse pointer is a ✛.

3 ● Click on the first bullet of slide 2 in the Outline tab when the mouse pointer is a ⟨⊹⟩.

Having Trouble?
If you accidentally drag selected text, it will move. To return it to its original location, click ⟨↺⟩ Undo on the Quick Access toolbar immediately.

● Type **Your Name, Volunter** (this word is intentionally misspelled) **Coordinator.**

Your screen should be similar to Figure 1.11

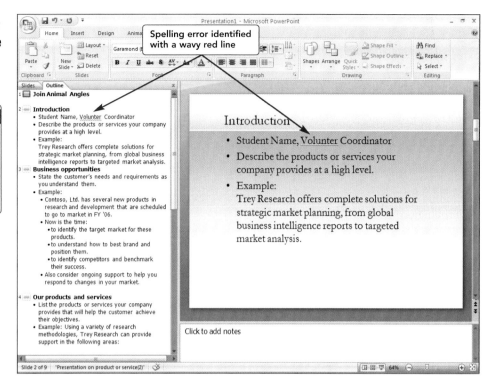

Figure 1.11

As soon as you pressed a key, the selected text was deleted and replaced with the text you typed. Also, as you enter text, the program checks each word for accuracy. In this case, a spelling error was located.

Correcting Errors

PowerPoint identified the word as misspelled by underlining it with a wavy red line.

Concept 3

Spelling Checker

3 The **spelling checker** locates all misspelled words, duplicate words, and capitalization irregularities as you create and edit a presentation, and proposes possible corrections. This feature works by comparing each word to a dictionary of words. If the word does not appear in the **main dictionary** or in a **custom dictionary,** it is identified as misspelled. The main dictionary is supplied with the program; a custom dictionary is one you can create to hold words you commonly use, such as proper names and technical terms, but are not included in the main dictionary.

If the word does not appear in either dictionary, the program identifies it as misspelled by displaying a red wavy line below the word. You can then correct the misspelled word by editing it. Alternatively, you can display a list of suggested spelling corrections for that word and select the correct spelling from the list to replace the misspelled word in the presentation.

To quickly correct the misspelled word, you can select the correct spelling from a list of suggested spelling corrections displayed on the shortcut menu.

1 **Right-click on the misspelled word in the Outline tab to display the shortcut menu.**

Your screen should be similar to Figure 1.12

Shortcut menu appears

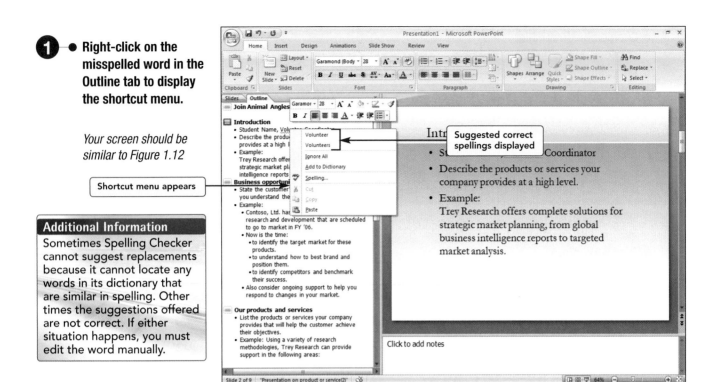

Figure 1.12

The shortcut menu displays two suggested correct spellings. The menu also includes several related menu options described below.

Option	Effect
Ignore All	Instructs PowerPoint to ignore the misspelling of this word throughout the rest of this session.
Add to Dictionary	Adds the word to the custom dictionary list. When a word is added to the custom dictionary, PowerPoint will always accept that spelling as correct.
Spelling	Opens the Spelling dialog box to check the entire presentation.

You will replace the word with the correct spelling and then enter the information for the second bullet.

2 Choose "Volunteer."

- **Select the text in the second bullet on slide 2 in the Outline tab.**
- **Press** Delete**.**
- **Select the text in the Example bullet in the Outline tab.**
- **Type volunter (this word is intentionally misspelled) opportunities.**

Your screen should be similar to Figure 1.13

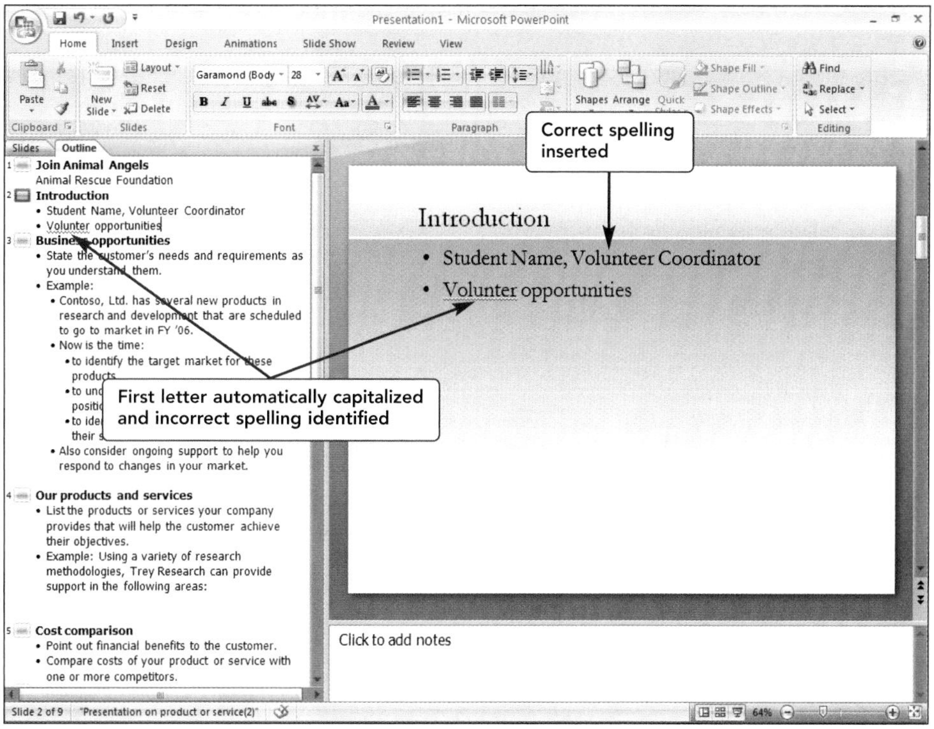

Figure 1.13

Additional Information

Bulleted items in a presentation are capitalized in sentence case format. Ending periods, however, are not included.

Notice that the first letter of "Volunter" was automatically capitalized. This is part of the AutoCorrect feature of PowerPoint. Also notice that the incorrect spelling is indicated. As before, we could correct the spelling using the shortcut menu; however, this time we will use another approach.

Concept 4

AutoCorrect

4 The **AutoCorrect** feature makes some basic assumptions about the text you are typing and, based on these assumptions, automatically corrects the entry. The AutoCorrect feature automatically inserts proper capitalization at the beginning of sentences and in the names of days of the week. It also will change to lowercase letters any words that were incorrectly capitalized due to the accidental use of the Caps Lock key. In addition, it also corrects many common typing and spelling errors automatically.

One way the program makes corrections automatically is by looking for certain types of errors. For example, if two capital letters appear at the beginning of a word, the second capital letter is changed to a lowercase letter. If a lowercase letter appears at the beginning of a sentence, the first letter of the first word is capitalized. If the name of a day begins with a lowercase letter, the first letter is capitalized.

Another way the program makes corrections is by automatically replacing a misspelled word with the correct spelling in situations where the spelling checker offers only one suggested spelling correction. Autocorrect also checks all words against the AutoCorrect list, a built-in list of words that are commonly spelled incorrectly or typed incorrectly. If it finds the entry on the list, the program automatically replaces the error with the correction. For example, the typing error "aboutthe" is automatically changed to "about the" because the error is on the AutoCorrect list. You also can add words to the AutoCorrect list that you want to be corrected automatically. Any such words are added to the list on the computer you are using and will be available to anyone who uses the machine after you.

Editing in the Slide Pane

You will correct the spelling of Volunter in the Slide pane because the text in the Outline tab is small and it is easier to work with it in the slide. Simply clicking on the slide pane makes it the active area.

1 ● **Click anywhere in the bulleted text in the Slide pane.**

Your screen should be similar to Figure 1.14

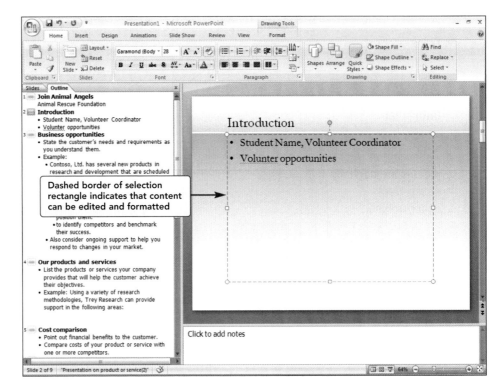

Figure 1.14

Additional Information

A solid-border selection rectangle indicates that you can format the box itself. Clicking the dashed-line border changes it to a solid border.

Notice the bulleted list placeholder is surrounded with a **selection rectangle.** The dashed-line border of the selection rectangle indicates that you can enter, delete, select, and format the object inside the placeholder. Because this placeholder contains text, an insertion point is displayed to show your location in the text and to allow you to select and edit the text. Additionally, the mouse pointer appears as a ⌶ to be used to position the insertion point.

Now, you will correct the spelling of the word. You can position the insertion point anywhere within the text by clicking on the location where you want it to appear.

2 • **Click between the "t" and the "e" in the misspelled word in the slide pane.**

• **Type e.**

• **Click at the end of the line.**

Your screen should be similar to Figure 1.15

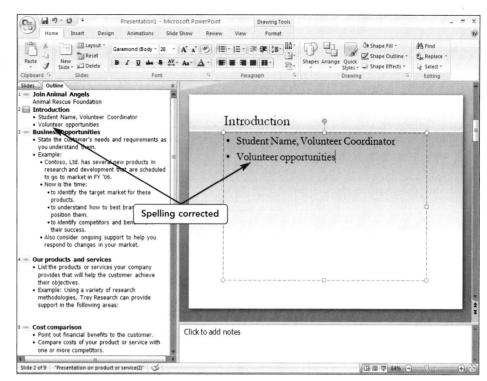

Figure 1.15

The spelling has been corrected and the word is no longer identified as misspelled.

Deleting a Slide

You are now ready to enter the text for the next slide in your presentation by entering the three main topics of discussion. As you look at the suggested content for slide 3, you decide to delete the slide and use slide 4 instead.

1 ● In the Outline tab, click anywhere on slide 3.

● Click 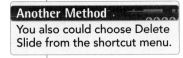 in the Slides group of the Home tab.

Another Method
You also could choose Delete Slide from the shortcut menu.

● In the Outline tab, click anywhere on the new slide 3.

Your screen should be similar to Figure 1.16

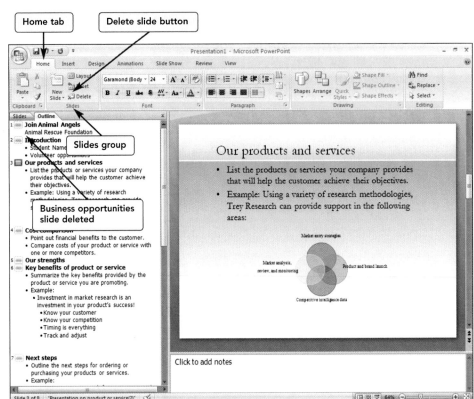

Figure 1.16

The slide is deleted and all following slides are renumbered.

Selecting and Editing Text

You want to enter a new title, Topics of Discussion, with three bulleted items describing the topics to be discussed. Two placeholder bullets with sample text are displayed. You will edit these and add a third bullet. To indicate which placeholder to work with, you click on it to select it.

1 ● Click on the sample title text in the Slide pane to select the title placeholder.

● Triple-click on the sample text to select the entire line.

● Type **Topics of Discussion**.

● Click anywhere on the bulleted list placeholder.

● Drag to select all the text in the placeholder.

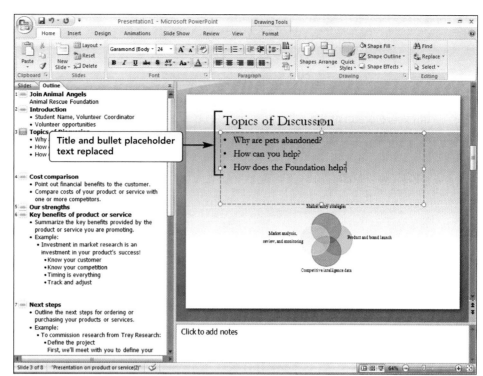

Figure 1.17

Another Method

You also can click [Select ▾] and choose Select All in the Editing Group on the Home tab or the shortcut key [Ctrl] + A to select everything in the placeholder box.

Finally, you want to delete the graphic element on the slide. Notice the graphic does not appear in the Outline tab.

● Type **Why are pets abandoned?**.

● Press [←Enter].

● Type **How can you help?**.

● Press [←Enter].

● Type **How does the Foundation help?**.

Having Trouble?

If you accidentally insert an extra bullet and blank line, press [Backspace] twice to remove them.

Your screen should be similar to Figure 1.17

2
- Click on the graphic in the Slide pane to select it.
- Click ✂ in the Clipboard group of the Home tab.

Your screen should be similar to Figure 1.18

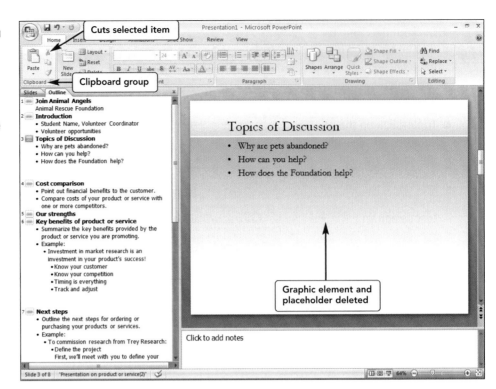

Figure 1.18

The placeholder and its contents have been deleted.

Moving Bulleted Items

You realize that you entered the topics in the wrong order. You want the last item to be the second item in the list. A bulleted point can be moved easily by selecting it and dragging it to a new location. You will move the bulleted item on the current line up one line.

1
- Select all the text in the third bulleted item in the Slide pane.

- Drag the selection to the beginning of the second bulleted item and release the mouse button.

Additional Information
The mouse pointer appears as 🔲 when you drag to move the item.

Your screen should be similar to Figure 1.19

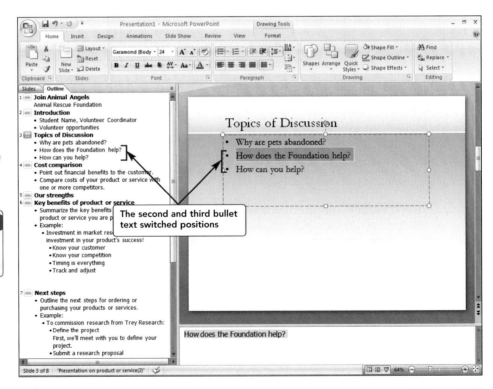

Figure 1.19

The third bullet is now the second bulleted item in the list. You also can drag and move bulleted items in the Outline tab in the same manner.

Moving among Slides

Next, you want to add text for the next few slides. Because you plan to do most of the editing in the Slide pane, you will switch to the Slides tab and increase the width of the tabs pane. This tab makes it easy to move from one slide to another.

1 ● Open the Slides tab.

● Point to the right border of the tabs pane. With the mouse pointer shaped as ←‖→ drag to the right to increase the width of the pane as in Figure 1.20.

● Click on slide 4 in the Slides tab to display it in the Slide pane.

Your screen should be similar to Figure 1.20

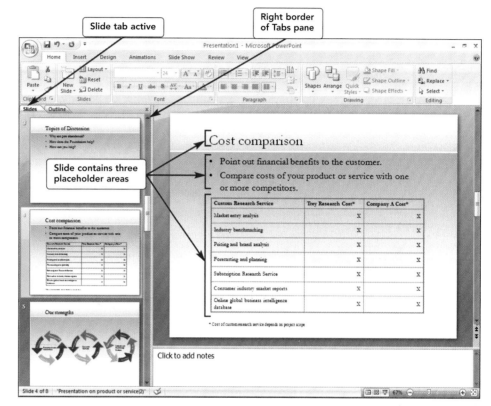

Figure 1.20

This slide contains three placeholder areas: title, bullets, and a table. You decide to take a quick look at the other slides in the presentation before deciding which slides to use. In addition to clicking on the slide in the Outline and Slides tabs, the following features can be used to move to other slides in Normal view.

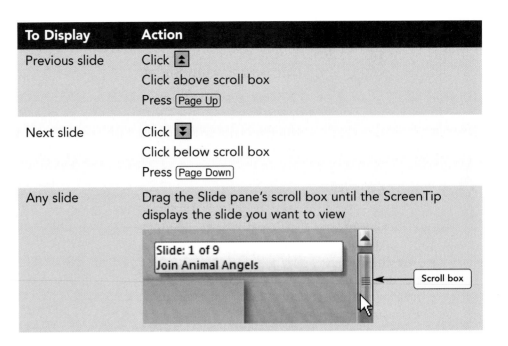

To Display	Action
Previous slide	Click ⏶
	Click above scroll box
	Press (Page Up)
Next slide	Click ⏷
	Click below scroll box
	Press (Page Down)
Any slide	Drag the Slide pane's scroll box until the ScreenTip displays the slide you want to view

Slide: 1 of 9
Join Animal Angels

Scroll box

2 ● Click ⏷ Next Slide to display slide 5.

Having Trouble?

The ⏶ Previous Slide and ⏷ Next Slide buttons are located at the bottom of the Slide pane's vertical scroll bar.

● Press (Page Down) to display slide 6.

● Click below the scroll box twice to display slides 7 and 8.

Your screen should be similar to Figure 1.21

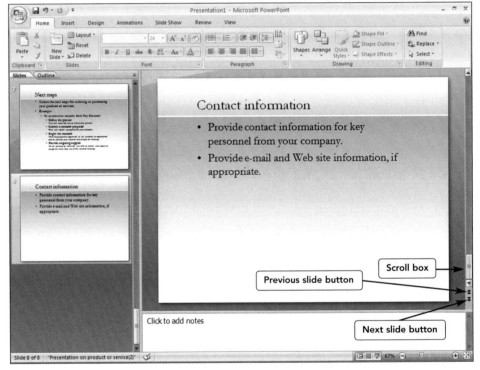

Figure 1.21

After looking at all the sample slides, you decide to use slide 6 as the basis for the next three slides in the presentation.

Moving and Copying Slides

You will move slide 6 above slide 4 and then make two copies of this slide.

1 ● Select slide 6 in the Slides tab.

● Drag it above slide 4 in the Slides tab.

● Click ▣ Copy in the Clipboard group on the Home tab.

● Click [Paste] in the Clipboard group two times.

● Select slide 4 in the Slides tab.

Your screen should be similar to Figure 1.22

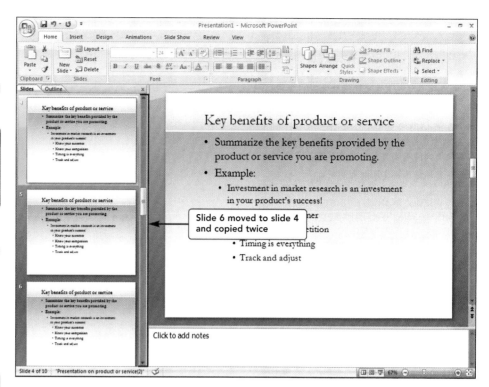

Figure 1.22

There are now three slides with the same content. The copied slides are inserted directly below the slide that was selected.

Now you are ready to enter the text for the next three slides.

2
- Replace the sample title text in slide 4 with **Why are Pets Abandoned?**.

- Delete all the text in the bullet text placeholders and enter the following bullets:

Poor or deteriorating health

Maintenance expenses

Change in lifestyle

Behavioral problems

Moving to a new location

Your screen should be similar to Figure 1.23

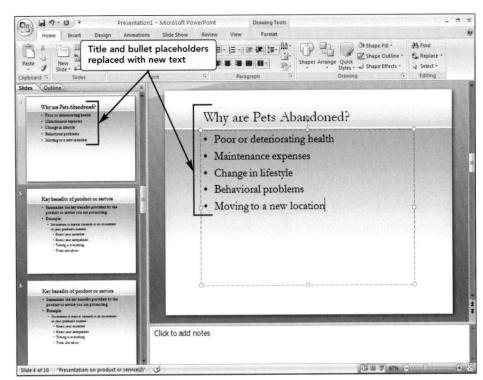

Figure 1.23

In the next slide, you will enter information about how people can help the Animal Rescue Foundation.

3
- Select slide 5.

- Replace the sample title text with **How Can You Help?**.

- Select all the text in the bulleted text placeholder.

- Type **Donate your time and talent**.

- Press ⏎Enter.

Your screen should be similar to Figure 1.24

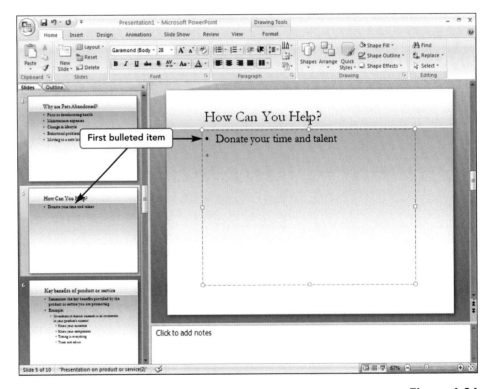

Figure 1.24

Demoting and Promoting Bulleted Items

You want the next bulleted item to be indented below the first bulleted item. Indenting a bulleted point to the right **demotes** it, or makes it a lower or subordinate topic in the outline hierarchy.

1 • **Press** Tab⇆.

• **Type** Become a foster parent.

• **Press** ←Enter.

• **Type** Work at adoption fairs.

• **Press** ←Enter.

Your screen should be similar to Figure 1.25

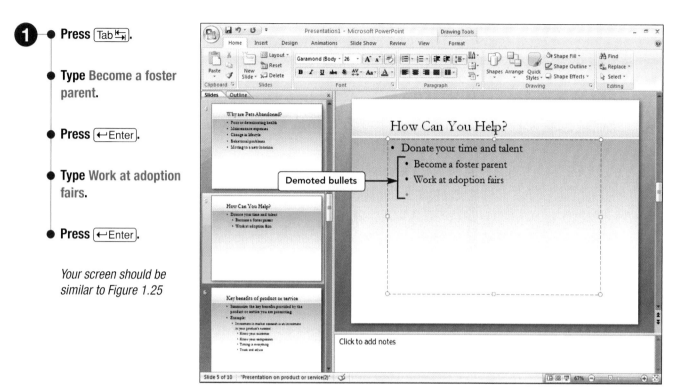

Figure 1.25

When you demote a bulleted point, PowerPoint continues to indent to the same level until you cancel the indent. Before entering the next item, you want to remove the indentation, or **promote** the line. Promoting a line moves it to the left, or up a level in the outline hierarchy.

2 ● Press ⇧Shift + Tab⭾.

● Type **Donate new or used items.**

● Press ←Enter.

● **Enter the next two bulleted items:**

  Crates and pads

  Collars, leads, and other items

  Your screen should be similar to Figure 1.26

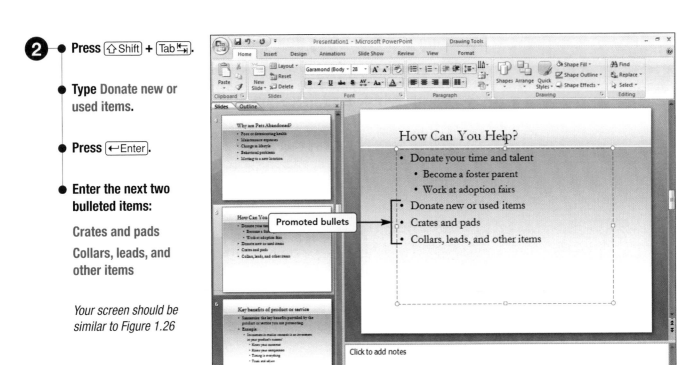

Figure 1.26

You also can promote or demote bulleted items after the text has been entered. The insertion point must be at the beginning of the line to be promoted or demoted or all the text must be selected. You will demote the last two bulleted items.

3 ● **Select the two bulleted items "Crates and pads" and "Collars, leads, and other items."**

● Press Tab⭾.

● **Move to the end of "Collars, leads, and other items."**

● Press ←Enter.

  Your screen should be similar to Figure 1.27

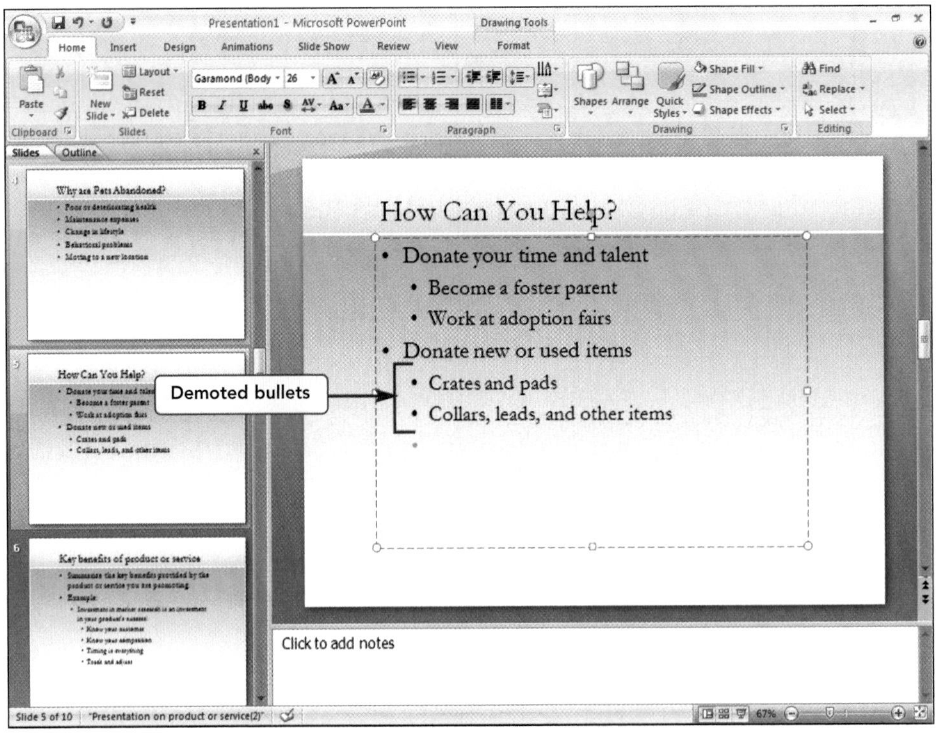

Figure 1.27

The last two items have been demoted. Next you will add more items to the bulleted list.

4
- Type **Provide financial support.**

- Press ⏎Enter.

- **Enter the following three bulleted items:**

  Send a donation
  Sponsor a foster pet
  Sponsor an adoption

- **Promote the "Provide financial support" bullet.**

Your screen should be similar to Figure 1.28

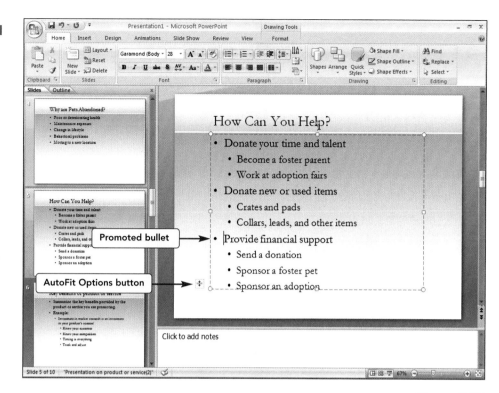

Figure 1.28

As you continued entering more bulleted items, the slide has become very full. Also notice that the ⬦ AutoFit Options button appears at the bottom left corner of the placeholder. It contains options that allow you to control the AutoFit feature and to handle any over-spilling text. The AutoFit feature will automatically adjust the line spacing and text size as needed to display the content inside the placeholder appropriately. Currently, this feature is off in this template.

5
- Click ⬦ AutoFit Options.

- Select **AutoFit Text to Placeholder.**

Your screen should be similar to Figure 1.29

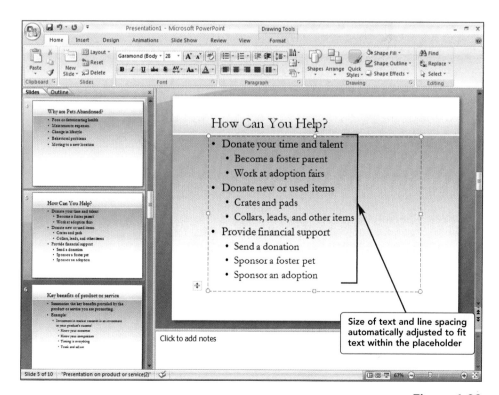

Figure 1.29

Editing a Presentation **PP1.31**

PowerPoint 2007

Now that the AutoFit Text to Placeholder option is on, the text size and line spacing of the bulleted items have been reduced to display the text more comfortably on the slide. If you were to add more text or increase or decrease the size of the placeholder, the AutoFit feature would continue to adjust the text size and spacing.

Splitting Text between Slides

Generally, when creating slides, it is a good idea to limit the number of bulleted items on a slide to six. It also is recommended that the number of words on a line should not exceed five. In this case, because there are 10 bulleted items on this slide, you decide to split the slide content between two slides.

1
- Click ⸬ AutoFit Options.

- Choose Split Text Between Two Slides.

- Scroll the tabs pane so that slides 5 and 6 are visible.

Your screen should be similar to Figure 1.30

New slide inserted and text split between slides

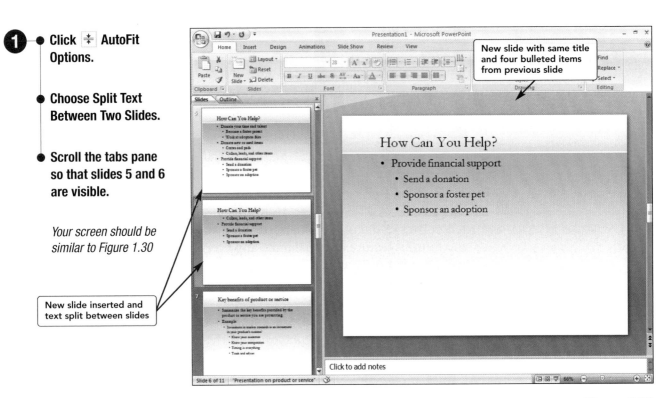

Figure 1.30

A new slide containing the same title as the previous slide and four of the bulleted items from the previous slide are inserted into the presentation. You will edit the slide title of slide 6.

Having Trouble?

You may have noticed that in the tabs pane slide 5 still displays the four bullet items. Do not be concerned. The four bullets have been removed; however, the tabs pane has not been updated to reflect the change.

2 ● **Replace the title text with** More Ways To Help!.

Your screen should be similar to Figure 1.31

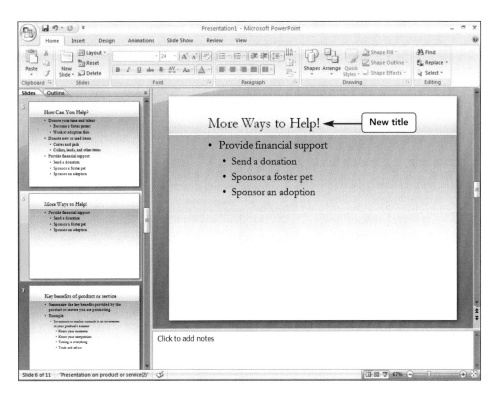

Figure 1.31

Saving, Closing, and Opening a Presentation

You have just been notified about an important meeting that is to begin in a few minutes. Before leaving for the meeting, you want to save the presentation. As you enter and edit text to create a new presentation, the changes you make are immediately displayed onscreen and are stored in your computer's memory. However, they are not permanently stored until you save your work to a file on a disk. After a presentation is saved as a file, it can be closed and opened again at a later time to be edited further.

As a backup against the accidental loss of work caused by a power failure or other mishap, Office 2007 includes an **AutoRecover** feature. When this feature is on, as you work you may see a pulsing disk icon briefly appear in the status bar. This icon indicates that the program is saving your work to a temporary recovery file. The time interval between automatic saving can be set to any period you specify; the default is every 10 minutes. When you start up again, the recovery file containing all changes you made up to the last time it was saved by AutoRecover is opened automatically. You then need to save the recovery file. If you do not save it, it is deleted when closed. While AutoRecover is a great feature for recovering lost work, it should not be used in place of regularly saving your work.

Saving the Presentation

You will save the work you have done so far on the presentation. The Save or Save As commands on the 🄫 Office Button menu are used to save files. The

Save command or the 🖫 Save button on the Quick Access toolbar will save the active file using the same file name by replacing the contents of the existing file with the document as it appears on your screen. The Save As command allows you to save a file with a new file name and/or to a new location. This action leaves the original file unchanged. When a presentation is saved for the first time, either command can be used. It is especially important to save a new presentation very soon after you create it because the AutoRecover feature does not work until a file name has been specified.

● Click **[Save]** Save on the Quick Access toolbar.

Your screen should be similar to Figure 1.32

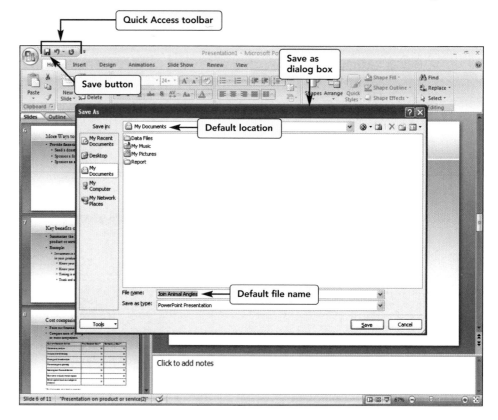

Figure 1.32

The Save As dialog box is displayed, in which you specify the location to save the file and the file name. The Save In list box displays the default location where files are stored. The File Name text box displays the title from the first slide as the default file name. You will change the location to the location where you save your files and the file name. Notice that the default name is highlighted, indicating that it is selected and will be replaced as you type the new name.

2 Type Volunteer.

● Open the Save In list box and select the location where you will save your files.

Your screen should be similar to Figure 1.33

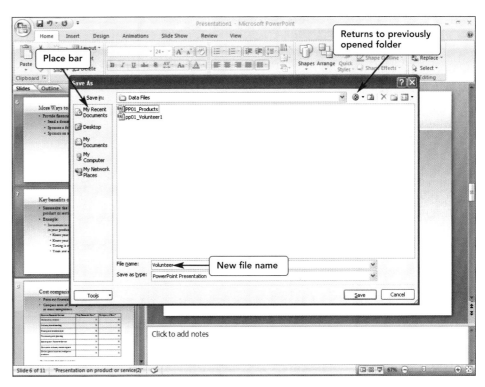

Figure 1.33

The large list box displays the names of any PowerPoint files (if any) stored in that location. Only PowerPoint presentation files are listed, because the selected file type in the Save As Type list box is Presentation. Presentation files have a default file extension of .pptx.

You also can select the save location from the Places bar along the left side of the dialog box. The icons bring up a list of recently accessed files and folders, the contents of the My Documents and Favorites folders, the Windows desktop, and folders that reside on a network or Web through the My Network Places. Selecting a folder from one of these lists changes to that location. You also can click the [Back ▾] button in the toolbar to return to folders that were previously opened during the current session.

 **Click** [Save] **Save.**

Your screen should be similar to Figure 1.34

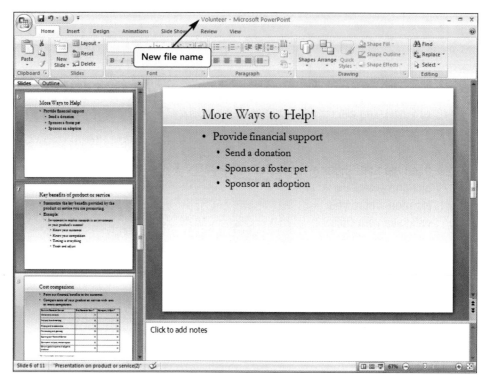

New file name

Figure 1.34

The new file name is displayed in the window title bar. The presentation is now saved in a new file named Volunteer. The view in use at the time the file is saved also is saved with the file.

Closing a Presentation

You are now ready to close the file.

Click 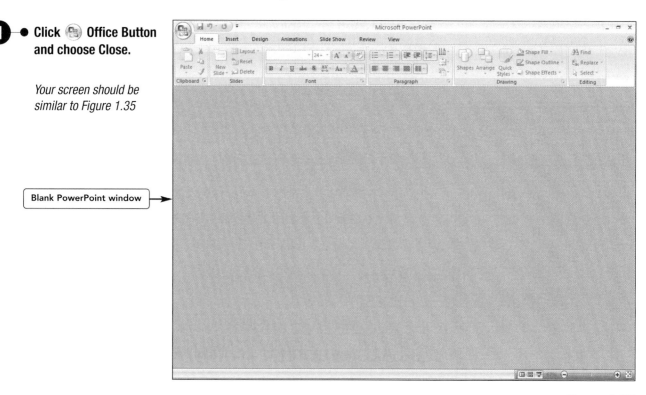 **Office Button and choose Close.**

Your screen should be similar to Figure 1.35

Blank PowerPoint window

Figure 1.35

The presentation is closed, and an empty workspace is displayed. Always save your slide presentation before closing a file or leaving the PowerPoint program. As a safeguard against losing your work if you forget to save the presentation, PowerPoint will remind you to save any unsaved presentation before closing the file or exiting the program.

Note: If you are ending your lab session now, choose 🔘 Office Button, then choose ✕ Exit PowerPoint to exit the program.

Opening an Existing Presentation

After returning from your meeting, you continued to work on the presentation. You revised the content of several of the slides and added information for several new slides. Then you saved the presentation using a new file name. You will open this file to see the changes and will continue working on the presentation.

1 ● Click 🔘 **Office Button and choose Open.**

Another Method
The keyboard shortcut to open a file is ⌃ Ctrl + O.

● **If necessary, select the location containing your data files from the Look In drop-down list box.**

● **Select** pp01_Volunteer1.

Your screen should be similar to Figure 1.36

Additional Information
The 🔘 Office Button/New command opens a blank new presentation. You also can quickly open a recently used file by selecting it from the Recent Documents list in the 🔘 Office Button menu.

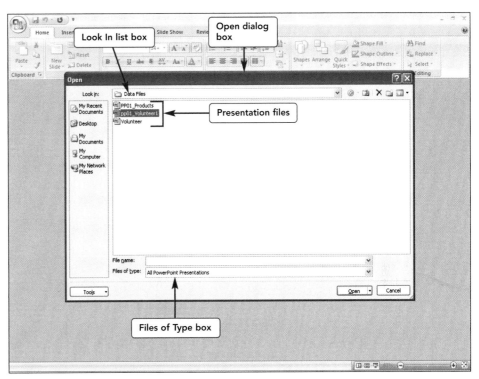

Figure 1.36

In the Open dialog box, you specify the location and name of the file you want to open. The Look In drop-down list box displays the last specified location, in this case the location where you saved the Volunteer presentation. The large list box displays the names of PowerPoint presentation files only, as specified by the setting in the Files of Type box. As in the Save As dialog box, the Places bar can be used to quickly access recently used files.

You will open the selected file next.

2 • Click [Open ▾].

• Open the Outline tab.

• Replace Student Name in slide 1 with your name.

• Scroll the Outline tab to see the additional content that has been added to the presentation.

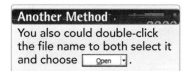

Another Method
You also could double-click the file name to both select it and choose [Open ▾].

Your screen should be similar to Figure 1.37

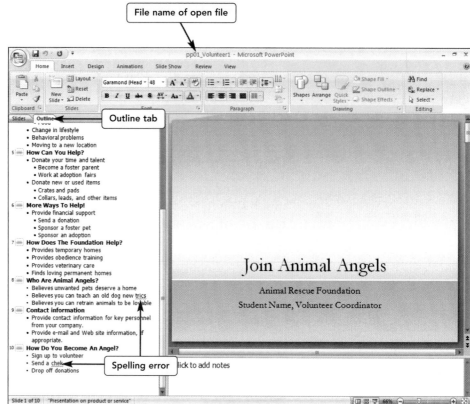

Figure 1.37

The presentation now contains 10 slides, and all the sample text has been replaced with text for the volunteer recruitment presentation, except for slide 10.

Checking Spelling

As you entered the information on the additional slides, you left some typing errors uncorrected. To correct the misspelled words and grammatical errors, you can use the shortcut menu to correct each individual word or error, as you learned earlier. However, in many cases you may find it more efficient to wait until you are finished writing before you correct any spelling or grammatical errors. Rather than continually breaking your train of thought to correct errors as you type, you can check the spelling on all slides of the presentation at once by running the spelling checker.

1 Open the Review Tab.

● Click [ABC Spelling] .

Another Method

The keyboard shortcut to check spelling is [F7].

Your screen should be similar to Figure 1.38

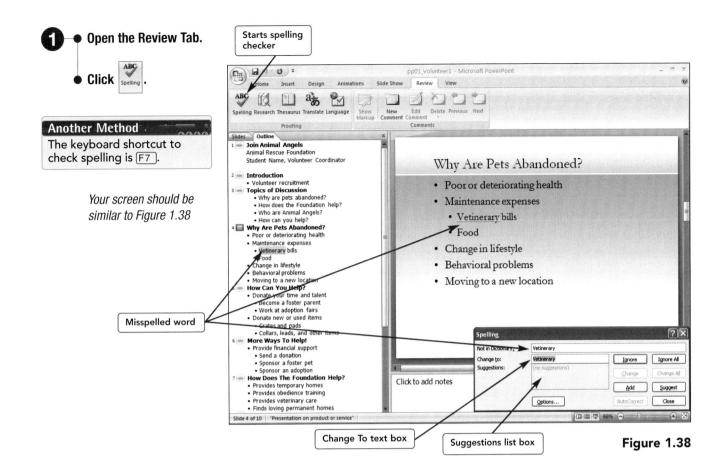

Starts spelling checker

Misspelled word

Change To text box

Suggestions list box

Figure 1.38

The program jumps to slide 4; highlights the first located misspelled word, "Vetinerary," in the Outline pane; and opens the Spelling dialog box. The Spelling dialog box displays the misspelled word in the Not in Dictionary text box. The Suggestions list box typically displays the words the spelling checker has located in the dictionary that most closely match the misspelled word.

In this case, the spelling checker does not display any suggested replacements because it cannot locate any words in the dictionaries that are similar in spelling. If there are no suggestions, the Not in Dictionary text box simply displays the word that is highlighted in the text. When none of the suggestions is correct, you must edit the word yourself by typing the correction in the Change To text box.

Additional Information

The spelling checker identifies many proper names and technical terms as misspelled. To stop this from occurring, use the Add Words To option to add those names to the custom dictionary.

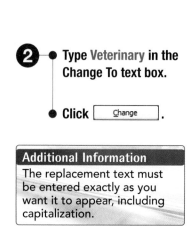

2 ● Type **Veterinary** in the Change To text box.

● Click [Change] .

Additional Information

The replacement text must be entered exactly as you want it to appear, including capitalization.

Additional Information

You also can edit words directly in the presentation and then click [Resume] to continue checking spelling.

Your screen should be similar to Figure 1.39

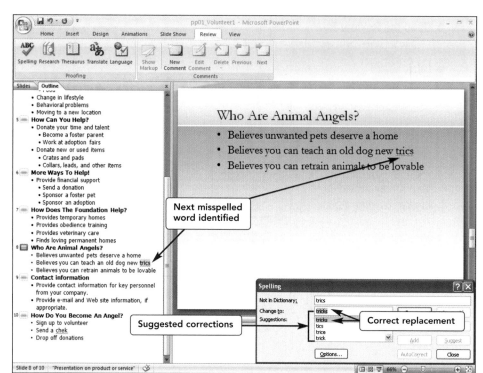

Figure 1.39

The corrected replacement is made in the slide. After the Spelling dialog box is open, the spelling checker continues to check the entire presentation for spelling errors. The next misspelled word, "trics," is identified. In this case, the suggested replacement is correct.

3 ● Click [Change] .

Having Trouble?

If necessary, move the dialog box to see the located misspelled word.

---

4 ● Correct any other located spelling errors as needed.

● Click ⬜ OK ⬜ in response to the message telling you that the spelling check is complete.

● Choose ⬛ Office Button, then Save As to save the revised presentation as Volunteer1 to your solution file location.

Your screen should be similar to Figure 1.40

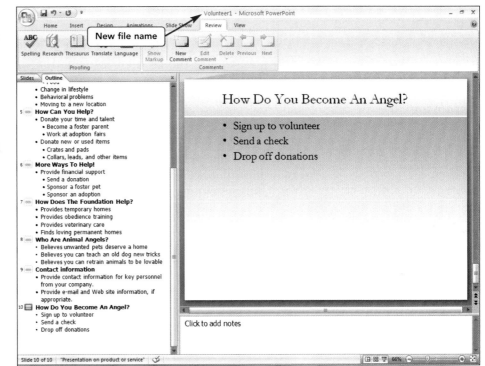

Figure 1.40

You also can use spelling checker in other views. The located errors are highlighted in the Slide pane rather than in the Outline tab.

Working with Slides

To get a better overall picture of all slides in the presentation, you will switch to Slide Sorter view.

1 ● Click ⬛ Slide Sorter.

● Set the zoom to 90%.

Your screen should be similar to Figure 1.41

Having Trouble?
Do not be concerned if your screen displays a different number of slides per row. This is a function of your monitor settings.

Additional Information
The current slide does not change when you switch views.

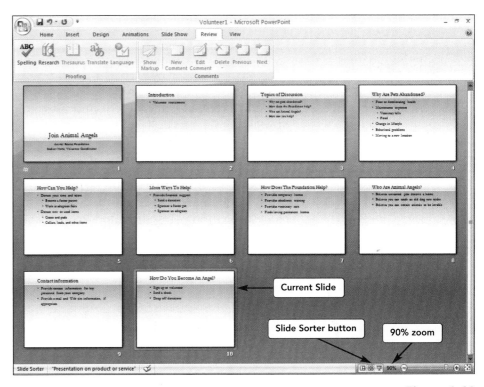

Figure 1.41

Viewing the slides side by side helps you see how your presentation flows. You realize that the second slide is no longer necessary because you added your name to the opening slide. You also decide to delete slide 9 because you plan to add the contact information to slide 10. As you continue to look at the slides, you can now see that slides 7 and 8 are out of order and do not follow the sequence of topics in the Topics of Discussion slide.

Selecting and Deleting Slides

You will delete slides 2 and 9. In this view, it is easy to select and work with multiple slides at the same time. To select multiple slides, hold down Ctrl while clicking on each slide to select it.

① ● Select slide 2, hold down Ctrl, and click on slide 9.

● Press Delete.

Additional Information
You can use the shortcut key Delete to delete a slide in Slide Sorter view and in the Slides tab. However, in the Outline tab and the Slide pane, using Delete deletes text or placeholder content.

Your screen should be similar to Figure 1.42

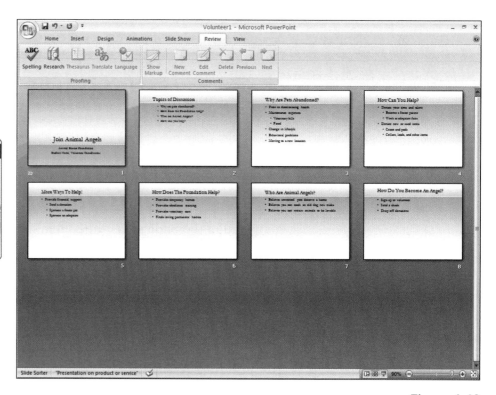

Figure 1.42

The slides have been deleted, and all remaining slides have been appropriately renumbered.

Moving Slides

Now you want to correct the organization of the slides by moving slides 6 and 7 before slide 4. To reorder a slide in Slide Sorter view, you drag it to its new location using drag and drop. As you drag the mouse, an indicator line appears to show you where the slide will appear in the presentation. When the indicator line is located where you want the slide to be placed, release the mouse button. You will select both slides and move them at the same time.

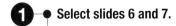

1 • Select slides 6 and 7.

• Point to either selected slide and drag the mouse until the indicator line is displayed before slide 4.

Additional Information

The mouse pointer appears as ⬚ when you drag to move a slide.

• Release the mouse button.

Another Method

You also can use the 📋 Cut and 📋 Paste commands in the Clipboard group on the Home tab to move slides in Slide Sorter view.

Your screen should be similar to Figure 1.43

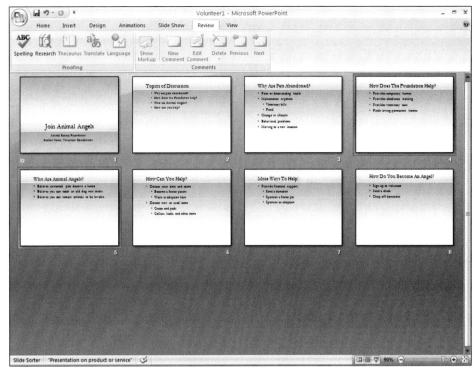

Figure 1.43

The slides now appear in the order you want them.

Inserting Slides

During your discussion with the foundation director, it was suggested that you add a slide showing the history of the organization. To include this information in the presentation, you will insert a new slide after slide 4.

1 ● **Click in the space before slide 5.**

● **Open the Home tab.**

● **Click** 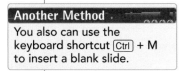 **in the Slides group.**

● **Switch to Normal view and open the Slides tab.**

Your screen should be similar to Figure 1.44

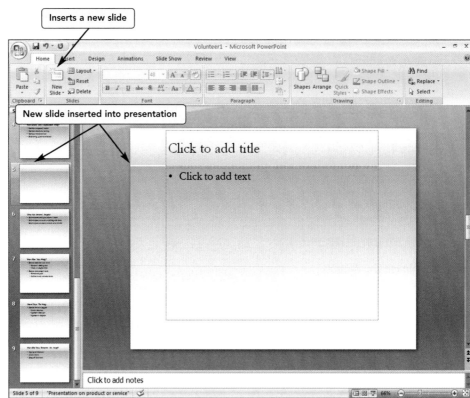

Figure 1.44

A blank new slide is inserted. It has the same design elements as the other slides in the presentation.

Selecting the Slide Layout

The new slide is inserted with the default Title and Text layout. You need to change the layout to accommodate the changes you discussed with the director.

Concept 5

Layout

5 **Layouts** define the position and format for objects and text that will be added to a slide. A layout contains placeholders for the different items such as bulleted text, titles, charts, graphics, and so on. For example, there are text layouts that include placeholders for a title and bulleted text, and content layouts that include placeholders for a table, diagram, chart, or clip art. Many layout elements that can be included on a slide are shown in the following diagram.

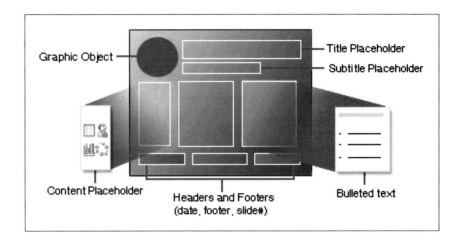

You can change the layout of an existing slide by selecting a new layout. If the new layout does not include placeholders for objects that are already on your slide (for example, if you created a chart and the new layout does not include a chart placeholder), you do not lose the information. All objects remain on the slide and the selected layout is automatically adjusted by adding the appropriate type of placeholder for the object. Alternatively, as you add new objects to a slide, the layout automatically adjusts by adding the appropriate type of placeholder. You also can rearrange, size, and format placeholders on a slide any way you like to customize the slide's appearance.

To make creating slides easy, use the predefined layouts. The layouts help you keep your presentation format consistent and, therefore, more professional.

PowerPoint includes 11 predefined layouts. The number of layouts that are available varies with the template you are using.

1 Click [Layout ▾] in the Slides group.

Your screen should be similar to Figure 1.45

Eleven layouts associated with the current template

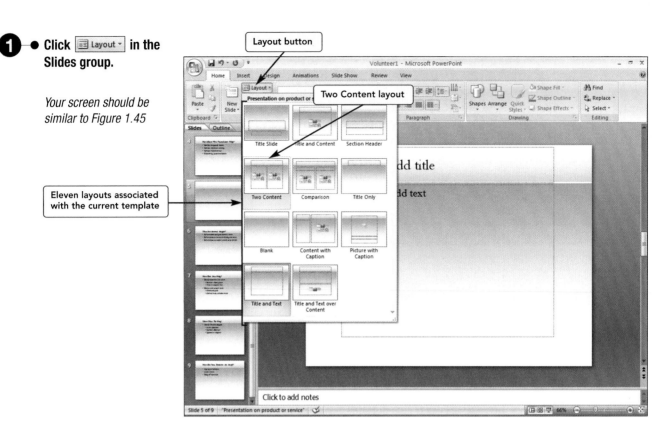

Figure 1.45

The 11 layouts associated with the current template are displayed. Because this slide will contain two columns of text about the history of the organization, you will use the Two Content layout.

2 Select Two Content.

Your screen should be similar to Figure 1.46

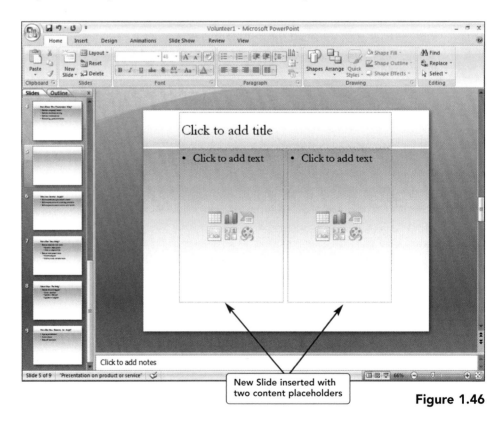

New Slide inserted with two content placeholders

Figure 1.46

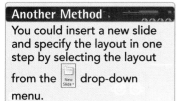
The slide displays the three placeholders created by the Two Content layout. Unlike the template slides, the placeholders on the inserted slide do not contain sample text. When you select the placeholder, you can simply type in the text without having to select or delete any sample text.

You will add text to the slide presenting a brief history of the Animal Rescue Foundation. First, you will enter the slide title and then the list of dates and events.

3
- Click in the title placeholder.

- Type **Animal Rescue Foundation History.**

- Click in the left text placeholder.

- Type **Year.**

- Press ⏎Enter.

- Continue entering the information shown below. Remember to press ⏎Enter to create a new line.

  1990
  1991
  1992
  2000

- In the same manner, enter the following text in the right text placeholders:

  Event
  Founded by Steve Dow
  Built first shelter
  Began volunteer program
  Rescued 1000 animals!

  Your screen should be similar to Figure 1.47

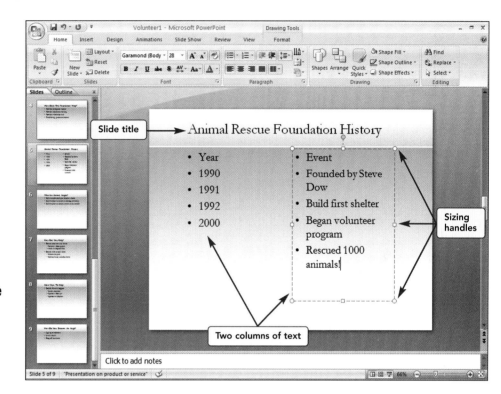

Figure 1.47

The left placeholder is too big for its contents and the right is too small, forcing some items to wrap to a second line. To correct the size, you can adjust the size of the placeholders.

Sizing a Placeholder

The four circles and squares that appear at the corners and sides of a selection rectangle are **sizing handles** that can be used to adjust the size of the placeholder. Dragging the corner sizing handles will adjust both the height and width at the same time, whereas the center handles adjust the associated side borders. When you point to the sizing handle, the mouse pointer appears as ↖, indicating the direction in which you can drag the border to adjust the size.

1 On the right placeholder, drag the left-center sizing handle to the left until each item appears on one line.

- Select the left text placeholder and drag the right-center sizing handle to the left (see Figure 1.48).

Your screen should be similar to Figure 1.48

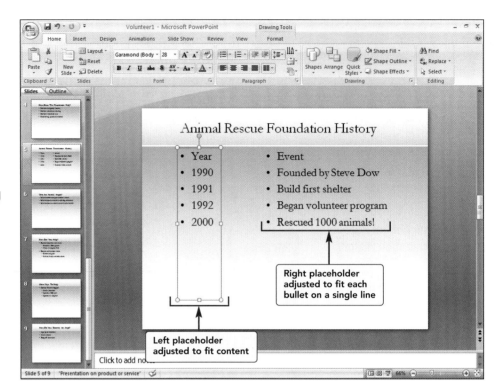

Figure 1.48

Moving a Placeholder

Next, you want to move the Year column placeholder closer to the Event column. Then you want to move both placeholders so they appear more centered in the space. An object can be moved anywhere on a slide by dragging the selection rectangle. The mouse pointer appears as 🔀 when you can move a placeholder. As you drag the placeholder, a dotted outline is displayed to show your new location.

1 • Point to one edge of the Year column selection rectangle (not a handle) until the mouse pointer appears as 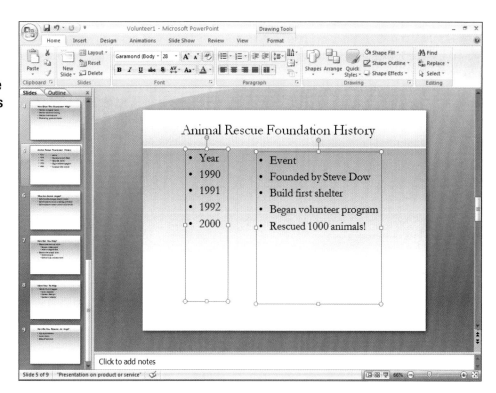 and drag the selected placeholder to the right, closer to the Event column.

• With the left placeholder still selected, hold down [Ctrl] while clicking on the right placeholder to select both.

• Drag the selected placeholders to the left to their new location as shown in Figure 1.49.

• Save your changes to the presentation using the same file name.

Your screen should be similar to Figure 1.49

Figure 1.49

Rehearsing a Presentation

Now that the slides are in the order you want, you would like to see how the presentation would look when viewed by an audience. Rather than set up the presentation as you would to present it for an audience, a simple way to rehearse a presentation is to view it electronically on your screen as a slide show. A **slide show** displays each slide full screen and in order. While the slide show is running, you can plan what you want to say to supplement the information provided on the slides.

Using Slide Show View

When you view a slide show, each slide fills the screen, hiding the PowerPoint application window, so you can view the slides as your audience would. You will begin the slide show starting with the first slide.

1 • Select slide 1 in the Slides tab.

• Click 🖵 Slide Show (in the Status bar).

Additional Information

Using 🖵 Slide Show runs the slide show beginning with the currently selected slide.

Another Method

You also can use [From Beginning] or

[From Current Slide] on the Slide Show tab or the shortcut keys [F5] and [⇧Shift] + [F5] respectively to start the slide show.

Your screen should be similar to Figure 1.50

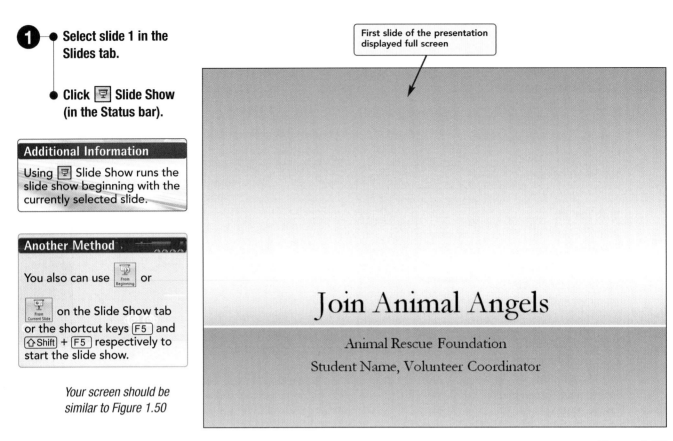

First slide of the presentation displayed full screen

Join Animal Angels

Animal Rescue Foundation
Student Name, Volunteer Coordinator

Figure 1.50

The presentation title slide is displayed full screen, as it will appear when projected on a screen using computer projection equipment. Did you notice that the first slide displayed with a special effect? This feature was included in the template as part of the template design. You will learn about special effects in Lab 2.

The easiest way to see the next slide is to click the mouse button. You also can use the keys shown below to move to the next or previous slide.

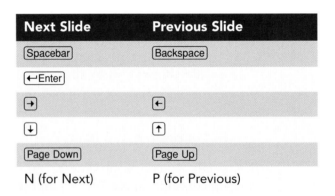

Next Slide	Previous Slide
Spacebar	Backspace
←Enter	
→	←
↓	↑
Page Down	Page Up
N (for Next)	P (for Previous)

You also can select Next, Previous, or Last Viewed from the shortcut menu. Additionally, moving the mouse pointer in Slide Show displays the Slide Show toolbar in the lower-left corner of the window. Clicking ◀ or ➡ moves to the previous or next slide and 📄 opens the shortcut menu.

2 • Click to display the next slide.

• Using each of the methods described, slowly display the entire presentation.

• When the last slide displays a black window, click again to end the slide show.

Additional Information

You can press [Esc] or use End Show on the shortcut menu at any time to end the slide show.

Your screen should be similar to Figure 1.51

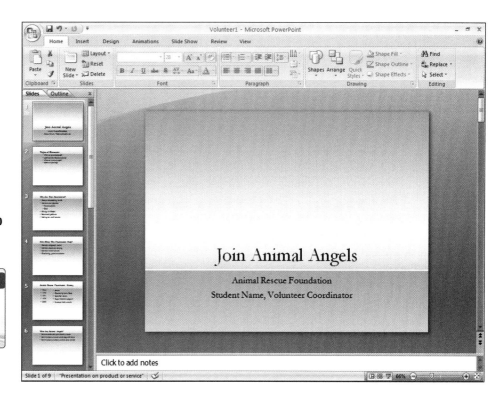

Figure 1.51

After the last slide is displayed, the program returns to the view you were last using, in this case Normal view.

Formatting Slide Text

While looking at the slide show, you decide that the title slide needs to have more impact. You also want to remove the bullets from the items on the history slide. Enhancing the appearance of the slide to make it more readable or attractive is called **formatting.** The design template you are using already includes many formatting features.

Applying different formatting to characters and paragraphs can greatly enhance the appearance of the slide. **Character formatting** features affect the selected characters only. They include changing the character style and size, applying effects such as bold and italics, changing the character spacing, and adding animated text effects. **Paragraph formatting** features affect an entire paragraph. A paragraph is text that has a carriage return from pressing [←Enter] at the end of it. Each item in a bulleted list, title, and subtitle is a paragraph. Paragraph formatting features include the position of the paragraph or its alignment between the margins, paragraph indentation, spacing above and below a paragraph, and line spacing within a paragraph.

Changing Fonts

First, you will improve the appearance of the presentation title by changing the font of the title text.

Concept 6

Font and Font Size

6   A **font,** also commonly referred to as a **typeface,** is a set of characters with a specific design. The designs have names such as Times New Roman and Courier. Using fonts as a design element can add interest to your presentation and give your audience visual cues to help them find information quickly.

There are two basic types of fonts: serif and sans serif. **Serif fonts** have a flair at the base of each letter that visually leads the reader to the next letter. Two common serif fonts are Roman and Times New Roman. Serif fonts generally are used for text in paragraphs. **Sans serif fonts** do not have a flair at the base of each letter. Arial and Helvetica are two common sans serif fonts. Because sans serif fonts have a clean look, they are often used for headings in documents. It is good practice to use only two or three different fonts in a presentation because too many can distract from your presentation content and can look unprofessional.

Each font has one or more sizes. **Font size** is the height and width of the character and is commonly measured in **points,** abbreviated pt. One point equals about 1/72 inch, and text in most documents is 10 pt or 12 pt.

Several common fonts in different sizes are shown in the following table.

Font Name	Font Type	Font Size
Calibri	Sans serif	This is 10 pt. **This is 16 pt.**
Courier New	Serif	This is 10 pt. This is 16 pt.
Garamond	Serif	This is 10 pt. This is 16 pt.

To change the font before typing the text, use the command and then type. All text will appear in the specified setting until another font setting is selected. To change a font setting for existing text, select the text you want to change and then use the command. If you want to apply font formatting to a word, simply move the insertion point to the word and the formatting is automatically applied to the entire word.

1 ● Select the text "Join Animal Angels" in the Slide pane on slide 1.

Your screen should be similar to Figure 1.52

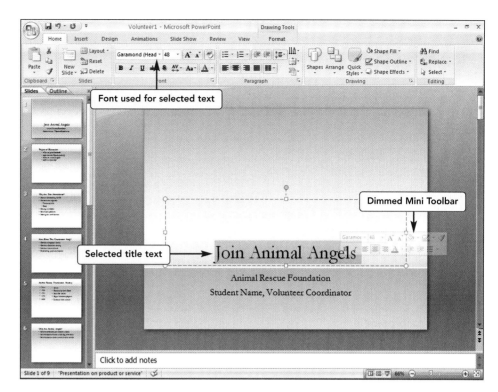

Figure 1.52

The PowerPoint Mini Toolbar appears dimmed whenever you select text. If you want to use it, point to it and it is no longer dimmed. It includes a variety of text formatting options that are also available on the Ribbon. Because the Mini Toolbar appears next to the selected text, it is often quicker and more convenient to choose commands from the Mini toolbar.

You want to change the font to a design that has a less serious appearance.

2 ● Point to the Mini Toolbar.

● Open the Garamon ▾ 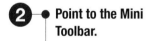 Font drop-down list.

● Scroll the list and choose Comic Sans MS.

Your screen should be similar to Figure 1.53

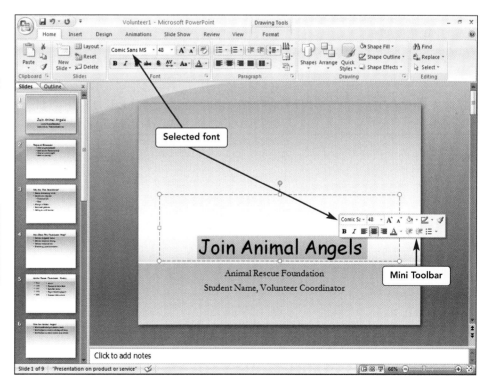

Figure 1.53

Formatting Slide Text   **PP1.53**

PowerPoint 2007

The text has changed to the new font style, and the Font button displays the font name used in the current selection.

Changing Font Size

The title text is also a little smaller than you want it to be.

1 ● Click  Increase Font Size in the Mini Toolbar twice.

Another Method

You also could use click A in the Font group of the Home tab, use the keyboard shortcut Ctrl + ⇧Shift + > or select a size from the 48 ▼ Font Size drop-down menu in the Font group of the Home tab to increase the font size.

Your screen should be similar to Figure 1.54

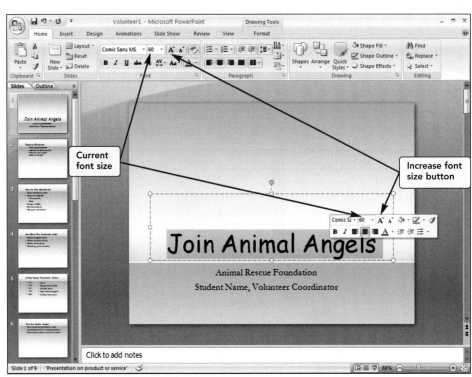

Figure 1.54

Additional Information

Use A Decrease Font Size or Ctrl + ⇧Shift + < to incrementally decrease the point size of selected text.

Additional Information

If a selection includes text in several different sizes, the smallest size appears in the Font Size button followed by a + sign.

The font size increased from 48 points to 54 points and then to 60 points. The Font Size button displays the point size of the current selection.

Adding and Removing Bullets

Next, you want to remove the bullets from the items on the history slide. You can quickly apply and remove bullets using ≡ ▼ Bullets in the Paragraph group on the Home tab. This button applies the bullet style associated with the design template you are using. Because the placeholder items already include bullets, using this button will remove them.

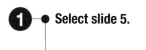

1 • Select slide 5.

• Select both content placeholders.

• Click 📋 ▾ **Bullets** from the Paragraph group in the Home tab.

Your screen should be similar to Figure 1.55

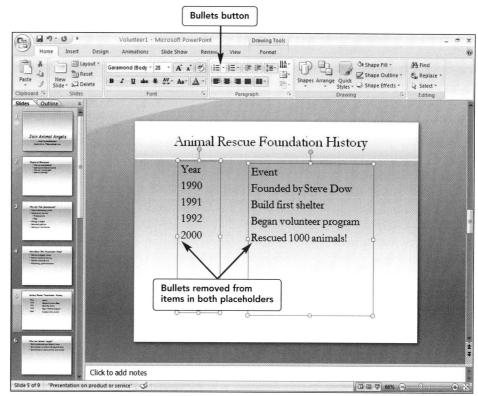

Figure 1.55

The bullets are removed from all the items in both placeholders. Now, however, you think it would look better to add bullets back to the four items under each column heading.

2 • Select the four years in the left column.

• Click 📋 ▾ **Bullets** from the Paragraph group in the Home tab.

• Apply bullets to the four events in the right column.

• Click outside the selected object to deselect it.

• Save the presentation again.

Your screen should be similar to Figure 1.56

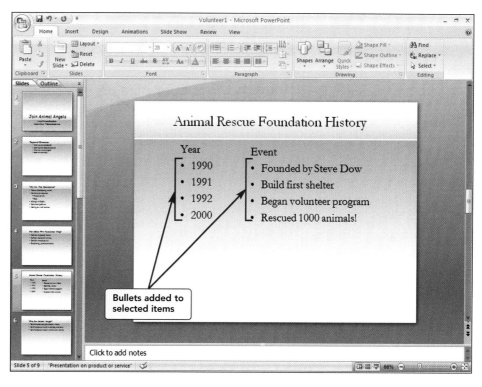

Figure 1.56

Bullets appear before the selected text items only.

Working with Graphics

Finally, you want to add a picture to the title slide. A picture is one of several different graphic objects that can be added to a slide.

Concept 7

Graphics

7 A **graphic** is a nontext element or object, such as a drawing or picture, that can be added to a slide. A graphic can be a simple **drawing object** consisting of shapes such as lines and boxes. A drawing object is part of your presentation document. A **picture** is an image such as a graphic illustration or a scanned photograph. Pictures are graphics that were created from another program and are inserted in a slide as embedded objects. An **embedded object** becomes part of the presentation file and can be opened and edited using the **source program**, the program in which it was created. Any changes made to the embedded object are not made to the original picture file because they are independent. Several examples of drawing objects and pictures are shown below.

Photograph

Graphic illustration

Drawing object

Add graphics to your presentation to help the audience understand concepts, to add interest, and to make your presentation stand out from others.

Graphic files can be obtained from a variety of sources. Many simple drawings called **clip art** are available in the Clip Organizer, a Microsoft Office tool that arranges and catalogs clip art and other media files stored on the computer's hard disk. The Clip Organizer's files, or clips, include art, sound, animation, and movies you can add to a presentation. Additionally, you can access Microsoft's Clip Art and Media Web site for even more graphics.

Digital images created using a digital camera are one of the most common types of graphic files. You also can create graphic files using a scanner to convert any printed document, including photographs, to an electronic format. Most images that are scanned and inserted into documents are stored as Windows bitmap files (.bmp). All types of graphics, including clip art, photographs, and other types of images, can be found on the Internet. These files are commonly stored as .jpg or .pcx files. Keep in mind that any images you locate on the Internet may be protected by copyright and should only be used with permission. You also can purchase CDs containing graphics for your use.

Inserting a Graphic from a File

You want to add a graphic to the opening slide. You want to see how a digital photograph of a litter of puppies you recently received from one of the foster parents would look. The Insert tab includes commands that are designed to enhance a presentation by adding features such as shapes and illustrations to movies and sounds.

1
- Select slide 1.

- Open the Insert tab.

- Click [Picture] in the Illustrations group.

- Change the location to your data file location.

Your screen should be similar to Figure 1.57

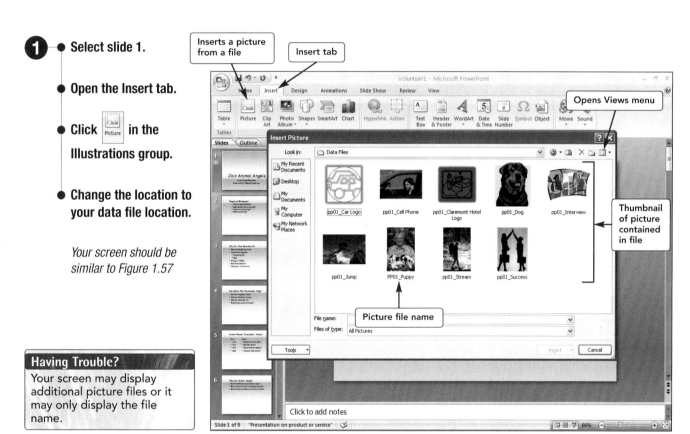

Figure 1.57

The Insert Picture dialog box is similar to the Open and Save dialog boxes, except that the only types of files listed are files with picture file extensions. A thumbnail preview of each picture is displayed above the file name.

2 ● **Select** pp01_Puppy.

● **Click** [Insert |▼].

*Your screen should be
similar to Figure 1.58*

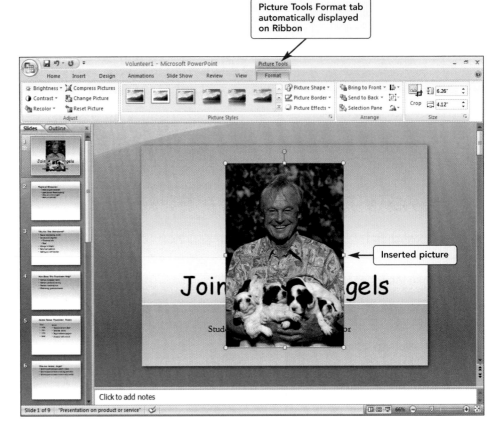

Picture Tools Format tab
automatically displayed
on Ribbon

Inserted picture

Figure 1.58

The picture is inserted in the center of the slide on top of the text. It is a
selected object and can be sized and moved like any other selected object.
The Picture Tools Format tab is automatically displayed in the Ribbon, in
anticipation that you may want to modify the graphic.

Inserting a Graphic from the Clip Organizer

Although you like the picture of the puppies, you want to check the Clip
Art Gallery to see what pictures of animals are available.

Open the Insert tab.

Click [Clip Art].

Your screen should be similar to Figure 1.59

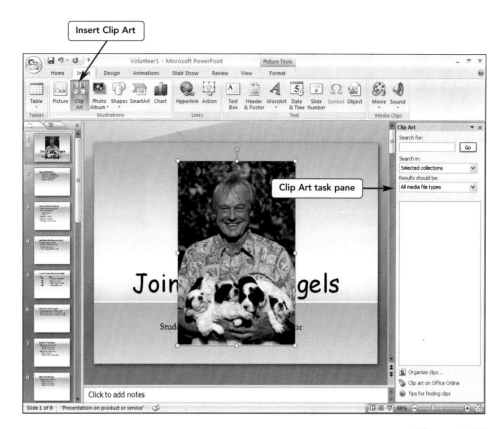

Figure 1.59

In the Clip Art task pane, you specify the locations to search and the type of media files, such as clip art, movies, photographs, or sound, to display in the search results. You want to find clip art or photographs of dogs since there are more dogs in foster care than any other type.

2 If necessary, select any existing text in the Search For text box.

- In the Search For text box, type animals.

- If All Collections is not displayed in the Search In text box, select Everywhere from the drop-down list.

- Open the Results Should Be drop-down list.

- Select Clip Art and deselect the other options.

Having Trouble?
Click the box next to an option to select or deselect (clear the checkmark).

- Click outside the drop-down list to close it.

- Click [Go].

Your screen should be similar to Figure 1.60

Having Trouble?
If your thumbnails appear in a single column, increase the width of your task pane by dragging the left edge of the pane until two columns are displayed.

Having Trouble?
Do not worry if the thumbnails displayed on your screen do not match these shown in Figure 1.60 since the online clip art is continuously changing.

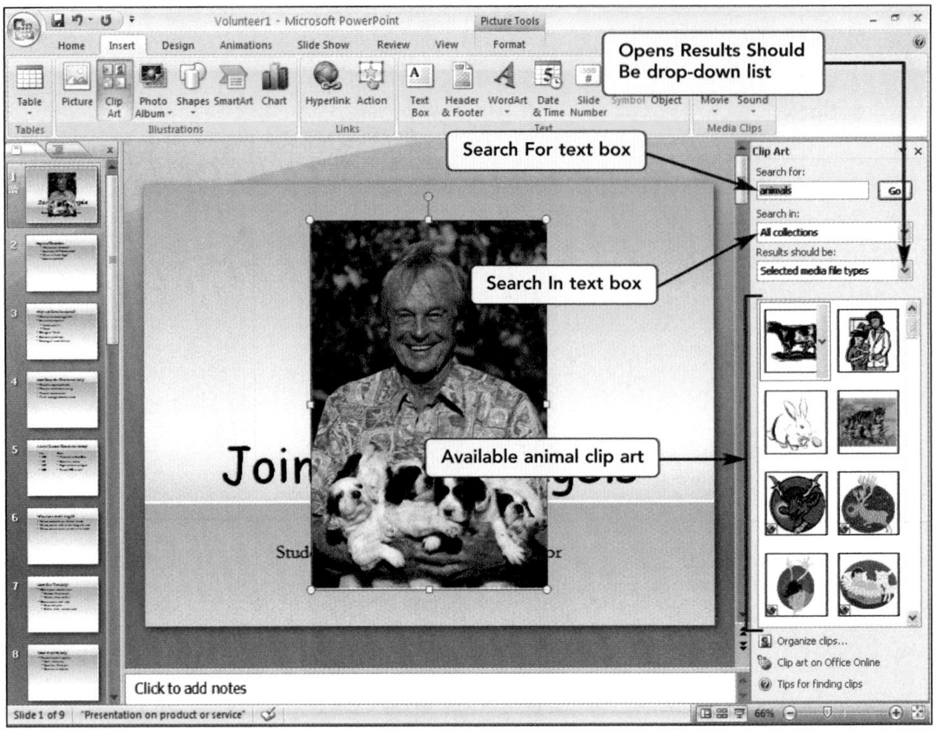

Figure 1.60

The program searches all locations on your computer and, if an Internet connection is established, searches Microsoft's Clip Art and Media Web site for clip art and graphics that match your search term. The Results area displays thumbnails of all located graphics. The pictures stored on your computer in the Microsoft Clip Art gallery appear first in the results list, followed by the Office Online clip art.

Pointing to a thumbnail displays a ScreenTip containing the **keywords** associated with the picture and information about the picture properties. It also displays a drop-down list bar that accesses the item's shortcut menu. The shortcut menu commands are used to work with and manage the items in the Clip Organizer. Because it is sometimes difficult to see the graphic in the thumbnail, you can preview it in a larger size.

3 ● Scroll the list to view additional images.

● Point to any graphic and click ⌄ to open the thumbnail menu.

● Choose Preview/ Properties.

Your screen should be similar to Figure 1.61

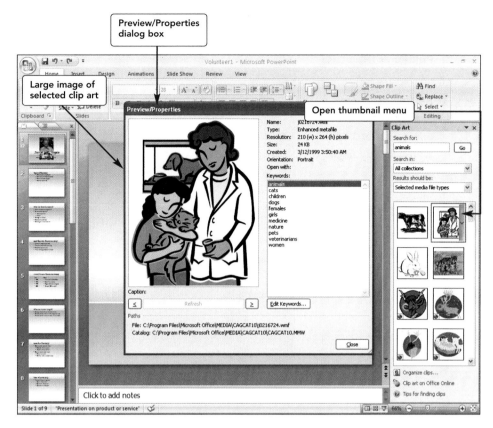

Figure 1.61

Having Trouble?
Do not worry if your preview image does not match Figure 1.61. It will only match if you selected the same graphic in the results area.

The Preview/Properties dialog box displays the selected graphic larger so it is easier to see. It also displays more information about the properties associated with the graphic. Notice the search word you entered appears as one of the keywords associated with the graphic.

After looking at the results, you decide to redefine your search. You want to find graphics of dogs only. To do this, you will use a more specific keyword, in this case "dogs", to narrow the scope of the search to locate graphics associated with that keyword.

4
- Click [Close] to close the Preview/Properties dialog box.

- Replace the word "animals" in the Search For text box with the word **dogs**.

- Click [Go].

Your screen should be similar to Figure 1.62

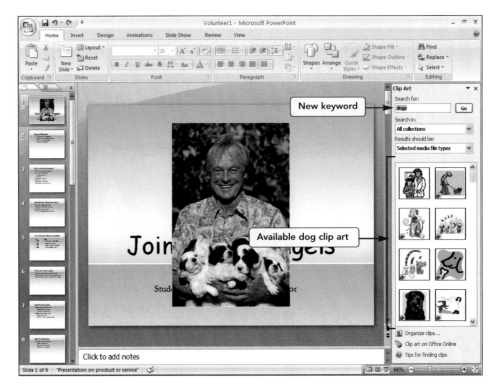

Figure 1.62

Fewer graphics were located because the term you used was more specific. Now you will scroll the list of graphics to find one you like.

5
- Scroll the list to locate the graphic shown in Figure 1.63.

- Click on the graphic to insert it in the slide.

Another Method
You also could choose Insert from the thumbnail's shortcut menu to insert the graphic.

Your screen should be similar to Figure 1.63

Having Trouble?
If this graphic is not available in the Clip Organizer, close the Clip Art task pane and click [Picture] from the Illustrations group on the Insert tab. Then insert pp01_Dog from your data file location.

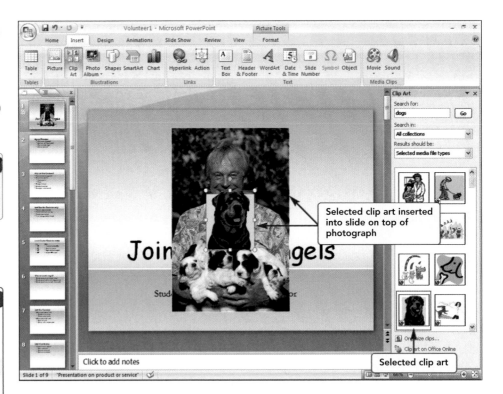

Figure 1.63

The second graphic is inserted on the slide on top of the photograph object. As objects are added to a slide, they automatically stack in individual layers.

Concept 8

Stacking Order

8 Stacking order is the order in which objects are inserted into different layers of the slide. As each object is added to the slide, it is added to the top layer. Adding objects to separate layers allows each object to be positioned precisely on the page, including in front of and behind other objects. As objects are stacked in layers, they may overlap. To change the stacking order, the Picture Tools tab is used. The Picture Tools tab will appear whenever a picture object is selected.

Additional Information

Sometimes it is easy to lose an object behind another. If this happens, you can press [Tab↹] to cycle forward or [⇧Shift] + [Tab↹] to cycle backward through the stacked objects until the one you want is selected.

Because the photograph was the first object added to the slide, it is on the bottom layer of the stack. Although the clip art looks good, you think the photo shows the enjoyment gained from volunteering better.

6 ● If necessary, select the clip art.

● Press [Delete] to remove the selected object.

Enhancing Graphics

When a graphic object is inserted into a slide, it can be manipulated in many ways. For example, you can move, size, or crop it; change colors; add borders; change the shape; and add effects such as shadows and reflections.

Sizing and Cropping a Graphic

Additional Information

Be careful when increasing the size of a picture (bitmap) image as it can lose sharpness and appear blurry if enlarged too much.

First you need to size and position the picture on the slide. A graphic object is sized and moved just like a placeholder. You want to decrease the graphic size slightly and position it in the space above the title.

1 ● Click on the graphic to select it.

● Drag the bottom right corner sizing handle inward to decrease its size to that shown in Figure 1.64.

● Drag the graphic to position it as shown in Figure 1.64.

Your screen should be similar to Figure 1.64

Figure 1.64

Although this is better, you decide it is not the right shape for the space. You will remove the upper part of the picture by cropping it to show the puppies only. This will make the picture smaller and rectangular shaped.

2 ● Open the Picture Tools Format tab.

● Click  from the Size group.

Additional Information
The mouse pointer appears as ⬚ when it is used to crop a picture

● Point to the upper-left corner of the photo and when the mouse pointer changes to a ┌, drag down to just above the puppies.

● Click  from the Size group to turn off this feature.

● Size and move the picture as in Figure 1.65.

Your screen should be similar to Figure 1.65

Figure 1.65

Adding a Picture Style

Next, you want to enhance the graphic by applying a picture style to it. **Picture styles** are combinations of border, shadow, and shape effects that can be applied in one simple step. You also can create your own picture style effects by selecting specific style elements, such as borders and shadows, individually using the [🔲 Picture Shape ▾], [🖼 Picture Border ▾], and [🔲 Picture Effects ▾] buttons.

1 ● Click ⊡ **More in the Picture Styles group to open the Picture Styles gallery.**

● **Point to several styles to see the Live Preview.**

Your screen should be similar to Figure 1.66

Figure 1.66

Additional Information

The Live Preview feature is also available with many other formatting features. It does not appear if you use the Mini Toolbar to apply formatting.

When you point to a style, the style name appears in a ScreenTip and the selected graphic displays how the selected picture style will look with your graphic if chosen. This is the **Live Preview** feature of PowerPoint. As you can see, many are not appropriate. However, you decide that the Metal Rounded Rectangle style will enhance the graphic and the slide.

2 ● Select ⬚ **the Metal Rounded Rectangle style.**

Your screen should be similar to Figure 1.67

Figure 1.67

As you look at the picture, you decide to remove the rectangle and instead use an oval shape with a black border.

● Click 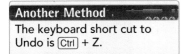 Undo in the Quick Access toolbar.

Another Method
The keyboard short cut to Undo is Ctrl + Z.

Your screen should be similar to Figure 1.68

Figure 1.68

Additional Information
If you click ↶ Undo multiple times, you remove the last actions one by one in sequence.

Using Undo reverses your last action. Notice that the Undo button includes a drop-down list button. Clicking this button displays a list of the most recent actions that can be reversed, with the most recent action at the top of the list. When you select an action from the drop-down list, you also undo all actions above it in the list.

4
- Select the ⬭ Metal Oval style.

- Click 📝 Picture Border ▾ on the Picture Styles group.

Your screen should be similar to Figure 1.69

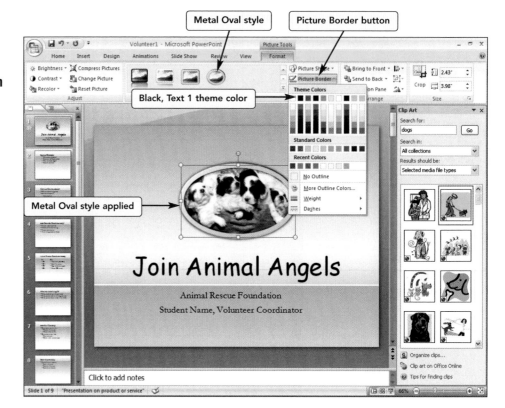

Figure 1.69

A drop-down gallery of Picture Border colors is displayed. You will change the border color to black.

5
- Click the Black, Text 1 from the Theme Colors group.

- Click outside the graphic to deselect the object.

- Close the Clip Art task pane.

- Save the presentation again.

- Run the slide show from the first slide.

Additional Information
You will learn about Themes in Lab 2.

With the addition of the graphic, the title slide will make a much better impression.

Previewing and Printing the Presentation

Although you still plan to make many changes to the presentation, you want to provide a copy of the slides to the foundation director to get feedback regarding the content and layout. Although your presentation looks good on your screen, it may not look good when printed. Previewing the presentation allows you to see how it will look before you waste time and paper printing it out. Many times, you will want to change the print and layout settings to improve the appearance of the output.

Previewing the Presentation

Shading, patterns, and backgrounds that look good on the screen can make printed handouts unreadable, so you want to preview how the printout will look before making a copy for the director.

1 ● **Click** ⊕ **Office Button and select Print.**

● **Choose Print Preview from the Print submenu.**

Your screen should be similar to Figure 1.70

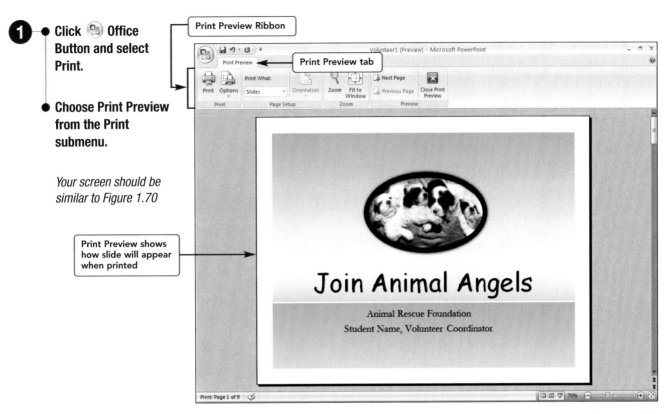

Figure 1.70

The Print Preview window displays the first slide in the presentation as it will appear when printed using the selected printer. It is displayed in color if your selected printer is a color printer; otherwise, it appears in grayscale (shades of gray). Even if you have a color printer, you can print the slides in grayscale or pure black and white. The Print Preview tab is used to modify the default print settings. You will print the slides in black and white.

Additional Information

Use grayscale when your slides include patterns whose colors you want to appear in shades of gray.

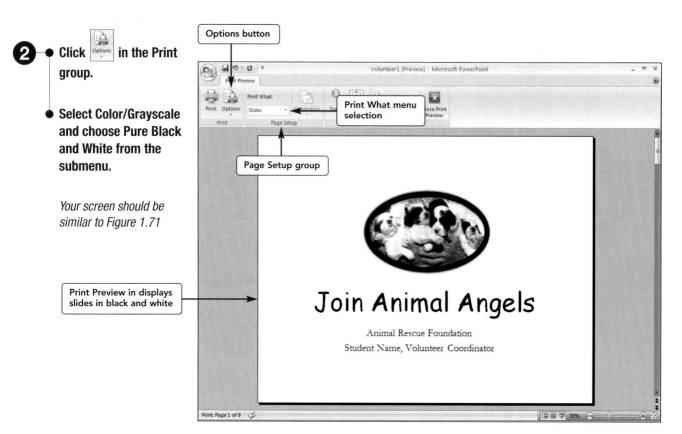

2 • Click [Options] in the Print group.

• Select Color/Grayscale and choose Pure Black and White from the submenu.

Your screen should be similar to Figure 1.71

Figure 1.71

The preview shows how the slide will look when printed in black and white.

Specifying Printed Output

The Preview window displays a single slide on the page as it will appear when printed. This is the default print setting. You can change the type of printed output using the Print What menu selection. The output types are described in the table below. Only one type of output can be printed at a time.

Output Type	Description
Slides	Prints one slide per page.
Handouts	Prints multiple slides per page.
Notes Pages	Prints the slide and the associated notes on a page.
Outline View	Prints the slide content as it appears in Outline view.

Additional Information
You will learn about notes in Lab 2.

You want to change the print setting to Handouts to print several slides on a page.

1 • **Click** Slides ▾
Print What in the Page Setup group and choose Handouts (6 Slides Per Page).

Your screen should be similar to Figure 1.72

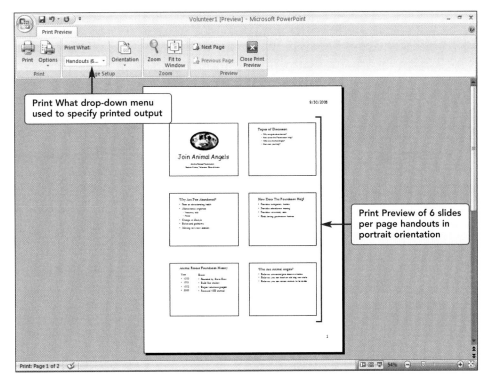

Print What drop-down menu used to specify printed output

Print Preview of 6 slides per page handouts in portrait orientation

Figure 1.72

Changing Page Orientation

You also want to change the orientation or the direction the output is printed on a page. The default orientation for handouts is **portrait.** This setting prints across the width of the page. You will change the orientation to **landscape** so that the slides print across the length of the paper. Then you will preview the other pages.

1 • **Click** Orientation **in the Page Setup group and choose Landscape.**

• **Click** Next Page **in the Preview group.**

Your screen should be similar to Figure 1.73

The second page of handouts in landscape orientation

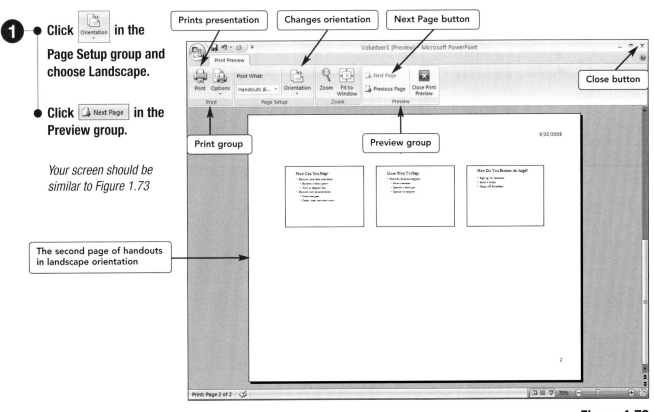

Prints presentation

Changes orientation

Next Page button

Close button

Print group

Preview group

Figure 1.73

The last three slides in the presentation are displayed on the second page in landscape orientation.

Printing the Presentation

Now, you are ready to print the handouts.

1 ● Click 🖶 in the Print group.

Another Method
The menu equivalent to print is 🔘 Office Button/Print and the keyboard shortcut is Ctrl + P.

Your screen should be similar to Figure 1.74

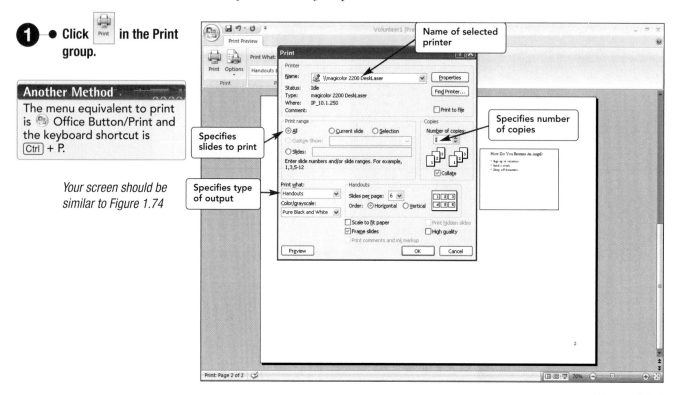

Figure 1.74

Note: Please consult your instructor for printing procedures that may differ from the following directions.

The Name text box in the Printer section displays the name of the selected printer. You may need to specify the printer you will be using. (Your instructor will provide the printer to select.) The Print Range settings specify the slides to print. The default setting, All, prints all the slides, while Current Slide prints only the slide you are viewing. The Slides option is used to specify individual slides or a range of slides to print by entering the slide numbers in the text box. The Copies section is used to specify the number of copies of the specified print range. The default is to print one copy.

At the bottom of the dialog box, PowerPoint displays many of the same options to control color output, number of slides per page, and orientation. The options you specified in the Print Preview window are already selected. The Frame Slides option is selected by default and displays a border around each slide.

2 ● If you need to select a different printer, open the Name drop-down list and select the appropriate printer.

● If necessary, make sure your printer is on and ready to print.

● Click [OK].

● Click  .

A printing progress bar appears in the status bar, indicating that the program is sending data to the Print Manager, and your handouts should be printing. Your printed output should be similar to that shown in the Case Study at the beginning of the lab.

Exiting PowerPoint

You have finished working on the presentation for now and will exit the PowerPoint program.

1 ● Click ⊠ Close in the title bar.

● If asked to save the file again, click [Yes].

> **Another Method**
> The menu equivalent to exit PowerPoint is 🗔 Office Button/⊠ Exit PowerPoint .

Focus on Careers

EXPLORE YOUR CAREER OPTIONS

Account Executive

Sales is an excellent entry point for a solid career in any company. Account Executive is just one of many titles that a sales professional may have; Field Sales and Sales Representative are two other titles. Account executives take care of customers by educating them on the company's latest products, designing solutions using the company's product line, and closing the deal to make the sale and earn their commission. These tasks require the use of effective PowerPoint presentations that educate and motivate potential customers. The salary range of account executives is limited only by his/her ambition; salaries range from $30,000 to more than $120,540. To learn more about this career, visit the Web site for the Bureau of Labor Statistics of the U.S. Department of Labor.

LAB 1
Creating a Presentation

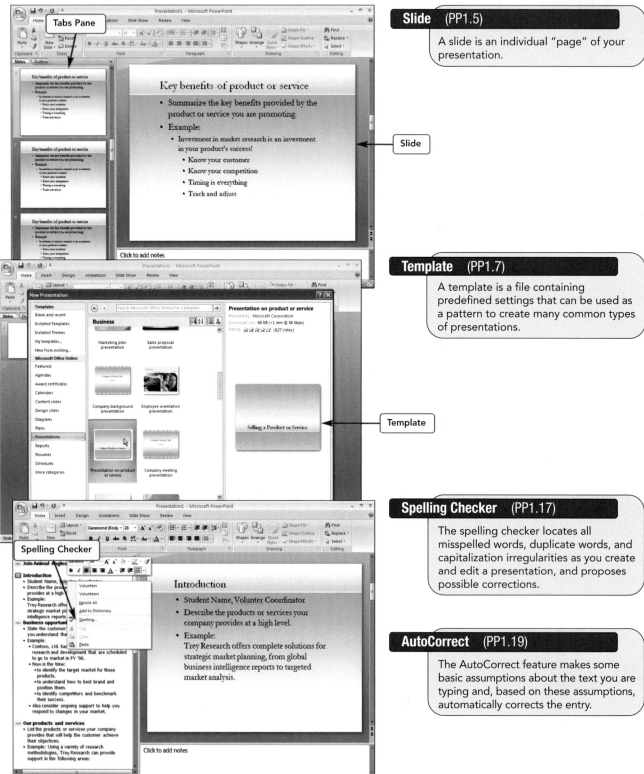

Slide (PP1.5)

A slide is an individual "page" of your presentation.

Template (PP1.7)

A template is a file containing predefined settings that can be used as a pattern to create many common types of presentations.

Spelling Checker (PP1.17)

The spelling checker locates all misspelled words, duplicate words, and capitalization irregularities as you create and edit a presentation, and proposes possible corrections.

AutoCorrect (PP1.19)

The AutoCorrect feature makes some basic assumptions about the text you are typing and, based on these assumptions, automatically corrects the entry.

Layout (PP1.45)

Layouts define the position and format for objects and text that will be added to a slide. A layout contains placeholders for the different items such as bulleted text, titles, charts, and so on.

Font and Font Size (PP1.52)

A font, also commonly referred to as a typeface, is a set of characters with a specific design. The designs have names such as Times New Roman and Courier. Each font has one or more sizes.

Graphics (PP1.56)

A graphic is a nontext element or object, such as a drawing or picture, that can be added to a slide

Stacking Order (PP1.63)

Stacking order is the order in which objects are inserted into different layers of the slide.

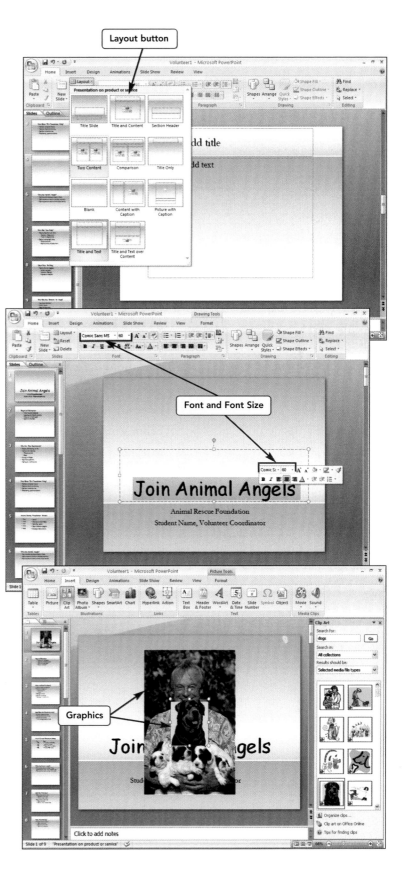

key terms

AutoCorrect   PP1.19

AutoRecover   PP1.33

character formatting   PP1.51

clip art   PP1.56

current slide   PP1.11

custom dictionary   PP1.17

default settings   PP1.6

demote   PP1.29

drawing object   PP1.56

embedded object   PP1.56

font   PP1.52

font size   PP1.52

formatting   PP1.51

graphic   PP1.56

keyword   PP1.60

landscape   PP1.70

layout   PP1.45

Live Preview   PP1.66

main dictionary   PP1.17

Notes pane   P1.10

object   PP1.15

Outline tab   P1.10

paragraph formatting   PP1.51

picture   PP1.56

picture style   P1.65

placeholder   PP1.15

placeholder text   P1.9

point   PP1.52

portrait   PP1.70

promote   PP1.29

sans serif font   PP1.52

selection rectangle   PP1.20

serif font   PP1.52

sizing handles   PP1.47

slide   PP1.5

Slide pane   P1.10

slide show   PP1.49

Slides tab   P1.10

source program   PP1.56

spelling checker   PP1.17

stacking order   PP1.63

template   PP1.7

thumbnail   PP1.8

typeface   PP1.52

view   PP1.9

workspace   PP1.5

command summary

Command	Shortcut	Action
🏢 Office Button		
New		Opens New Presentation dialog box
Open	Ctrl + O	Opens existing presentation
Save	Ctrl + S	Saves presentation
Save As	F12	Saves presentation using new file name and/or location
Print/Print	Ctrl + P	Opens Print dialog box
Print/Print Preview		Displays preview of presentation
Close		Closes presentation
✕ Exit PowerPoint		Closes PowerPoint
Quick Access Toolbar		
💾 Save	Ctrl + S	Saves presentation
↩ ▾ Undo	Ctrl + Z	Reverses last action
Home tab		
Clipboard group		
Paste	Ctrl + V	Pastes item from Clipboard
✂ Cut	Ctrl + X	Cuts selection to Clipboard
📋 Copy	Ctrl + C	Copies selection to Clipboard
Slides group		
New Slide ▾	Ctrl + M	Inserts new slide with selected layout
📑 Layout ▾		Changes layout of a slide
✖ Delete		Deletes selected slide
Font group		
Eras Medium ITC ▾ Font		Changes font type
48 ▾ Size		Changes font size
Paragraph group		
☰ ▾ Bullets/Bullets and Numbering/Bulleted		Formats bullets and numbers

Command	Shortcut	Action
Editing group		
[🔽 Select ▾] /Select All	Ctrl + A	Selects everything in the placeholder box
Insert tab		
Illustrations group		
[Clip Art]		Inserts clip art
[Picture]		Inserts a picture from file
Slide Show tab		
Start Slide Show group		
[From Beginning]	F5	Displays presentation starting with the first slide
[From Current Slide]	⇧ Shift + F5	Displays presentation starting with the current slide
Review tab		
Proofing group		
[Spelling]	F7	Spell-checks presentation
View tab		
Presentation Views group		
[Normal]		Switches to Normal view
[Slide Sorter]		Switches to Slide Sorter view
[Slide Show]		Runs slide show
Picture Tools Format tab		
Size group		
[Crop]		Crops picture to remove unwanted parts

command summary

Command	Shortcut	Action
Picture Styles group		
⊟ More		Applies an overall visual style to picture
📷 Picture Shape ▾		Changes shape of drawing
📝 Picture Border ▾		Applies a border style to picture
🖼 Picture Effects ▾		Applies a visual effect to picture
Print Preview tab		
Page Setup group		
Slides ▾ Print What		Specifies what is to be printed
Orientation		Sets either Portrait or Landscape layout

screen identification

1. In the following PowerPoint screen, letters identify important elements. Enter the correct term for each screen element in the space provided.

Possible answers for the screen identification are:

Clip art	Ribbon	**A.** _____	**I.** _____
Current slide	Selection handle	**B.** _____	**J.** _____
File name	Slide pane	**C.** _____	**K.** _____
Group	Slide tab	**D.** _____	**L.** _____
Object	Status bar	**E.** _____	**M.** _____
Office Button	Subtitle	**F.** _____	**N.** _____
Outline tab	Tab	**G.** _____	**O.** _____
Notes pane	Thumbnail	**H.** _____	**P.** _____

matching

Match the item on the left with the correct description on the right.

1. AutoRecover _____ **a.** define the position and format for objects and text that will be added to a slide

2. demote _____ **b.** sample text that suggests the content for the slide

3. embedded object _____ **c.** becomes part of the presentation file and can be opened and edited using the source program

4. font size _____ **d.** program that automatically saves work to a temporary file

5. layout _____ **e.** displays each slide as a thumbnail

6. Notes pane _____ **f.** height and width of the character commonly measured in points

7. placeholder text _____ **g.** small image

8. slide _____ **h.** includes space to enter notes that apply to the current slide

9. Slides tab _____ **i.** indent a bulleted point to the right

10. thumbnail _____ **j.** individual page of a presentation

multiple choice

Circle the correct response to the questions below.

1. When the spelling checker is used, you can create a(n) _____ dictionary to hold words that you commonly use but are not included in the main dictionary.
   a. custom
   b. official
   c. personal
   d. common

2. If you want to provide copies of your presentation to the audience showing multiple slides on a page, you would print _____.
   a. slides
   b. handouts
   c. note pages
   d. outline area

3. The _____ feature makes some basic assumptions about the text you are typing and, based on these assumptions, automatically corrects the entry.
   a. spell checker
   b. grammar checker
   c. template
   d. AutoCorrect

4. The step in the development of a presentation that focuses on determining the length of your speech, the audience, the layout of the room, and the type of audiovisual equipment available is _____.

   a. planning
   b. creating
   c. editing
   d. enhancing

5. _____ displays a miniature of each slide to make it easy to reorder slides, add special effects such as transitions, and set timing between slides.

   a. publish
   b. slide sorter
   c. template
   d. normal view

6. A _____ is a file containing predefined settings that can be used as a pattern to create many common types of presentations.

   a. graphic
   b. slide
   c. presentation
   d. template

7. If you want to work on all aspects of your presentation, switch to _____ view, which displays the Slide pane, Outline pane, and Note pane.

   a. Slide Sorter
   b. Outline
   c. Slide
   d. Normal

8. A _____ is a nontext element or object, such as a drawing or picture, that can be added to a slide.

   a. slide
   b. graphic
   c. text box
   d. template

9. A(n) _____ is an onscreen display of your presentation.

   a. outline
   b. handout
   c. slide show
   d. slide

10. A font, also commonly referred to as (a) _____, is a set of characters with a specific design.

   a. typeface
   b. font size
   c. graphic
   d. Times New Roman

Circle the correct answer to the following questions.

1.	Font is commonly measured in pixels.	True	False
2.	An embedded file cannot be edited in the source program.	True	False
3.	A slide is a set of characters with a specific design.	True	False
4.	All drawing objects are inserted into the same layer of the presentation.	True	False
5.	The page orientation can be landscape or portrait.	True	False
6.	Graphics are objects, such as charts, drawings, pictures, and scanned photographs, that provide visual interest or clarify data.	True	False
7.	Content templates focus on the design of a presentation.	True	False
8.	A layout contains placeholders for the different items such as bulleted text, titles, charts, and so on.	True	False
9.	You can rely on AutoRecover to save your document for you.	True	False
10.	Font size is the height and width of the character and is commonly measured in points.	True	False

fill-in

Complete the following statements by filling in the blanks with the correct terms.

1. _____ order is the order objects are inserted in the different layers of the slide.

2. _____ is a PowerPoint feature that advises you of misspelled words as you add text to a slide and proposes possible corrections.

3. A _____ is an individual "page" of your presentation.

4. A _____ is text or graphics that appears at the bottom of each slide.

5. A _____ is a miniature of a slide.

6. An embedded object is edited using the _____ program.

7. The default orientation for handouts is _____.

8. A _____ is a file containing predefined settings that can be used as a pattern to create many common types of presentations.

9. _____ define the position and format for objects and text that will be added to a slide.

10. The size of a _____ can be changed by dragging its sizing handles.

Hands-On Exercises

rating system
★ Easy
★★ Moderate
★★★ Difficult

step-by-step

Triple Crown Presentation ★

1. Logan Thomas works at Adventure Travel Tours. He is working on a presentation about lightweight hiking to be presented to a group of interested clients. Logan recently found some new information to add to the presentation. He also wants to rearrange some slides and make a few other changes to improve the appearance of the presentation. The handouts of your completed presentation will be similar to those shown here.

   a. Open the file pp01_Triple Crown. Run the slide show.

   b. Enter your name and today's date in the subtitle on slide 1.

   c. Spell-check the presentation, making the appropriate corrections.

   d. Change the layout of slide 5 to Title Only.

   e. Move slide 6 before slide 5.

   f. Insert the picture pp01_Jump on slide 4. Size and position it appropriately.

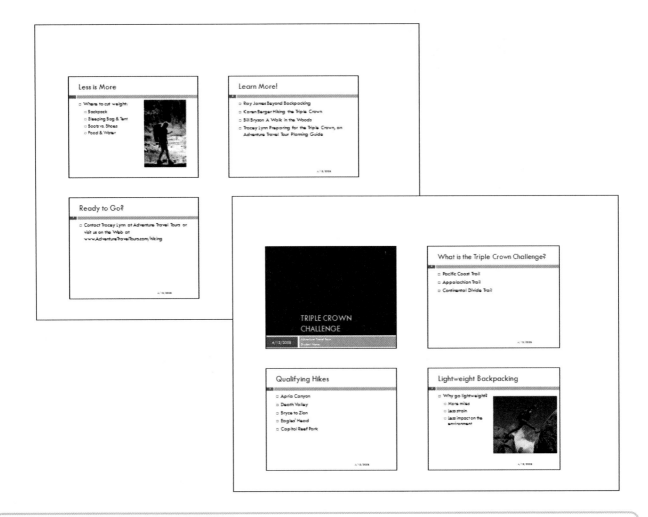

g. Select slide 4. Open the Outline tab and click at the end of the bullet "Less impact on the environment" in the Tabs pane. Press ⏎Enter and promote the new bullet twice. Enter the title **Less is More**.

h. Insert the picture pp01_Stream in the content placeholder.

i. Change the layout of slide 7 to Title and Content layout. Add the following text in the text placeholder: **Contact Tracey Lynn at Adventure Travel Tours or visit us on the Web at www.AdventureTravelTours.com/hiking**.

j. Run the slide show.

k. Save the presentation as Triple Crown Presentation. Print the slides in landscape orientation as handouts (four per page).

Writing Effective Resumes ★★

2. Assume that you work for the career services center of a major university and are working on a presentation to help students create effective resumes and cover letters. You are close to finishing the presentation but need to clean it up and enhance it a bit before presenting it. The handouts of your completed presentation will be similar to those shown here.

a. Open the PowerPoint presentation pp01_Resume.

b. Run the Spelling Checker and correct any spelling errors.

c. On slide 1: Display in normal view.

Change title font size to 44 pt.

Change subtitle font size to 36 pt.

Insert, size, and position the picture from file pp01_Success.

d. On slide 2, replace "Student Name" with your name.

e. On slide 5, capitalize the first word of each bulleted item.

f. On slide 6, split the slide content into two slides.

g. On slide 10, reorganize the bulleted items so that "Types of cover letters" is the first item.

h. To match the slide order with the way the topics are now introduced, move slide 13 before slide 11.

i. On slide 13: Break each bulleted item into two or three bullets each as appropriate.

Capitalize the first word of each bulleted item.

Remove any commas and periods at the end of the bullets.

j. Save the presentation as Resume1.

k. Run the slide show.

l. Print the slides as handouts (nine per page in landscape orientation) and close the presentation.

Driving Safety ★★

3. Assume that you are a paramedic and have been asked to give a lecture to high school students about the danger of distracted driving. You have already organized statistics and data for the presentation, but now you need to add clip art, edit, and finalize the presentation. The handouts of your completed presentation will be similar to those shown here.

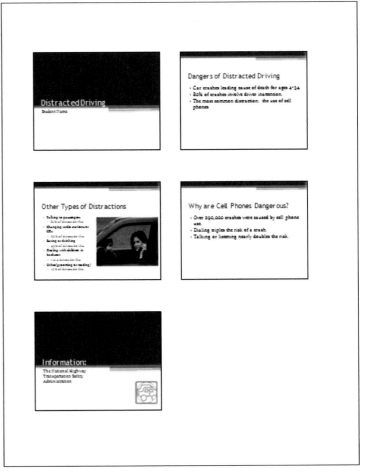

a. Open the PowerPoint presentation pp01_Distracted Driving.

b. Run spell check and correct any errors.

c. On slide 1, replace "Student Name" with your name.

d. On slide 4:

Change the layout to Two Content.

Insert, size, and position the picture from file pp01_Cell Phone into the right content area.

e. Move slide 4 in front of slide 3.

f. On slide 3:

Promote bullet 1.

Demote the last bullet.

g. On slide 5, insert the picture from file pp01_Car Logo and position it in the lower-right corner of the slide.

h. Save the presentation as Distracted Driving.

i. Run the slide show.

j. Print the slides as handouts and close the presentation.

Employee Orientation ★ ★ ★

4. As the front desk manager of Claremont Hotel, you want to make a presentation to your new employees about all of the amenities your hotel offers its guests as well as information on activities and dining in the area. The purpose of this presentation is to enable employees to answer the many questions that are asked by the guests about both the hotel and the town. The handouts of your completed presentation will be similar to those shown here.

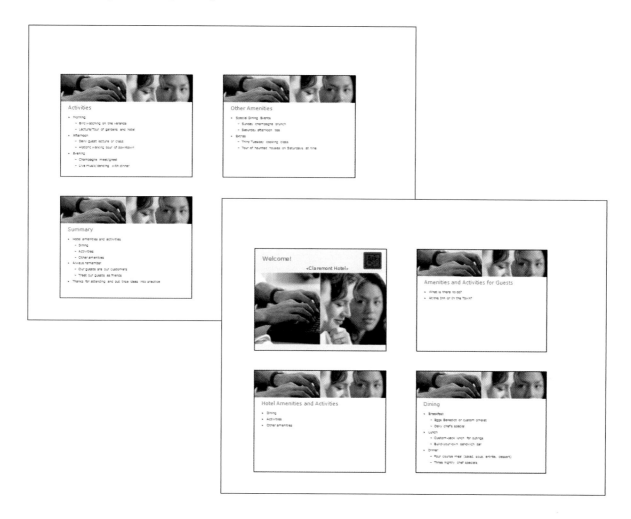

a. Open pp01_Claremont Hotel, which uses the Employee Orientation Presentation template from Microsoft Online.

b. On slide 1:

Enter **Claremont Hotel** as the company name, right-align this subtitle, and set the font color to red and size 24.

Insert, size, and position the picture from file pp01_Claremont Logo.

c. On slide 2:

Enter **Amenities and Activities for Guests** as the title.

Enter the sample bulleted text What is there to do? as the first bullet.

Enter **At the Hotel or In the Town?** as the second bullet.

Remove the remaining placeholders.

d. Insert a new slide after slide 2. In this slide:

> Set the layout to Title and Content.
>
> Enter **Hotel Amenities and Activities** as the title.
>
> Enter **Dining** as the first bullet.
>
> Enter **Activities** as the second bullet.
>
> Enter **Other amenities** as the third bullet.

e. Insert a new slide after slide 3. In this slide:

> Set the layout to Title and Content.
>
> Enter **Dining** as the title.
>
> Enter **Breakfast** as the first bullet under Dining.
>
> Enter **Eggs Benedict or custom omelet** and demote to appear as the first bullet under Breakfast.
>
> Enter **Daily chef's special** as the second bullet under Breakfast.
>
> Enter **Lunch** and promote to appear as the second bullet under Dining.
>
> Enter **Custom-pack lunch for outings** and demote to appear as the first bullet under Lunch.
>
> Enter **Build-your-own sandwich bar** as the second bullet under Lunch.
>
> Enter **Dinner** and promote to appear as the third bullet under Dining.
>
> Enter **Four course meal (salad, soup, entrée, dessert)** as the first bullet under Dinner.
>
> Enter **Three nightly chef specials** as the second bullet under Dinner.

f. Insert a new slide after slide 4. In this slide:

> Set the layout to Title and Content.
>
> Enter **Activities** as the title.
>
> Enter **Morning** as the first bullet under Activities.
>
> Enter **Bird watching on the veranda** and demote to appear as the first bullet under Morning.
>
> Enter **Lecture/Tour of gardens and hotel** as the second bullet under Morning.
>
> Enter **Afternoon** and promote to appear as the second bullet Activities.
>
> Enter **Daily guest lecture or class** as the first bullet under Afternoon.
>
> Enter **Historic walking tour of downtown** as the second bullet under Afternoon.
>
> Enter **Evening** and promote to appear as the third bullet under Activities.
>
> Enter **Champagne meet/greet** and demote to appear as the first bullet under Evening.
>
> Enter **Live music/dancing with dinner** as the second bullet under Evening.

g. Insert a new slide after slide 5. In this slide:

> Set the layout to Title and Content.
>
> Enter **Other Amenities** as the title.
>
> Enter **Special Dining Events** as the first bullet under Other Amenities.
>
> Enter **Sunday champagne brunch** and demote to appear as the first bullet under Special Dining Events.
>
> Enter **Saturday afternoon tea** as the second bullet under Special Dining Events.

Enter **Extras** and promote to appear as the second bullet for Other Amenities.

Enter **Third Tuesday cooking class** and demote to appear as the first bullet under Extras.

Enter **Tour of haunted houses on Saturdays at nine** as the second bullet under Extras.

h. Delete slides 7 through 13.

i. On slide 7:

Enter **Hotel amenities and activities** as the first bullet under Summary.

Enter **Dining** and demote to appear as the first bullet under Hotel amenities and activities.

Enter **Activities** as the second bullet under Hotel amenities and activities.

Enter **Other amenities** as the third bullet under Hotel amenities and activities.

Enter **Always remember** and promote to appear as the second bullet under Summary.

Enter **Our guests are our customers** and demote to appear as the first bullet under Always remember.

Enter **Treat our guests as friends** as the second bullet under Always remember.

Enter **Thanks for attending and put these ideas into practice** and promote to appear as the third bullet under Summary.

Delete any remaining placeholders.

j. Save the presentation as **Claremont Hotel Orientation**.

k. Run the slide show.

l. Print the slides as handouts (six per page in landscape orientation).

Interviewing Basics ★ ★ ★

5. Jane DuBois works in a job recruitment office. She has just started preparing a presentation on interviewing skills for her new recruits. Jane has organized the topics to be presented and located a graphic that will complement the talk. She is now ready to use PowerPoint to create her presentation. The handouts of your completed presentation will be similar to those shown on the next page.

a. Open the Training Presentation-General template in file pp01_Interviewing.

b. On slide 1,

Enter **Interviewing Basics** as the title and change the font to 72.

Enter your name as the presenter.

Insert, size, and position the picture from file pp01_Interview.

c. On slide 2:

Enter **Interviewing basics and beyond** as bullet 1.

Enter **First impressions last** as bullet 2.

Enter **An interviewer's guide to interviews** as bullet 3.

Delete the tip at the bottom of the slide.

d. On slide 3:

Enter **Today's Lesson** as the title.

Enter **Lesson 1: Before you go** as the first bullet under Today's Lesson.

Enter **Preparing your resume, learn about employer, practice** as the first bullet under Lesson 1: Before you go.

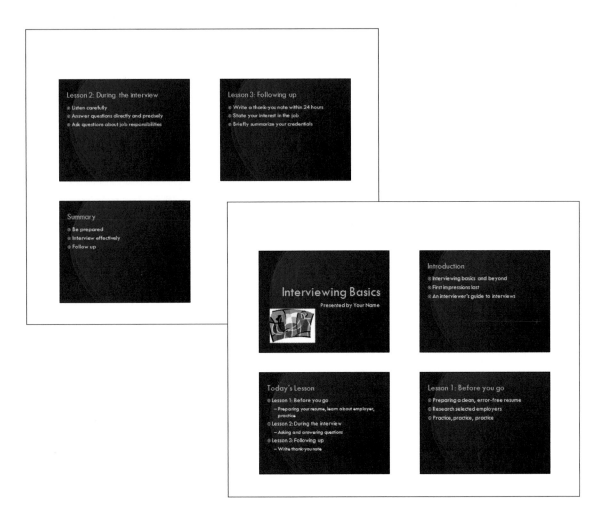

Enter **Lesson 2: During the interview** as the second bullet under Today's Lesson.

Enter **Asking and answering questions** as the first bullet under Lesson 2: During the interview.

Enter **Lesson 3: Following up** as the third bullet under Today's Lesson.

Enter **Write thank-you note** as the first bullet under Lesson 3: Following up.

e. On slide 4:

Enter **Lesson 1: Before you go** as the title.

Enter **Preparing a clean, error-free resume** as bullet 1.

Enter **Research selected employers** as bullet 2.

Enter **Practice, practice, practice** as bullet 3.

Delete the tip at the bottom of the slide.

f. Delete slides 5 and 6.

g. On slide 5:

Enter **Lesson 2: During the interview** as the title.

Enter **Listen carefully** as bullet 1.

Enter **Answer questions directly and precisely** as bullet 2.

Enter **Ask questions about job responsibilities** as bullet 3.

Delete the tip at the bottom of the slide.

h. Delete slides 6 and 7.

i. On slide 6:

Enter **Lesson 3: Following up** as the title.

Enter **Write a thank-you note within 24 hours** as bullet 1.

Enter **State your interest in the job** as bullet 2.

Enter as bullet 3 **Briefly summarize your credentials**.

Delete the tip at the bottom of the slide.

j. Delete slides 7 and 8.

k. On slide 7:

Enter **Summary** as the title.

Enter **Be prepared** as the first bullet under Summary.

Enter **Interview effectively** as the second bullet under Summary.

Enter **Follow up** as the third bullet under Summary.

Delete any unused placeholders.

l. Delete slide 8.

m. Save the presentation as Interviewing Basics.

n. Run the slide show.

o. Print the slides as handouts (six per page).

on your own

Internet Policy Presentation ★

1. You are working in the information technology department at International Sales Incorporated. Your manager has asked you to give a presentation on the corporation's Internet policy to the new hire orientation class. Create your presentation with PowerPoint, using the information in the file pp01_Internet Policy as a resource. Use a template of your choice. When you are done, run the spelling checker, then save your presentation as Internet Policy and print it.

Telephone Training Course ★★

2. You are a trainer with Super Software, Inc. You received a memo from your manager alerting you that many of the support personnel are not using proper telephone protocol or obtaining the proper information from the customers who call in. Your manager has asked you to conduct a training class that covers these topics. Using the pp01_Memo data file as a resource, prepare the slides for your class. When you are done, save the presentation as Phone Etiquette and print the handouts.

Car Maintenance Presentation ★★

3. You work as a field representative for a large auto parts manufacturer. A local organization has asked you to make a presentation on basic car maintenance. Using the Web or other resources, locate content and graphics for your presentation. Create the presentation using PowerPoint and save the presentation as Car Maintenance. Print the handouts.

Classroom Policies Presentation ★★★

4. You work in a local high school and have been asked to prepare a presentation on the rules and policies of your school. Using the Web or other resources, gather information and graphics about school policies. Using a template of your choice, create the presentation, save it as School Rules, and print the handouts.

Careers with Animals ★★★

5. You have been volunteering at the Animal Rescue Foundation. The director has asked you to prepare a presentation on careers with animals to present to local schools in hopes that some students will be inspired to volunteer at the foundation. Using the pp01_AnimalCareers data file as a resource, create the presentation. Add photos or clip art where appropriate. When you are done, save the presentation as Careers with Animals and print the handouts.

Modifying and Refining a Presentation

Objectives

After completing this lab, you will know how to:

 Find and replace text.

 Create and enhance a table.

 Duplicate and hide slides.

 Modify graphic objects and create a text box.

 Create and enhance Shapes.

 Create and animate SmartArt graphics.

 Change the theme.

 Modify slide masters.

⑨ Add and hide slide footers.

⑩ Add animation, sound, and transitions.

⑪ Control and annotate a slide show.

⑫ Add speaker notes.

⑬ Document a file.

⑭ Customize print settings.

Case Study

Animal Rescue Foundation

The Animal Rescue Foundation director was very impressed with your first draft of the presentation to recruit volunteers, and asked to see the presentation onscreen. While viewing it together, you explained that you plan to make many more changes to improve the appearance of the presentation. For example, you plan to use a different color theme and to include more art and other graphic features to enhance the appearance of the slides. You also explained that you will add more action to the slides using the special effects included with PowerPoint to keep the audience's attention.

The director suggested that you include more information on ways that

volunteers can help. Additionally, because the organization has such an excellent adoption rate, the director wants you to include a table to illustrate the success of the adoption program.

Office PowerPoint 2007 gives you the design and production capabilities to create a first-class onscreen presentation. These features include artist-designed layouts and color themes that give your presentation a professional appearance. In addition, you can add your own personal touches by modifying text attributes, incorporating art or graphics, and including animation to add impact, interest, and excitement to your presentation.

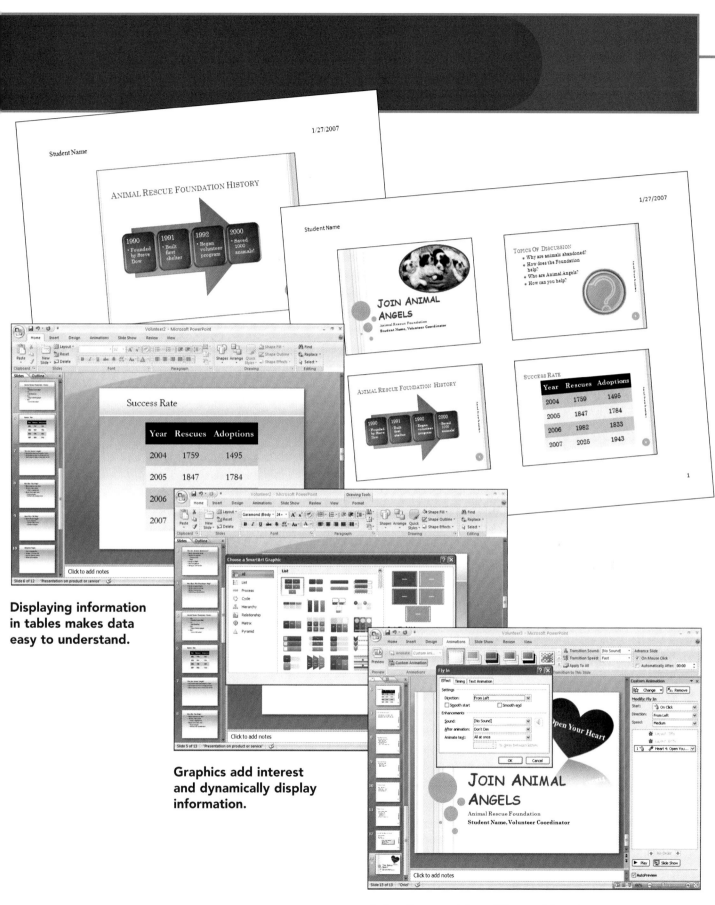

Displaying information in tables makes data easy to understand.

Graphics add interest and dynamically display information.

Animations and transitions add action to a slide show.

Concept Preview

The following concepts will be introduced in this lab:

1 **Find and Replace** To make editing easier, you can use the Find and Replace feature to find text in a presentation and replace it with other text.

2 **Table** A table is used to organize information into an easy-to-read format of horizontal rows and vertical columns.

3 **Alignment** Alignment controls the position of text entries within a space.

4 **Document Theme** A document theme is a predefined set of formatting choices that can be applied to an entire document in one simple step.

5 **Master** A master is a special slide or page that stores information about the formatting for all slides or pages in a presentation.

6 **Animations** Animations are special effects that add action to text and graphics so they move around on the screen during a slide show.

Replacing Text

After meeting with the Foundation director, you updated the content to include the additional information on ways that volunteers can help the Animal Rescue Foundation.

1
- Start Office PowerPoint 2007.

- Open the file pp02_Volunteer2.

- If necessary, switch to Normal view.

- Replace Student Name in slide 1 with your name.

- Scroll the Slides pane to view the content of the revised presentation.

Your screen should be similar to Figure 2.1

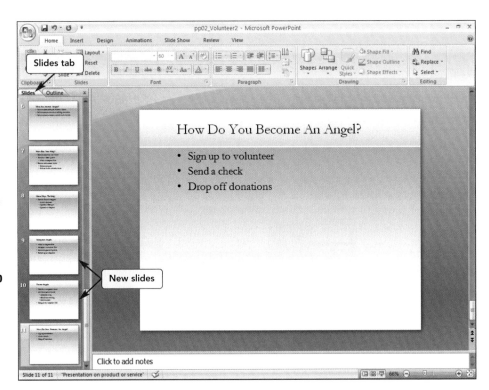

Figure 2.1

You added two new slides, 9 and 10, with more information about the Animal Angels volunteer organization, making the total number of slides in the presentation 11. As you reread the content of the presentation, you decide to edit the text by replacing the word "pet" in many locations with the word "animal."

Concept 1
Find and Replace

1   To make editing easier, you can use the **Find and Replace** feature to find text in a presentation and replace it with other text. The Find feature will locate and identify any text string you specify in the presentation by highlighting it. When used along with the Replace feature, not only will the string be identified, but it will be replaced with the replacement text you specify if you choose. For example, suppose you created a lengthy document describing the type of clothing and equipment needed to set up a world-class home gym, and then you decided to change "sneakers" to "athletic shoes." Instead of deleting every occurrence of "sneakers" and typing "athletic shoes," you can use the Find and Replace feature to perform the task automatically.

The Replace feature also can be used to replace a specified font in a presentation with another. When using this feature, however, all text throughout the presentation that is in the specified font to find is automatically changed to the selected replacement font.

The Find and Replace feature is fast and accurate; however, use care when replacing so that you do not replace unintended matches.

Using Find and Replace

You want to replace selected occurrences of the word "pet" with "animal" throughout the presentation. Because it is easier to read the text in the Slide pane, you will make that pane active before starting. Whichever pane is active at the time you begin using Find and Replace is the pane in which the located text will be highlighted.

1 ● Select slide 1 in the Slides tab and click in the Slide pane to make it active.

● If necessary, open the Home tab.

● Click 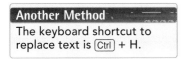 Replace in the Editing group.

Another Method
The keyboard shortcut to replace text is Ctrl + H.

Your screen should be similar to Figure 2.2

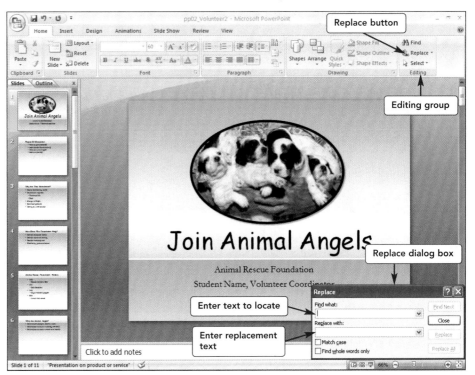

Figure 2.2

In the Replace dialog box, you first enter the text you want to locate in the Find what: text box. The two options described in the following table allow you to refine the procedure that is used to conduct the search.

Option	Effect on Text
Match Case	Distinguishes between uppercase and lowercase characters. When selected, finds only those instances in which the capitalization matches the text you typed in the Find what: box.
Find Whole Words Only	Distinguishes between whole and partial words. When selected, locates matches that are whole words and not part of a larger word. For example, finds "cat" only and not "catastrophe" too.

Then, the text you want to replace the located text is entered in the Replace with: text box. The replacement text must be entered exactly as you want it to appear in your presentation.

You want to find all occurrences of the complete word "pet" and replace them with the word "animal." You will not use either option because you want to locate all words regardless of case and because you want to find "pet" as well as "pets" in the presentation.

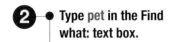

● Type **pet** in the Find what: text box.

Additional Information

After entering the text to find, do not press ←Enter or this will choose [Find Next] and the search will begin.

● Press Tab⇥ or click in the Replace with: text box.

● Type **animal** in the Replace with: text box.

● Click [Find Next].

● If necessary, move the dialog box so you can see the located text.

Your screen should be similar to Figure 2.3

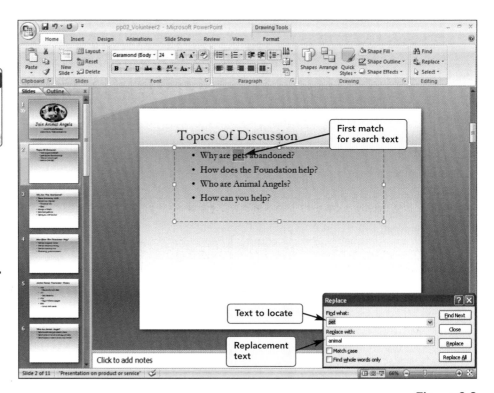

Figure 2.3

Immediately, the first occurrence of text in the presentation that matches the entry in the Find what: text box is located and highlighted in the Slide pane. You will replace the located word in slide 2 with the replacement text.

3 ● Click [Replace].

Your screen should be similar to Figure 2.4

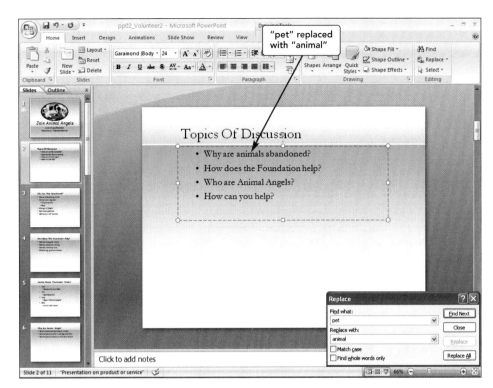

Figure 2.4

The located text is replaced with the replacement text and the next occurrence of text in the Find what: box is located. You could continue finding and replacing each occurrence. You will, however, replace all the remaining occurrences at one time. As you do, the replacement is entered in lowercase even when it replaces a word that begins with an uppercase character. You will correct this when you finish using replacing.

4 ● Click [Replace All] to continue.

● Click [OK] in response to the finished searching dialog box.

● Click [Close] to close the Replace dialog box.

● Edit the word "animals" to "Animals" in slide 3.

● Save the presentation as Volunteer2.

Your screen should be similar to Figure 2.5

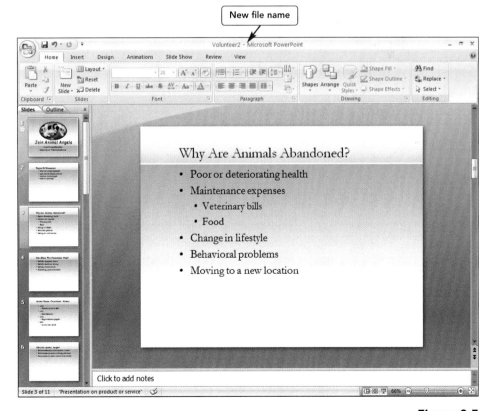

Figure 2.5

If you plan to change all occurrences, it is much faster to use the [Replace All]. Exercise care when using Replace All, however, because the search text you specify might be part of another word and you may accidentally replace text you want to keep.

Creating a Simple Table

During your discussion with the director, he suggested that you add a slide containing data showing the success of the adoption program. The information in this slide will be presented using a table layout.

Concept 2

Table

2 A **table** is used to organize information into an easy-to-read format of horizontal rows and vertical columns. The intersection of a row and column creates a **cell** in which you can enter data or other information. Cells in a table are identified by a letter and number, called a **table reference**. Columns are identified from left to right beginning with the letter A, and rows are numbered from top to bottom beginning with the number 1. The table reference of the top-leftmost cell is A1 because it is in the first column (A) and first row (1) of the table. The third cell in column 2 is cell B3. The fourth cell in column 3 is C4.

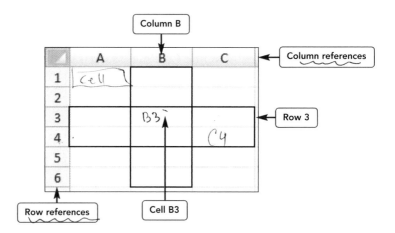

Tables are a very effective method for presenting information. The table layout organizes the information for readers and greatly reduces the number of words they have to read to interpret the data. Use tables whenever you can to make the information in your presentation easier to read.

The table you will create will display columns for the year, and for the number of rescues and adoptions. The rows will display the data for the past four years. Your completed table will be similar to the one shown on the next page.

Creating a Table Slide

To include this information in the presentation, you will insert a new slide after slide 5. Because this slide will contain a table showing the adoption data, you want to use the Title and Content layout.

Year	Rescues	Adoptions
2004	1759	1495
2005	1847	1784
2006	1982	1833
2007	2025	1943

---

1 ● Display slide 5.

● Open the [New Slide] drop-down menu from the Slides group on the Home tab.

● Choose the Title and Content layout.

Additional Information

PowerPoint remembers the last slide layout used while working in this presentation or during the current session and inserts it when you click [New Slide].

Your screen should be similar to Figure 2.6

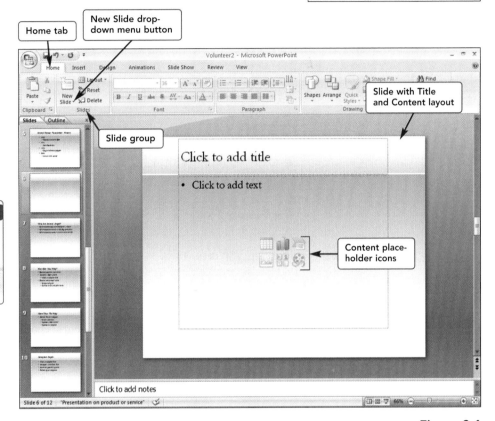

Figure 2.6

Inside the content placeholder are six icons shown below each representing the different types of content that can be inserted. Clicking an icon opens the appropriate feature to add the specified type of content.

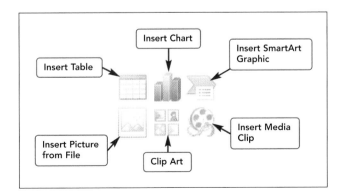

Inserting the Table

First, you will add a slide title and then you will create the table to display the number of adoptions and rescues.

1
- Enter the title Success Rate in the title placeholder.

- Click the 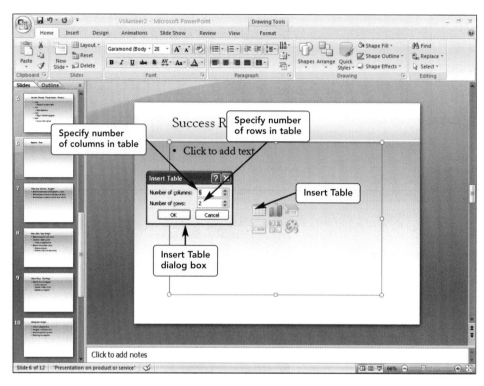 Insert Table icon in the center of the slide.

Your screen should be similar to Figure 2.7

Figure 2.7

In the Insert Table dialog box, you specify the number of rows and columns for the table.

2
- Specify 3 columns and 5 rows.

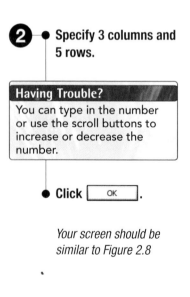

Having Trouble?
You can type in the number or use the scroll buttons to increase or decrease the number.

- Click [OK].

Your screen should be similar to Figure 2.8

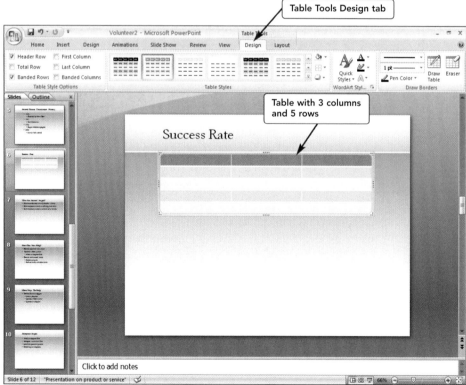

Figure 2.8

A basic table consisting of three columns and five rows is displayed as a selected object. In addition, the Table Tools Design tab opens in anticipation that you will want to modify the design of the table.

Entering Data in a Table

Now, you can enter the information into the table. The insertion point appears in the top-left corner cell, cell A1, ready for you to enter text. To move in a table, click on the cell or use Tab↹ to move to the next cell to the right and ⇧Shift + Tab↹ to move to the cell to the left. If you are in the last cell of a row, pressing Tab↹ takes you to the first cell of the next row. You also can use the ↑ and ↓ directional keys to move up or down a row. When you enter a large amount of text in a table, using Tab↹ to move rather than the mouse is easier because your hands are already on the keyboard.

 **Type** Year.

● **Press** Tab↹ **or click on the next cell to the right.**

Having Trouble?

Do not press ↵Enter to move to the next cell as this adds a new line to the current cell. If this happens, press ←Backspace to remove it.

Your screen should be similar to Figure 2.9

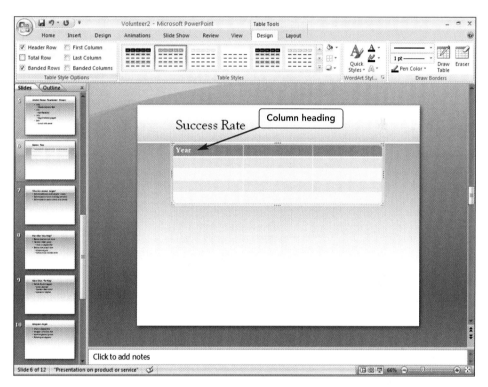

Figure 2.9

Next, you will complete the information for the table by entering the data shown below.

	Col. A	Col. B	Col. C
Row 1	Year	Rescues	Adoptions
Row 2	2004	1759	1495
Row 3	2005	1847	1784
Row 4	2006	1982	1833
Row 5	2007	2025	1943

2 ● **Add the remaining information shown above to the table.**

Your screen should be similar to Figure 2.10

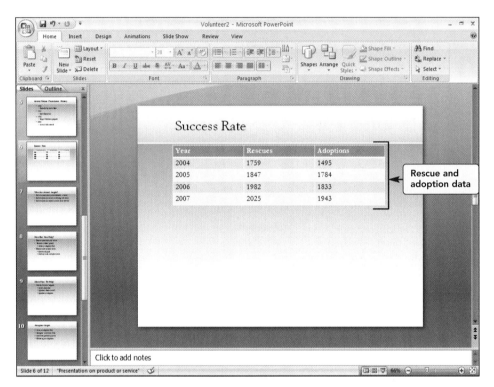

Figure 2.10

You are happy with the table but would like to increase the font size of the text to make it more readable on screen. The size of the font in a table can be changed like any other text on a slide. However, selecting text in a table is slightly different. The following table describes how to select different areas of a table.

Area to Select	Procedure
Cell	Drag across the contents of the cell.
Row	Drag across the row or click in front of the row when the mouse pointer is a ➡.
Column	Drag down the column or click in front of the row when the mouse pointer is a ⬇.
Multiple cells, rows, or columns	Drag through the cells, rows, or columns when the mouse pointer is a ⬈ or I.
	Or select the first cell, row, or column, and hold down ⇧Shift while clicking on another cell, row, or column.
Contents of next cell	Press Tab⇥.
Contents of previous cell	Press ⇧Shift + Tab⇥.
Entire table	Drag through all the cells or click anywhere inside the table and press Ctrl + A.

3 ● **Select all the text in the table.**

● **Open the Home tab.**

● **Click 𝐀˙ Increase Font Size in the Font group four times.**

Additional Information

Clicking 𝐀˙ increases the font size by units.

Your screen should be similar to Figure 2.11

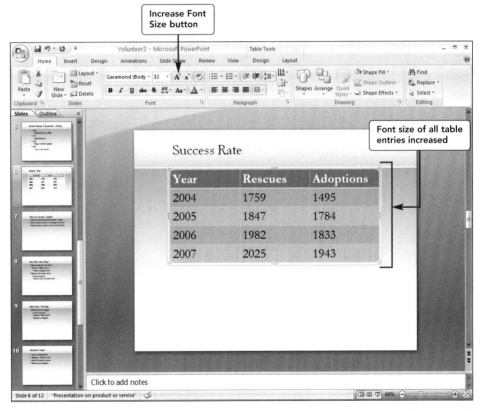

Figure 2.11

The font size has quickly been increased by four units, and at 32 points the text is much easier to read.

Sizing the Table and Columns

You now need to increase the overall size of the table and then adjust the size of the columns to fit their contents.

1 ● **Drag the lower-right-corner sizing handle down and outward to increase the table size as in Figure 2.12.**

Additional Information
The mouse pointer will appear in ↖ when you can drag the corner sizing handle.

Your screen should be similar to Figure 2.12

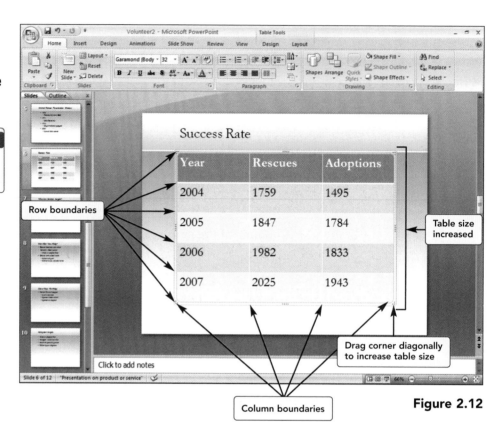

Figure 2.12

Additional Information
You also can double-click on the boundary line to automatically size the width to the largest cell entry.

To adjust the individual column width or row height, you drag the row and column boundaries. The mouse pointer appears as a ◄‖► when you can size the column and ╪ when you can size the row. The mouse pointer appears a ⁺↖ when you can move the entire table.

2 ● **Drag the right column boundary line of the year column to the left to reduce the column width as in Figure 2.13.**

● **Drag the boundary lines of the other two columns to the left to reduce the column widths as in Figure 2.13.**

● **Drag the entire table to center it in the slide as in Figure 2.13.**

Your screen should be similar to Figure 2.13

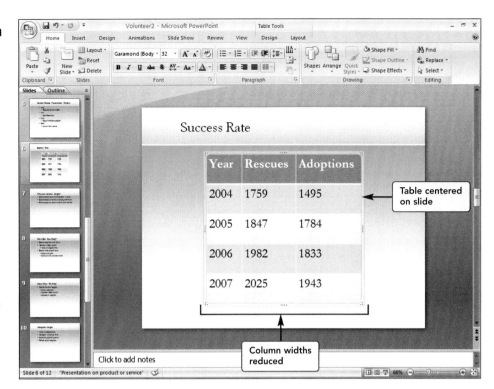

Figure 2.13

Now the columns are more appropriately sized to the data they display.

Aligning Text in Cells

The next change you want to make is to center the text and data in the cells. To do this, you can change the alignment of the text entries.

Concept 3

Alignment

3   **Alignment** controls the position of text entries within a space. You can change the horizontal placement of an entry in a placeholder or a table cell by using one of the four horizontal alignment settings: left, center, right, and justified. You also can align text vertically in a table cell with the top, middle, or bottom of the cell space.

Horizontal Alignment	Effect on Text	Vertical Alignment	Effect on Text
Left	Aligns text against the left edge of the placeholder or cell, leaving the right edge of text, which wraps to another line, ragged.	Top	Aligns text at the top of the cell space.
Center	Centers each line of text between the left and right edges of the placeholder or cell.	Middle	Aligns text in the middle of the cell space.
Right	Aligns text against the right edge of the placeholder or cell, leaving the left edge of multiple lines ragged.	Bottom	Aligns text at the bottom of the cell space.
Justified	Aligns text evenly with both the right and left edges of the placeholder or cell.		

The commands to change horizontal alignment are on the Home tab in the Paragraph group. However, using the shortcuts shown below or the Mini Toolbar is often much quicker.

Alignment	Keyboard Shortcut
Left	Ctrl + L
Center	Ctrl + E
Right	Ctrl + R
Justified	Ctrl + J

The data in the table is not centered within the cells. You want to center the cell entries both horizontally and vertically in their cell spaces.

1 ● Select the entire contents of the table.

● Right-click on the selection and click ☰ Center in the Mini Toolbar.

Another Method

You also could click ☰ Center in the Paragraph group of the Home tab.

● Open the 📄 Align Text drop-down menu in the Paragraph group and choose Middle.

Your screen should be similar to Figure 2.14

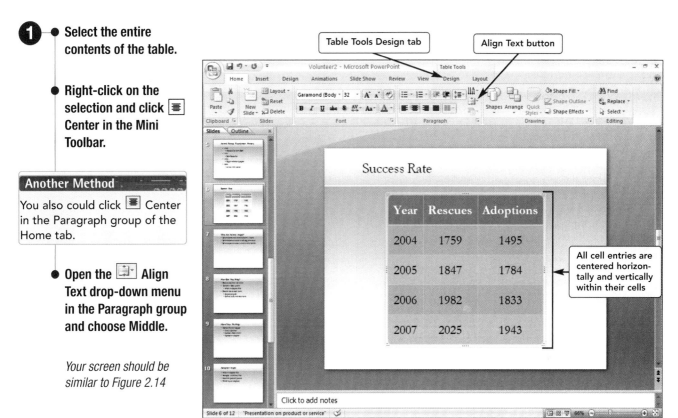

Figure 2.14

Changing the Table Style

Next, you will add a color and other formatting changes to the table. To quickly make these enhancements, you will apply a table style. Like picture styles, **table styles** are combinations of shading colors, borders, and visual effects such as shadows and reflections that can be applied in one simple step. You also can create your own table style effects by selecting specific style elements such as borders and shadows individually using the 🖌▾ Shading, ▦▾ Borders, and ▿▾ Effects commands from the Table Styles group on the Table Tool Design tab.

1 • Open the Table Tools Design tab.

• Click ⊡ More in the table styles group to display the Table Styles gallery.

• Select several table styles to see how they look in Live Preview.

• Choose Dark Style 2 from the gallery.

Having Trouble?
Scroll the gallery to see the Dark Styles at the bottom of the gallery.

• Click outside the table to see the new format.

• Save the file.

Your screen should be similar to Figure 2.15

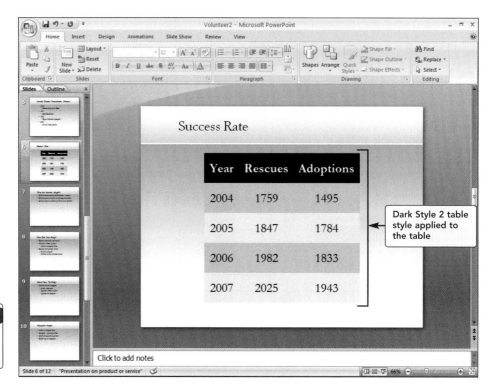

Figure 2.15

The style has been changed. New formatting has been applied to the table. The enhancements added to the table greatly improve its appearance. The table displays the information in an attractive and easy-to-read manner.

Modifying and Creating Graphic Objects

Now you are ready to enhance the presentation by adding several graphics. As you have seen, you can easily add clip art and photographs to slides. Many of the clip art graphics can be customized to your needs by changing colors and adding and deleting elements.

Changing the Slide Layout

First, you want to add a graphic to slide 2. Before adding the graphic, you will change the slide layout from the bulleted list style to a style that is designed to accommodate text as well as other types of content such as graphics.

1 ● Display slide 2.

● Click  Layout ▾ in the Slides group of the Home tab.

● Choose the Two Content layout.

Your screen should be similar to Figure 2.16

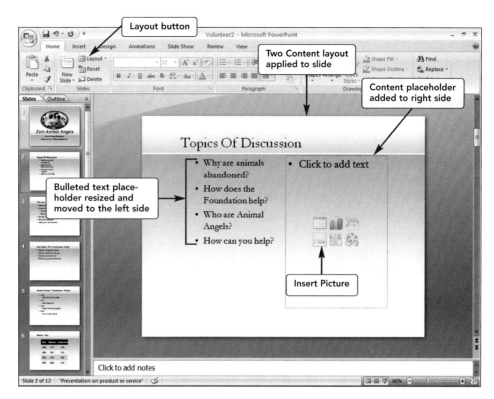

Figure 2.16

A content placeholder was added on the right side of the slide, and the bulleted text placeholder was resized and moved to the left side of the slide. You will add a clip art graphic of a question mark and then size the placeholder.

2 ● Click 🖼 Insert Picture in the content placeholder.

Additional Information
A ScreenTip identifies the content placeholder as you point to it.

● If necessary, change the Look In location to the location containing your data files.

● Locate and select the pp02_Question Mark clip art.

● Click Insert ▾.

● Increase the size of the graphic and position it as in Figure 2.17.

Your screen should be similar to Figure 2.17

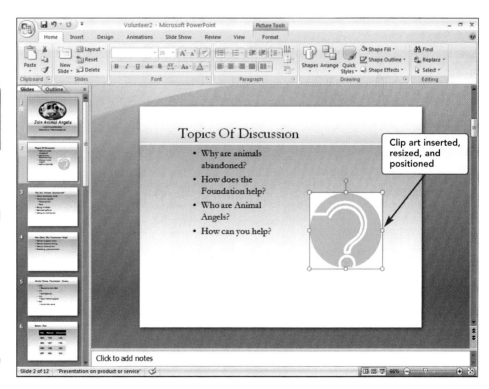

Figure 2.17

Enhancing a Picture

There are many effects you can use to improve the appearance of clip art. The first enhancement you would like to make is to change the color of the question mark so it coordinates with the slide design.

1
- With the clip art selected, click [Recolor] in the Adjust group of the Picture Tools Format tab.

- Float your mouse pointer over the choices in the Recolor gallery to see the Live Previews.

- Choose Accent color 2 Dark from the Dark Variations section.

Your screen should be similar to Figure 2.18

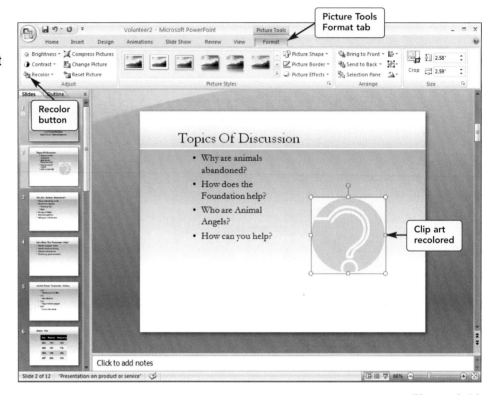

Figure 2.18

Next you will select a picture style.

2
- Click [▽] More in the Picture Styles group to display all the options in the Picture Styles gallery.

- Click the [⬭] Metal Oval picture style.

Your screen should be similar to Figure 2.19

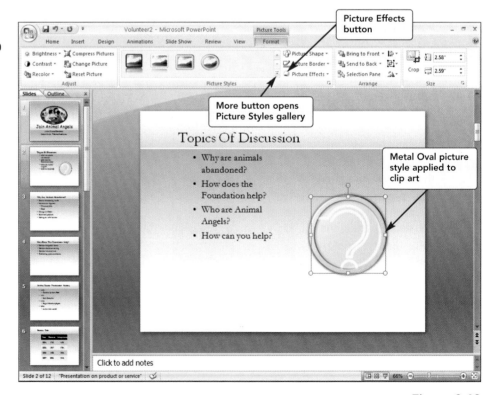

Figure 2.19

Although, you like how the picture style looks, you still feel the image needs some additional enhancements. You decide to look at adding a picture effect.

3
- **Click** Picture Effects ▾ .

- **Select Glow.**

- **Float the mouse pointer over the choices to see the Live Previews.**

- **Choose Accent color 2, 18 pt glow.**

- **Increase the width of the bulleted item placeholder until the text appears on a single line.**

- **Move the placeholder to the left until the bullets align with the title as shown in Figure 2.20.**

Your screen should be similar to Figure 2.20

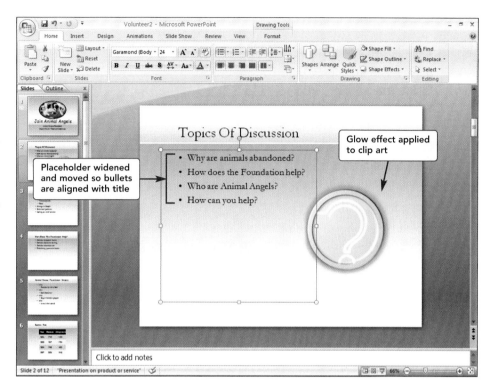

Figure 2.20

The glow adds just the right effect to the graphic and the bulleted list of items is now correctly aligned.

Duplicating a Slide

At the end of the presentation, you want to add a concluding slide. This slide needs to be powerful, because it is your last chance to convince your audience to join Animal Angels. To create the concluding slide, you will duplicate slide 1 and then create a graphic to complement the slide.

Duplicating a slide creates a copy of the selected slide and places it directly after the selected slide. You can duplicate a slide in any view, but in this case you will use the Slide Sorter view to duplicate slide 1 and move it to the end of the presentation.

1 Switch to Slide Sorter view.

● Select slide 1.

● Open the [New Slide] drop-down menu from the Slides group of the Home tab.

● Choose Duplicate Selected Slides.

● Move slide 2 to the end of the presentation.

Your screen should be similar to Figure 2.21

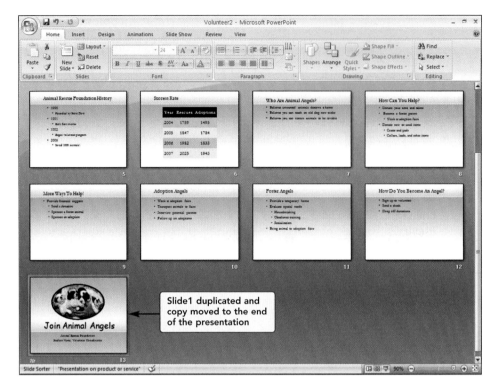

Figure 2.21

There are now 13 slides in the presentation.

Adding a Shape

Now you want to replace the graphic in the concluding slide with another of a heart. To quickly add a shape, you will use one of the ready-made shapes supplied with PowerPoint. These include such basic shapes as rectangles and circles, a variety of lines, block arrows, flowchart symbols, stars and banners, and callouts.

Additional Information

Most shapes also can be inserted from the Clip Organizer as well.

1 ● Double-click on slide 13 to display it in Normal view.

● Select the graphic and press [Delete].

● Click [Shapes] in the Drawing group of the Home tab.

Your screen should be similar to Figure 2.22

Another Method
You also can access the Shapes gallery by selecting [Shapes] on the Insert tab.

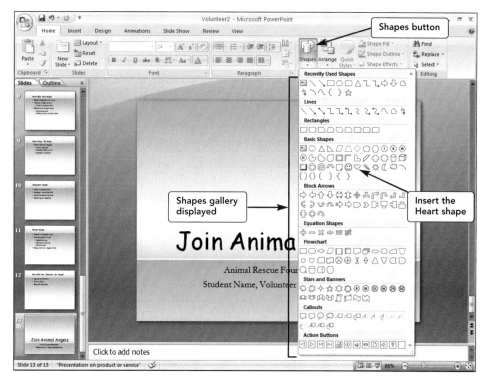

Figure 2.22

Additional Information
The selected shape will be added to the Recently Used Shapes section of the Shapes gallery.

Next, you need to select the shape you want from the Shapes gallery and then indicate where you want the shape inserted on the slide. When inserting a shape, the mouse pointer appears as + when pointing to the slide. Then, to insert the shape, click on the slide and drag to increase the size.

2 ● Click ♡ Heart in the Basic Shapes section.

● Click above the title on the slide and drag to insert and enlarge the heart.

● Size and position the heart as in Figure 2.23.

Additional Information
A shape can be sized and moved just like any other object.

Another Method
To maintain the height and width proportions of the shape, hold down [⇧ Shift] while you drag.

Your screen should be similar to Figure 2.23

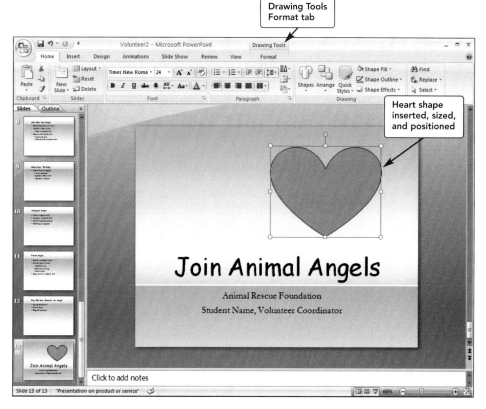

Figure 2.23

The heart shape is inserted and the Drawing Tools Format tab is available.

Enhancing a Shape

Next, you will enhance its appearance by selecting a shape style and adding a reflection. Just like the other styles in PowerPoint 2007, shape styles consist of combinations of colors, outlines, and effects.

1 ● **Open the Drawing Tools Format tab.**

● **Click ▾ More in the Shape Styles group to open the Shapes Styles gallery.**

● **Choose Moderate Effect – Accent 2 from the Shape Styles gallery.**

● **Click ⚉ Shape Effects ▾ .**

● **From the Reflection gallery, choose Half reflection, 4 pt offset.**

Your screen should be similar to Figure 2.24

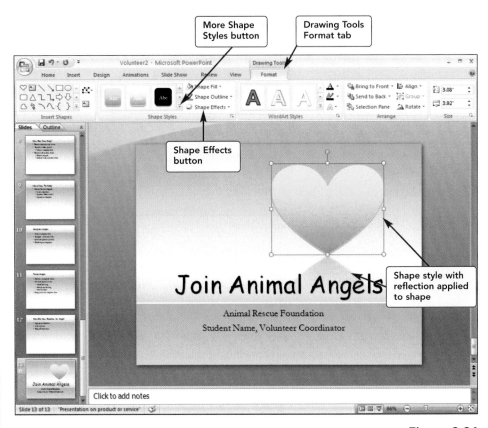

Figure 2.24

The addition of style and reflection effects greatly improves the appearance of the heart.

Adding Text to a Shape

Next, you will add text to the heart object. Text can be added to all shapes and becomes part of the shape; when the shape is moved, the text moves with it.

1 • **Right-click on the heart to open the shortcut menu, and choose Edit Text.**

• **Type** Open Your Heart.

Having Trouble?
If the inserted text does not fit into the heart shape, increase the size of the heart.

Your screen should be similar to Figure 2.25

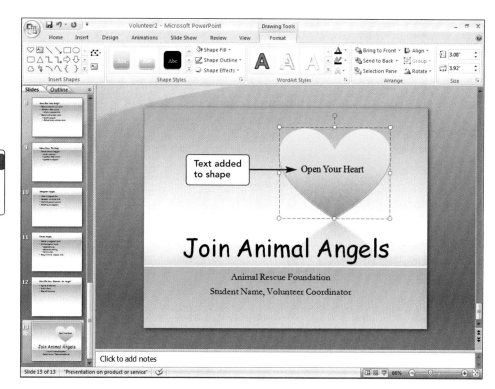

Figure 2.25

Next, you want to improve the appearance of the text by changing the format. Fonts and font size are two basic text attributes that you have used already. The table below describes some additional text formats and their uses. The Home tab and the Mini Toolbar contain buttons for many of the formatting effects.

Format	Example	Use
Bold, italic	***Bold Italic***	Adds emphasis
Underline	<u>Underline</u>	Adds emphasis
Superscript	"To be or not to be."[1]	Used in footnotes and formulas
Subscript	H_2O	Used in formulas
Shadow	Shadow	Adds distinction to titles and headings
Color	Color Color Color	Adds interest

You will use the Mini Toolbar to make all the formatting changes to the text.

2 ● Select the text in the
  Heart

● Click **B** Bold on the
  Mini Toolbar.

● Increase the font size
  to 28 points.

● Open the **A·** Font
  Color gallery and
  choose White,
  Background 1 in the
  Theme Colors section.

● Click **≡** Center.

*Your screen should be
similar to Figure 2.26*

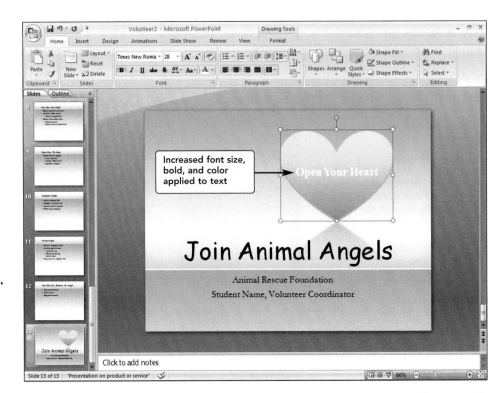

Figure 2.26

Rotating the Object

Additional Information

Holding down ⇧Shift while
using the rotate handle rotates
the object in 15-degree
increments.

Another Method

You also can use ⟲Rotate· in
the Arrange group of the
Drawing Tools Format tab to
rotate an object.

Finally, you want to change the angle of the heart. You can rotate an object
90 degrees left or right, flip it vertically or horizontally, or specify an exact
degree of rotation. You will change the angle of the heart to the right using

the ○ **rotate handle** for the selected object, which allows you to rotate

the object to any degree in any direction.

1 ● If necessary, select the graphic.

● Drag the rotate handle to the right slightly.

Your screen should be similar to Figure 2.27

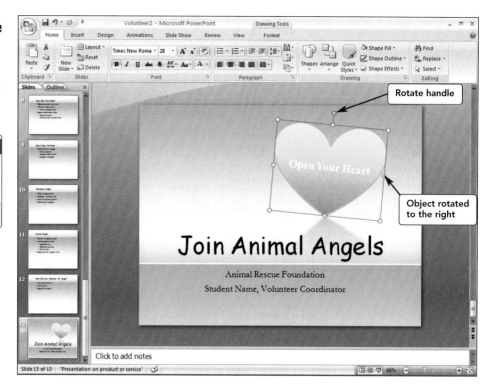

Figure 2.27

The graphic is a nice addition to the final slide of the presentation.

Converting Text to a SmartArt Graphic

The director liked the inclusion of the history of the foundation in the presentation but would like you to make that slide look more interesting. You decide to convert the bulleted list to a diagram using one of the Microsoft Office SmartArt graphics. **SmartArt** graphics help you quickly create a visual representation of textual information. Most SmartArt graphics are most effective when the number of shapes and amount of text are limited to key points. Larger amounts of text can distract from the visual appeal of the graphic and make it harder to convey the message.

1 ● Select slide 5.

● Select all of the bulleted text.

● Right-click on the selection and choose **Convert to SmartArt** from the shortcut menu.

Additional Information

The shortcut menu gallery of graphic shapes displays only those shapes that PowerPoint determined work best with bulleted lists.

● Choose **More SmartArt graphics.**

Your screen should be similar to Figure 2.28

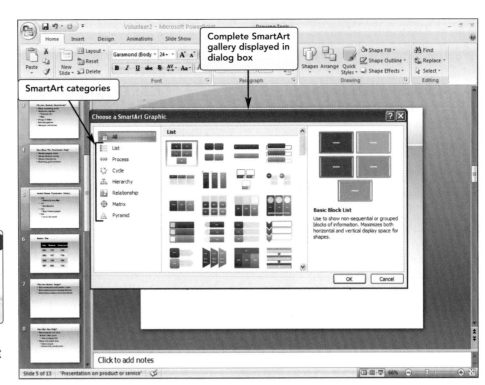

Figure 2.28

The complete gallery of SmartArt graphic designs is displayed. They are divided into categories by the type of graphic, such as Process, Cycle, or Hierarchy. Within each category are different layouts. The following table contains suggestions to help you decide what type of graphic to use to best illustrate the content. In addition, as you select each type, the dialog box displays an enlarged version of the graphic and a brief description of its use.

Purpose	Graphic Type
Show nonsequential information	List
Show steps in a process or timeline	Process
Show a continual process	Cycle
Show a decision tree	Hierarchy
Show proportional relationships	Pyramid
Illustrate connections	Relationship

Because the history slide content shows nonsequential events in time, you will use a layout in the Process category.

2
- Choose Process from the category list.

- Click on several different Process graphics and read the description.

- Choose Accent Process and click OK .

Your screen should be similar to Figure 2.29

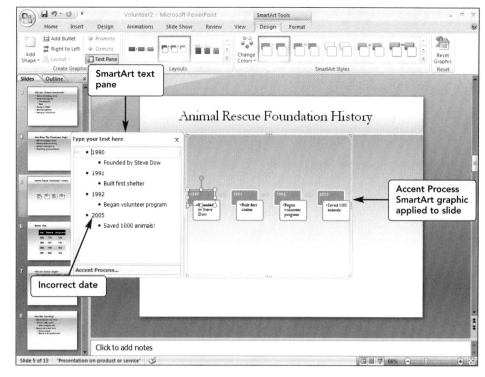

Figure 2.29

Additional Information

You also can copy text from another slide or program and paste it into the Text pane.

The selected text in the slide is automatically placed in the shapes and arranged in the SmartArt layout you choose. A Text pane opens next to the content placeholder. It is used to add or edit the text content of the SmartArt graphic. You notice the last date, 2005, is incorrect and should be 2000. You will change it in the text pane.

3
- Click on the 2005 bullet in the Text pane.

- Edit the date to 2000.

- Click × Close to close the Text pane.

Your screen should be similar to Figure 2.30

Additional Information

Clicking Text Pane along the left edge of the SmartArt graphic object opens the Text pane.

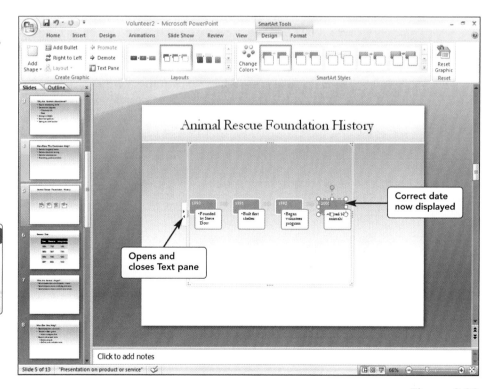

Figure 2.30

The text in the SmartArt graphic was automatically updated. Although you like the change to a diagram from the bulleted list, you decide to try another layout that may better visually represent the information.

4 ● Click ⬇ **More in the Layouts group.**

● **Point to several layouts to see the Live Preview.**

● **Choose Continuous Block Process.**

Your screen should be similar to Figure 2.31

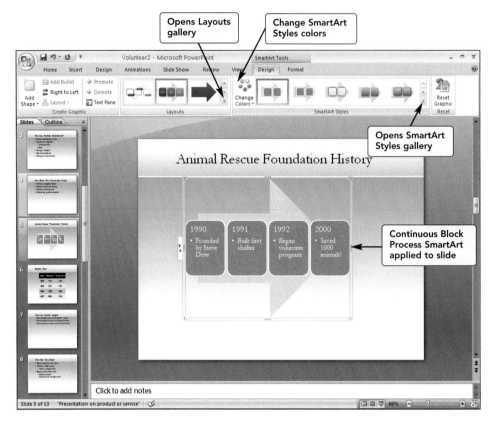

Figure 2.31

The new graphic design with the arrow in the background better suits the text. Next, you will change the colors and style of the SmartArt graphic. You want to use colors that are like those in the table in slide 6. Then you will use a SmartArt style, combinations of different formatting options such as edges, gradients, line styles, shadows, and three-dimensional effects, to enhance the SmartArt graphic. You can try different combinations of colors and styles until you find the one that suits your presentation.

5 ● **Click** Change Colors.

● **Choose Colorful Range – Accent Colors 4 to 5.**

● **Click** ▼ **More from the SmartArt Styles group.**

● **Point to several SmartArt designs to see the Live Preview.**

● **Choose Inset from the 3-D category.**

● **Click outside the graphic to deselect it.**

Your screen should be similar to Figure 2.32

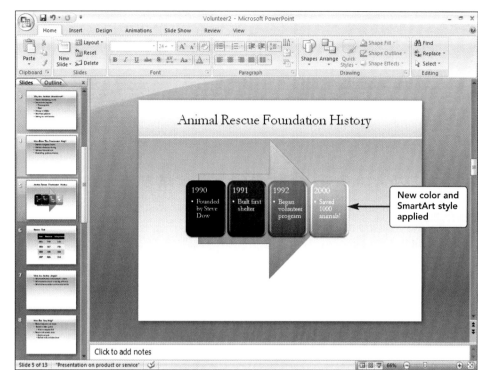

Figure 2.32

Inside figure: Animal Rescue Foundation History — 1990 • Founded by Steve Dow; 1991 • Built first shelter; 1992 • Began volunteer program; 2000 • Saved 1000 animals! — New color and SmartArt style applied

Additional Information

If, after making many formatting changes to a SmartArt graphic, you want to return to the original graphic design, use Reset Graphic.

The selected SmartArt style applies a combination of line, edge, and 3-D effects to all the shapes in the SmartArt graphic. You think the changes to the history slide greatly improve its appearance and readability.

Working with Text Boxes

On slide 12, you want to add the foundation's contact information. To make it stand out on the slide, you will put it into a text box. A **text box** is a container for text or graphics. The text box can be moved, resized, and enhanced in other ways to make it stand out from the other text on the slide.

Creating a Text Box

First you create the text box, and then you add the content.

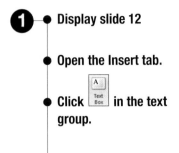

1
- Display slide 12
- Open the Insert tab.
- Click ⬛ in the text group.
- Click below the bullets and drag to the right.

Your screen should be similar to Figure 2.33

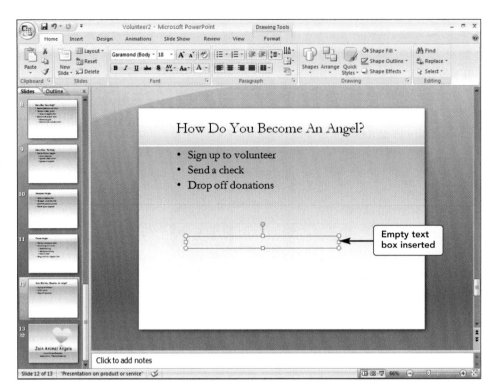

Figure 2.33

The text box is created and is a selected object. It is surrounded with a dashed border indicating you can enter, delete, select, and format the text inside the box.

Adding Text to a Text Box

The text box displays an insertion point, indicating that it is waiting for you to enter the text. As you type the text in the text box, it will resize automatically as needed to display the entire entry.

1 • Type the organization's name and address shown below in the text box.

Animal Rescue Foundation

1166 Oak Street

Lakeside, NH 03112

(603) 555-1313

• Select all the text and increase the font size to 24 points and bold.

Your screen should be similar to Figure 2.34

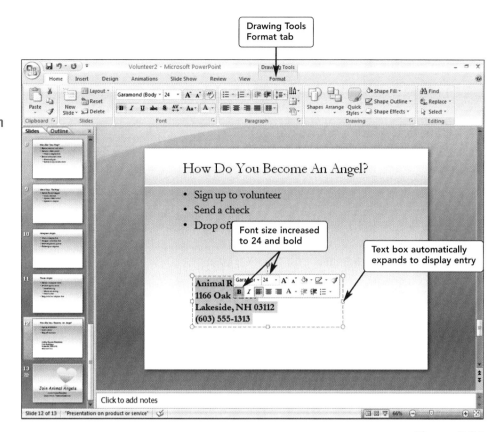

Figure 2.34

The text box resizes as you type and increase the font size.

Enhancing the Text Box

Like any other object, the text box can be sized and moved anywhere on the slide. It also can be enhanced by adding styles and effects. You want to change the color and add a border around the box to define the space. Then you will position it on the slide.

1 Deselect the text.

● Open the Drawing Tools Format tab.

● Open the Shape Styles gallery and choose Subtle Effect – Accent 4.

● Click 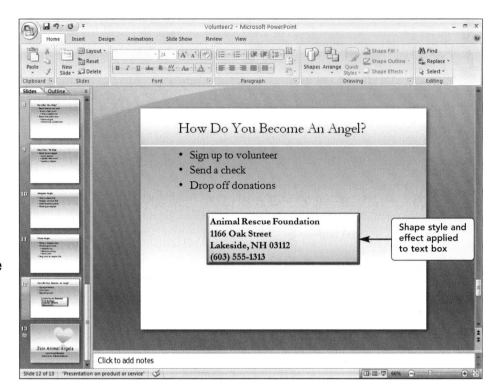.

● Choose Angle from the Bevel group.

● Move the text box to the position shown in Figure 2.35.

● Deselect the text box.

● Save the presentation.

Your screen should be similar to Figure 2.35

Figure 2.35

The information in the text box now stands out from the other information on the slide.

Changing the Presentation Design

When you first started this presentation, you used a PowerPoint template that included sample text as well as color and design elements. Now you are satisfied with the presentation's basic content and organization, but you would like to change its design style and appearance by applying a different document theme.

Concept 4

Document Theme

4 A **document theme** is a predefined set of formatting choices that can be applied to an entire document in one simple step. PowerPoint includes 20 named built-in themes. Each theme includes three subsets of components: colors, fonts, and effects. Each theme consists of 12 colors that are applied to specific elements in a document. Each font component includes different body and heading fonts. Each effects component includes different line and fill effects. You also can create your own custom themes by modifying an existing document theme and saving it as a custom theme. The default presentation uses the Office theme.

Using themes gives your documents a professional and modern look. Because themes are shared across 2007 Office applications, all your office documents can have the same uniform look.

Applying a Document Theme

A document theme can be applied to the entire presentation or to selected slides. You want to change the design for the entire presentation.

- **Display slide 1.**

- **Open the Design tab.**

- **Click ⊡ More in the Themes group to open the Themes gallery.**

- **Point to the Office Theme.**

  Your screen should be similar to Figure 2.36

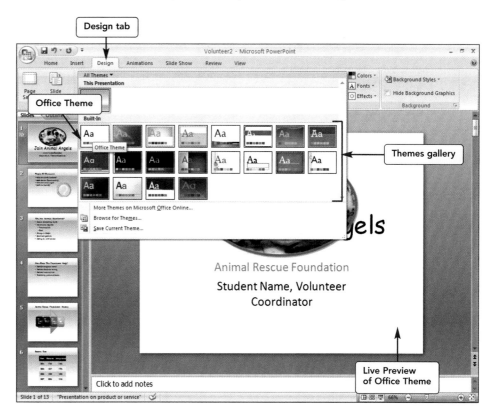

Figure 2.36

The Themes gallery displays samples of the document themes. The This Presentation area displays a preview of the theme that is currently used in the presentation. This is the theme associated with the presentation template you used to start the presentation. The Built-In area displays examples of the themes that are available in PowerPoint. The Live Preview shows how the presentation would look if the Office Theme were used. As you can see, the slide colors, background designs, font styles, and overall layout of the slide are affected by the theme.

You will preview several other themes, and then use the Oriel theme for the presentation.

2
● Preview several other themes.

● Choose the Oriel theme.

Your screen should be similar to Figure 2.37

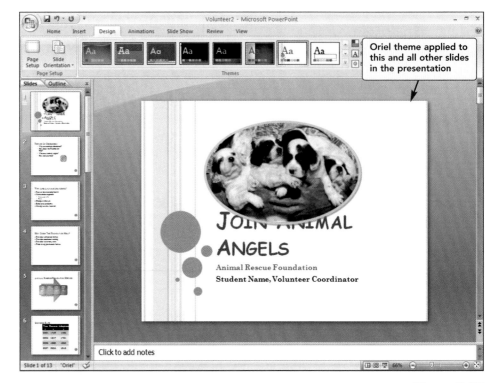

Oriel theme applied to this and all other slides in the presentation

Figure 2.37

The Oriel theme has been applied to all slides in the presentation. When a new theme is applied, the text styles, graphics, and colors that are included in the design replace the previous design settings. Consequently, the layout may need to be adjusted. For example, the photo on slide 1 will need to be repositioned and sized.

However, if you had made individual changes to a slide, such as changing the font of the title, these changes are not updated to the new theme design. In this case, the title font is still the Comic Sans MS that you selected; however, it has a smaller point size.

3 ● Use the Slides tab to select each slide and check the layout.

● Make the adjustments shown in the table below to the indicated slides.

After making the adjustments to slide 13, your screen should be similar to Figure 2.38

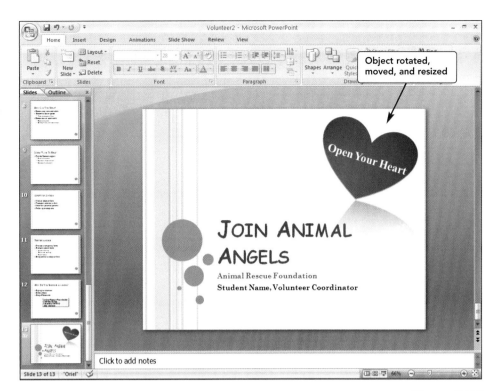

Figure 2.38

Slide	Adjustment
1	Reduce the size of the graphic slightly. Move the graphic to the upper right of the slide. Change the border color to the Blue-Gray, Text 2 theme color.
2	Adjust the size of the graphic. Recolor the graphic to Text color 2 Dark in the Dark Variations category.
5	Move and resize the SmartArt graphic.
7	Click 📋Reset in the slides group on the Home tab to reapply the theme bullet style to the text.
12	Click 📋Reset to reapply the theme bullet style to the text.
13	Rotate, move, and resize the heart to fit the upper-right area of the slide.

Changing the Theme Colors

To make the presentation livelier, you decide to try changing the colors associated with the selected theme. Although each theme has an associated set of colors, you can change the colors by applying the colors from another theme to the selected theme.

1
- Display slide 1 in Normal view.
- Open the Design tab.
- Click [Colors ▾] in the Themes group.

Your screen should be similar to Figure 2.39

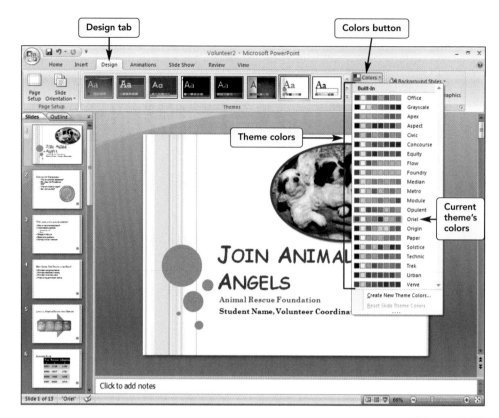

Figure 2.39

The colors used in each of the themes are displayed in the Built-In drop-down list. Each theme's colors consist of eight coordinated colors that are applied to different slide elements. The Oriel theme colors are selected because they are the set of colors associated with the Oriel theme. You want to see how the colors used in the Trek theme would look.

2
- Preview several other color themes.
- Select the Trek theme colors.

Your screen should be similar to Figure 2.40

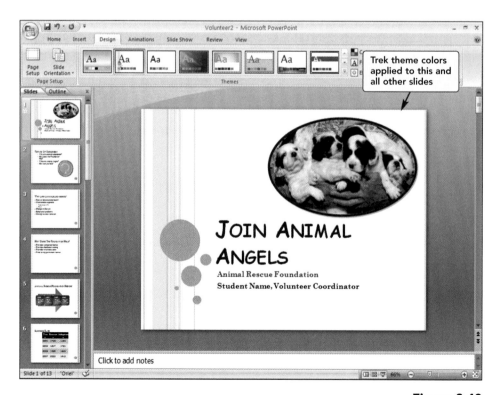

Figure 2.40

The slides are all converted to the colors used in the Trek theme. You like the slightly softer colors associated with the Trek theme. Using predefined theme colors gives your presentation a professional and consistent look.

Customizing Theme Colors

You like the Trek theme colors but think it could be improved by changing the title text color. You can customize theme colors by changing colors associated with the different elements. The new theme colors can then be saved as custom theme colors.

● **Click** **Colors**.

● **Choose Create New Theme Colors.**

Your screen should be similar to Figure 2.41

Figure 2.41

The dialog box identifies how the 12 Trek theme colors are applied to different elements of the slide. The sample box shows as example of how the selected colors are used in a slide. You will change the color of the background and title.

2
- Click **Text/Background
  – Dark 2** ◼ ▾.

- Choose **Red, Hyperlink**
  from the Theme Colors
  category.

- Type **Volunteer** in the
  Name text box.

- Click [Save].

- Save the presentation
  as Volunteer3.

*Your screen should be
similar to Figure 2.42*

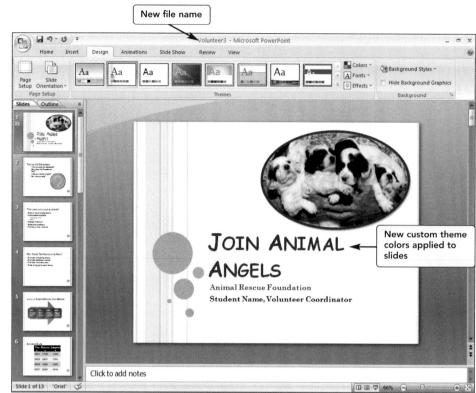

Figure 2.42

Additional Information
You can edit, delete, or
specify how to apply a theme
color by choosing the
appropriate option from the
theme color shortcut menu.

The new title color gives the presentation much more impact. In addition, the Volunteer custom theme colors will appear at the top of the available theme colors list. This makes it easy to reapply your custom color settings in the future. You saved the presentation with a new file name so you can show the director two different versions of the presentation.

Working with Master Slides

While viewing the slides, you think the slide appearance could be further improved by changing the bullet design on all slides. Although you can change each slide individually as you did in Lab 1, you can make the change much faster to all the slides by changing the slide master.

Concept 5

Master

5 A **master** is part of a template that stores information about the formatting for the three key components of a presentation—slides, speaker notes, and handouts. Each component has a master associated with it. The masters are described below.

Slide Master	Defines the format and layout of text and objects on a slide, text and object placeholder sizes, text styles, backgrounds, color themes, effects, and animation.
Handout Master	Defines the format and placement of the slide image, text, headers, footers, and other elements that will appear on every handout.
Notes Master	Defines the format and placement of the slide image, note text, headers, footers, and other elements that will appear on all speaker notes.

Any changes you make to a master affect all slides, handouts, or notes associated with that master. Each theme comes with its own slide master. When you apply a new theme to a presentation, all slides and masters are updated to those of the new theme. Using the master to modify or add elements to a presentation ensures consistency and saves time.

You can create slides that differ from the master by changing the format and placement of elements in the individual slide rather than on the master. For example, when you changed the font settings of the title on the title slide, the slide master was not affected. Only the individual slide changed, making it unique. If you have created a unique slide, the elements you changed on that slide retain their uniqueness even if you later make changes to the slide master. That is the reason that the title font did not change when you changed the theme.

Modifying the Slide Master

You will change the bullet style in the slide master so that all slides in the presentation will be changed.

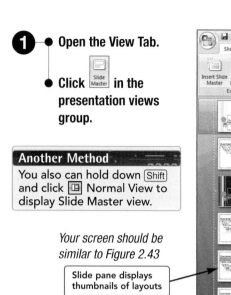

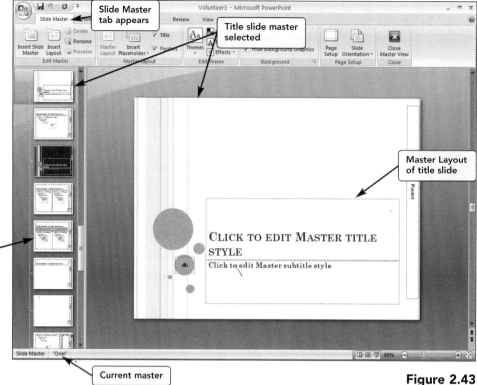

Figure 2.43

The view has changed to Slide Master view, and a new tab, Slide Master, is displayed. Slide Master view consists of two panes: the left pane, or Slide pane, displays thumbnails for each of the layouts associated with the Oriel slide master and the right pane displays the selected master slide. The status bar identifies the master you are viewing. The thumbnail for the title layout master is selected, and the slide pane displays the master slide.

You want to make changes to the slide master first.

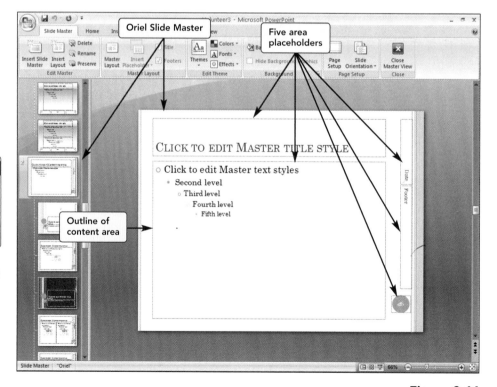

Figure 2.44

The slide master consists of five area placeholders that control the appearance of all slides: title, content, date, footer, and a shape. The title and content areas display sample text to show you how changes you make in these areas will appear. You make changes to the master slide in the same way that you change any other slide. You will modify the content area placeholder and change the current round bullet style to a picture bullet style.

3 ● **Click the outline of the content area on the slide to select it.**

● **Open the Home tab.**

● **Open the** 🔲▾ **Bullets drop-down menu.**

● **Choose Bullets and Numbering.**

● **Click** 🔲 Picture... 🔲**.**

Your screen should be similar to Figure 2.45

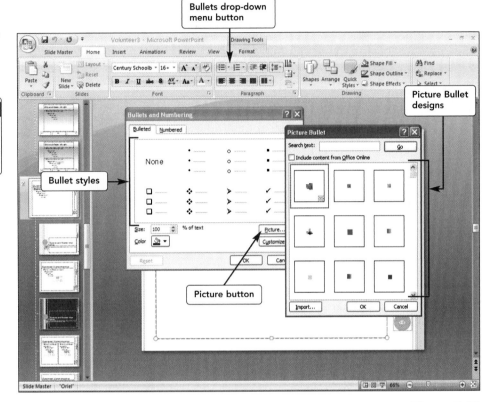

Figure 2.45

From the Picture Bullet dialog box, you select the bullet design you want to use from the bullet styles listed. You will use a round bullet design in a color that coordinates with the theme colors.

4 ● Scroll the gallery and choose ■ bullets, network blitz 15 ... (second column of the fourth row).

Having Trouble?
If this bullet style is not available, select another of your choice.

● Click [OK].

Your screen should be similar to Figure 2.46

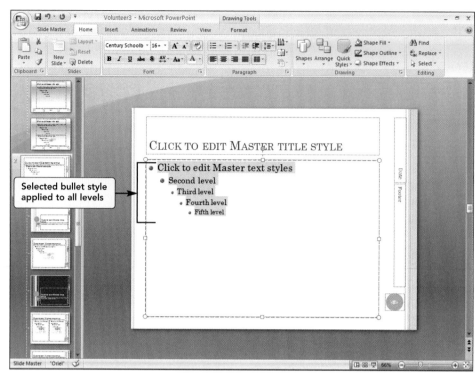

Figure 2.46

Additional Information
You can apply different bullet styles to each level by selecting each level individually.

The selected bullet style has been applied to all levels of items in the content area and to all slides under the main master slide that have bulleted items.

Now, you want to see how the changes you have made to the slide master have affected the actual slides in the presentation.

5 ● Click 🔠 Slide Sorter view.

● Increase the magnification to 100%.

Your screen should be similar to Figure 2.47

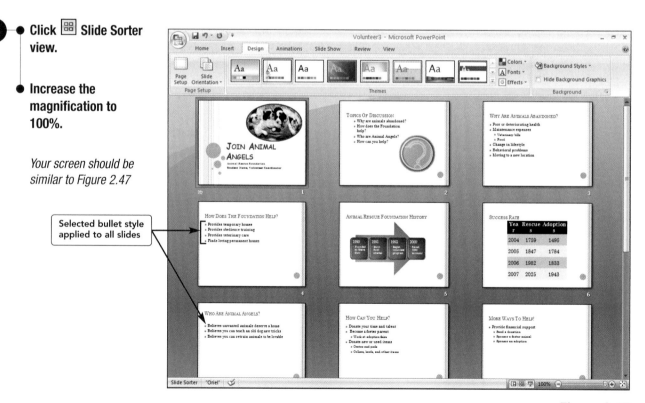

Figure 2.47

You can now see that the change you made to the bullet style in the slide master is reflected in all slides in the presentation. Using the slide master allows you to quickly make global changes to your presentation.

Adding Slide Footer Text

You also would like to include the name of the foundation and slide number in a footer on the slides. The slide master controls the placement and display of the footer information but does not control the information that appears in those areas.

1 ● **Open the Insert tab.**

● **Click** Header & Footer **in the Text group.**

● **If necessary, open the Slides tab.**

Your screen should be similar to Figure 2.48

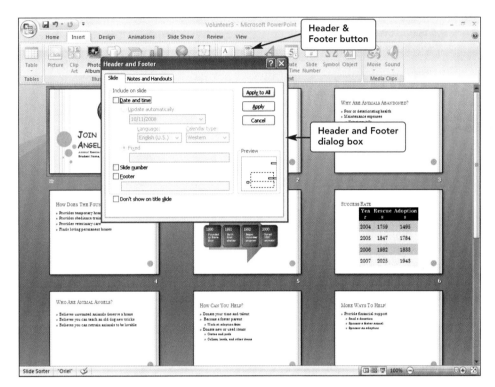

Figure 2.48

None of the options in the Include on Slide list are checked because there are currently no footers defined. The footer can appear on all slides or selected slides. You also can turn off the display of the footer information in title slides only. You would like to add the foundation name and the slide number to the footer of all slides, except the title slides.

2

● Select the Slide number option.

● Select the Footer option.

● Type **Animal Rescue Foundation** in the Footer text box.

● Select the Don't show on title slide option.

● Click [Apply to All].

Your screen should be similar to Figure 2.49

Additional Information

The [Apply] command button applies the settings to the current slide or selected slides only.

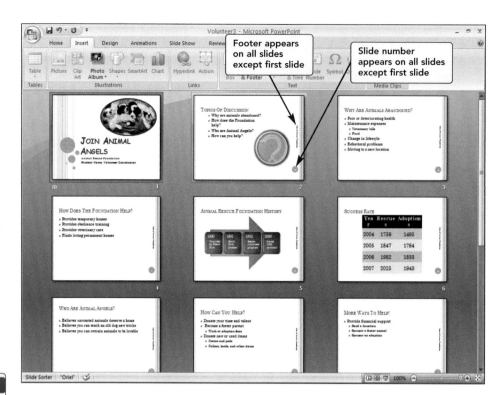

Figure 2.49

The text you entered is displayed in the Footer area placeholder and the slide number appears in the graphic circle. No footer information is displayed on the first or last slides in the presentation because they use the Title Slide layout.

As you run the slide show next, you will see that the footer does not display on the first or last slides. Also notice the use of the custom bullet throughout.

3

● Run the slide show beginning with slide 1.

● Click on each slide to advance through the presentation.

● Save the presentation.

As you ran the slide show, you probably noticed that slides 1 and 13, the title slides, displayed the text using a special animation effect. This effect was included in the template as part of the template design.

Note: If you are ending your session now, save the presentation and exit PowerPoint 2007. When you begin again, open this file.

Adding Animation Effects

You liked the animation effect that was included on the title slides and have several additional places in mind where using animation will make the presentation more interesting.

Concept 6

Animations

6 **Animations** are special effects that add action to text and graphics so they move around on the screen during a slide show. Animations provide additional emphasis for items or show the information on a slide in phases. There are two basic types of animations: object animations and transitions.

Object animations are used to display each bullet point, text, paragraph, or graphic independently of the other text or objects on the slide. You set up the way you want each element to appear (to fly in from the left, for instance) and whether you want the other elements already on the slide to dim or shimmer when a new element is added. For example, because your audience is used to reading from left to right, you could select animations that fly text in from the left. Then, when you want to emphasize a point, bring a bullet point in from the right. That change grabs the audience's attention.

Transitions control the way that the display changes as you move from one slide to the next during a presentation. You can select from many different transition choices. You may choose Dissolve for your title slide to give it an added flair. After that you could use Wipe Right for all the slides until the next to the last, and then use Dissolve again to end the show. As with any special effect, use slide transitions carefully.

When you present a slide show, the content of your presentation should take center stage. You want the animation effects to help emphasize the main points in your presentation—not draw the audience's attention to the special effects.

Animating an Object and Adding Sound Effects

You will begin by adding animation and sound to the shape object on the final slide.

1 ● **Display slide 13 in Normal view.**

● **Select the heart shape.**

● **Open the Animations tab.**

● **Click** [Custom Animation] **in the Animations group.**

Your screen should be similar to Figure 2.50

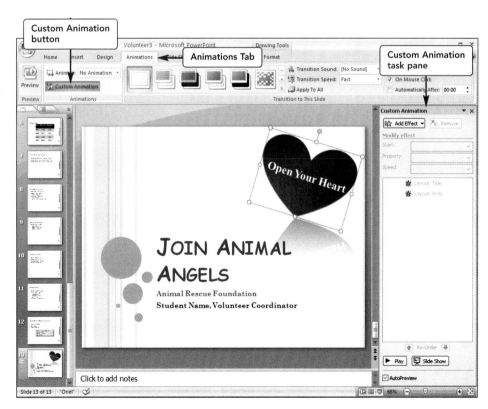

Figure 2.50

The Custom Animation task pane is used to assign animations and sound to objects on the slide. As you add animated items to a slide, each item is numbered. The number determines the order in which they display. A nonprinting numbered tag appears on the slide near each animated item that correlates to the effects in the list.

You will animate the shape object only. As you make selections, the Custom Animation list box will display the selected settings for the object and the effect will be demonstrated in the slide.

2
- If necessary, select the AutoPreview option.
- Click ⭐ Add Effect ▾.
- Select Entrance from the drop-down list.
- Choose 5. Fly In.
- From the Direction drop-down list, select From Left.
- From the Speed drop-down list, select Medium.
- Display the
  `1 🞲 🞲 Heart 4: Open You... ▾`
  drop-down list and select Effect Options.

Your screen should be similar to Figure 2.51

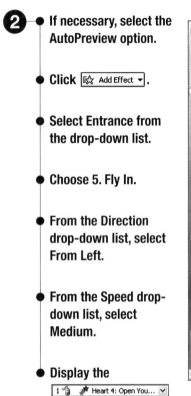

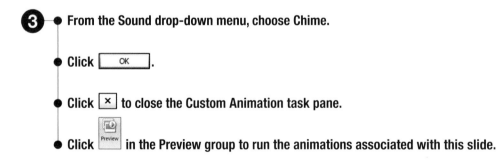

AutoPreview option

Figure 2.51

The Fly In dialog box includes the setting you already specified for the direction of the effect. You will use it to add a sound to the fly-in effect.

3
- From the Sound drop-down menu, choose Chime.
- Click ⬚ OK ⬚.
- Click ⬚×⬚ to close the Custom Animation task pane.
- Click 🞲Preview in the Preview group to run the animations associated with this slide.

Additional Information
You must have a speaker and a sound card to hear the sound.

The heart appeared using the fly-in effect, and the chime sound played as it will when the slide show is run.

Animating a SmartArt Graphic

Next, you will animate the SmartArt graphic. The entire graphic can be animated or the individual parts can be animated to show the information in phases.

1 ● **Display slide 5.**

● **Select the SmartArt shape.**

● **Open the**

Animate: No Animation ▾

drop-down list.

Your screen should be similar to Figure 2.52

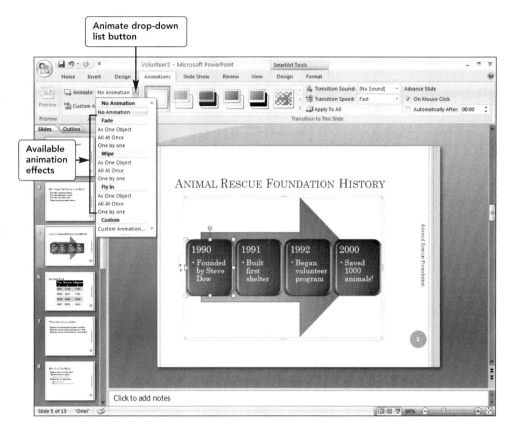

Figure 2.52

The animations that are displayed in the list are animations that are available for the layout of your SmartArt graphic. Animations for a SmartArt graphic are different than those for other graphic objects. This is because the animation plays in the order that the shapes appear. This order begins with the first item listed in the text pane and moves down. As you point to the different animations, a Live Preview demonstrates the effect.

2 ● Point to several animations to see the Live Preview.

● Choose One by One in the Fade group.

Your screen should be similar to Figure 2.53

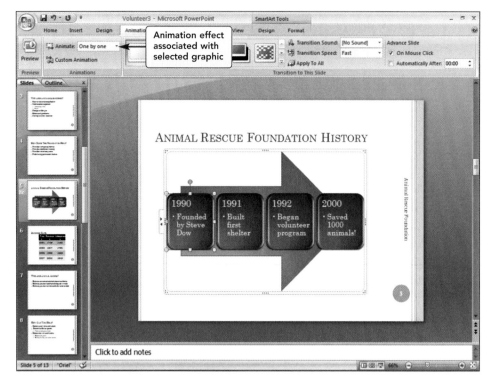

Figure 2.53

The underlying graphic, in this case the arrow, appeared first using a Fade effect. Then each box appeared in sequence also using the same effect.

Animating a Slide Master

The next effect you want to add to the slides is an animation effect that will display each bullet progressively on a slide. When the animation is applied to a slide, the slide initially shows only the title. The bulleted text appears as the presentation proceeds. You want to add this effect to all the slides that have bulleted items. To do this, you could add the effect to each slide individually. However, when there are many slides, it is faster to add the effect to the slide master so all slides based on the selected master slide layout display the effect.

1 ● Change to Slide Master view.

● Select the Oriel Title and Text Layout slide master.

Having Trouble?
Point to the slide master thumbnail to see the master slide layout name.

● Select the content placeholder.

● Open the Animations tab.

● Click .

● Click Add Effect and choose the Fly-in Entrance effect.

● Change the direction to Bottom-Left and speed to Medium.

● Close the task pane and return to Normal view.

Your screen should be similar to Figure 2.54

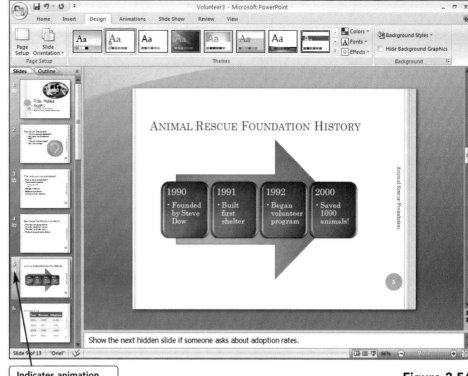

Indicates animation effect applied to slide

Figure 2.54

Notice the action icon ⭐ displayed next to the slides in the Slides tab. This indicates that an animation effect has been applied to the slide. To preview the animation, you can click the icon or 🖼️ Preview in the Animations tab.

2 ● Preview the animation on slide 3.

The preview demonstrates how each first-level bullet will appear one by one on the slide. The same effect has been applied to all slides using the Title and Text Layout. If a new slide were inserted using this layout, it would have the same animation effect.

Adding Transition Effects

Next, you want to add a transition effect to all the slides. Although you can add transitions in Normal view, you will use Slide Sorter view so you can preview the action on all the slides.

1
● Switch to Slide Sorter view.

● Click ⊽ More in the Transition to This Slide group to open the Transitions gallery.

Your screen should be similar to Figure 2.55

Additional Information
In Slide Sorter view, the animation icon appears below each slide.

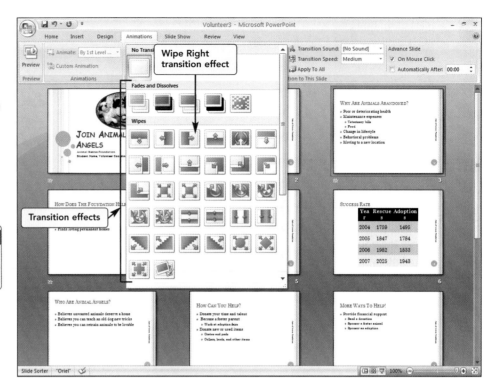

Figure 2.55

Additional Information
Use the No Transition option to remove transition effects.

There are five transition categories with each containing variations on the category effect. You want to use a simple transition effect that will display as each slide appears.

2
● Click  Wipe Right in the Wipes category.

Having Trouble?
If you want to see the transition effect again, click ▯ in the transition gallery in the Ribbon.

The selected slide displays the Wipe Right transition effect. This effect displays the next slide's content by wiping over the previous slide from the right with the new slide content. You want to try a similar effect in the Push and Cover category.

3
● Open the Transitions gallery again.

● Select Push Right from the Push and Cover category.

You like this effect too but think a little variety may be more effective. To do this, you decide to use the Random Transition effect, which will randomly run different transition effects, and apply the effect to all slides.

4 • Open the Transitions gallery again.

• Choose Random Transition from the Random category.

Having Trouble?
Scroll down to see the Random Transition option.

• Click **Apply to All** in the Transition to This Slide group.

Additional Information
You also could select all the slides or multiple slides and apply the transition to those slides only.

• Select all the slides and click 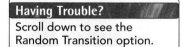 to see all animation effects.

Your screen should be similar to Figure 2.56

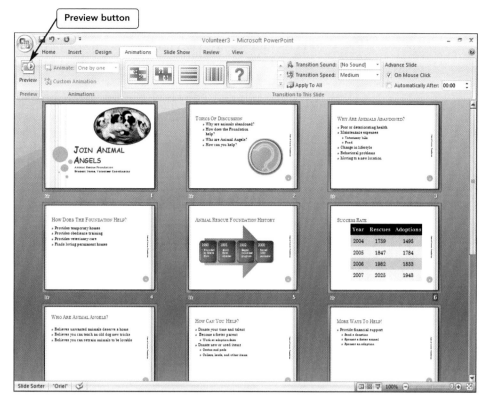

Figure 2.56

A variety of transitions were used as each slide was previewed.

5 • Switch to Normal view.

• Save the presentation.

You have made many changes to the presentation and want to run the show full screen to see the total effect.

Controlling the Slide Show

As much as you would like to control a presentation completely, the presence of an audience usually causes the presentation to change course. PowerPoint has several ways to control a slide show during the presentation. Before presenting a slide show, you should rehearse the presentation. To help with this aspect of the presentation, you can use the Rehearse Timings feature that records the time you spend on each slide as you practice your narration. If your computer is set up with a microphone, you could even record your narration with the Record Narration feature.

Navigating in a Slide Show

Running the slide show and practicing how to control the slide show help you to have a smooth presentation. For example, if someone has a question about a previous slide, you can go backward and redisplay it. You will try out some of the features you can use while running the slide show.

1 ● Start the slide show from the beginning.

● Click two times to display slides 2 and 3.

Your screen should be similar to Figure 2.57

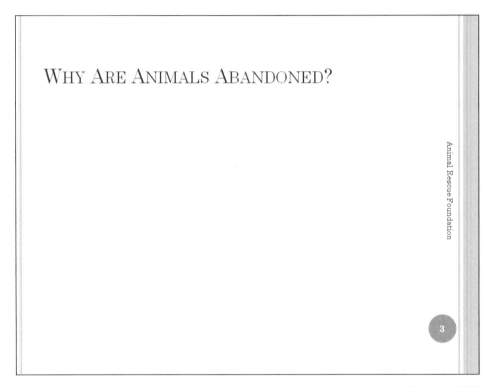

WHY ARE ANIMALS ABANDONED?

Animal Rescue Foundation

3

Figure 2.57

The first slide displayed the animation effect associated with the slide title. The second slide appeared using one of the transition effects. The third slide also appears with a transition effect and displays the title only.

When an animation is applied to the content area of a slide, the content items are displayed only when you click or use any of the procedures to advance to the next slide. This allows the presenter to focus the audience's attention and to control the pace of the presentation.

2 ● Continue to click or press [Spacebar] until slide 8, How Can You Help? appears.

● Press [←Backspace] (5 times).

Additional Information
You can return to the first slide in the presentation by holding down both mouse buttons for two seconds.

Your screen should be similar to Figure 2.58

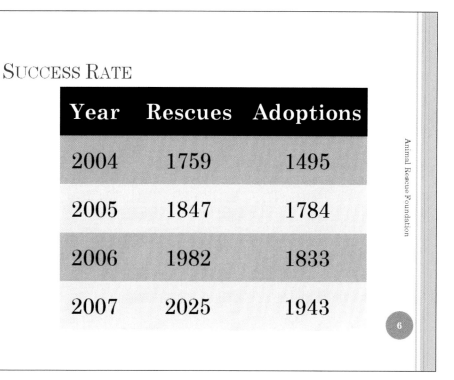

SUCCESS RATE

Year	Rescues	Adoptions
2004	1759	1495
2005	1847	1784
2006	1982	1833
2007	2025	1943

6

Animal Rescue Foundation

Figure 2.58

You returned the onscreen presentation to slide 6, but now, because the audience has already viewed slide 7, you want to advance to slide 8. To go to a specific slide number, you type the slide number and press [←Enter].

3 ● Type **8** and press [←Enter].

Another Method
You also can choose Go to Slide from the shortcut menu and select a slide to display.

● Click three times to display the bulleted items.

● Click again to display slide 9.

Your screen should be similar to Figure 2.59

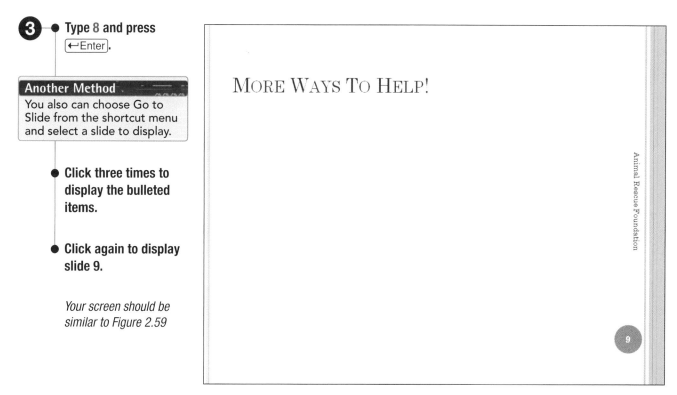

MORE WAYS TO HELP!

9

Animal Rescue Foundation

Figure 2.59

Slide 9, More Ways To Help, is displayed.

Sometimes a question from an audience member can interrupt the flow of the presentation. If this happens to you, you can black out the screen to focus attention onto your response.

4 ● Press b or B.

The screen goes to black while you address the topic. When you are ready to resume the presentation, you can bring the slide back.

5 ● Click, or press b.

● Click to display the bulleted items on slide 9.

Adding Freehand Annotations

During your presentation, you may want to point to an important word, underline an important point, or draw checkmarks next to items that you have covered. To do this, you can use the mouse pointer during the presentation. When you move the mouse, the mouse pointer appears and the Slide Show toolbar is displayed in the lower-left corner of the screen. The mouse pointer in its current shape ⌖ can be used to point to items on the slide. You also can use it to draw on the screen by changing the mouse pointer to a ballpoint pen, felt tip pen, or highlighter, which activates the associated freehand annotation feature.

1 ● Move the mouse on your desktop.

● Click ✏ to display the Pointer options menu.

Your screen should be similar to Figure 2.60

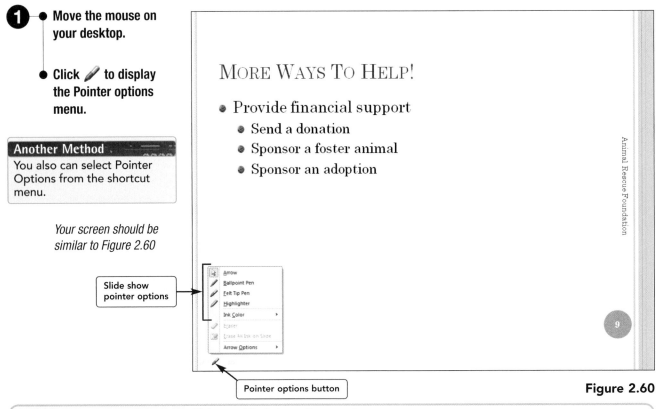

Figure 2.60

The mouse pointer and arrow options are described in the following table.

Pointer Options	Effect
Arrow	Displays the mouse pointer as an arrow.
Ballpoint Pen	Changes the mouse pointer to a diamond shape and turns on ballpoint pen annotation.
Felt Tip Pen	Changes the mouse pointer to a circle shape and turns on felt tip pen annotation.
Highlighter	Changes the mouse pointer to a bar shape and turns on highlighter.
Ink Color	Displays a color palette to select a color for the annotation tool.
Eraser	Erases selected annotations.
Erase All Ink on Slide	Removes all annotations from the slide.
Arrow Options	**(These options apply only if Arrow is selected.)**
Automatic	Hides the mouse pointer if it is not moved for 15 seconds. It reappears when you move the mouse. This is the default setting.
Visible	Displays the mouse pointer as an arrow and does not hide it.
Hidden	Hides the mouse pointer until another pointer option is selected.

You will try out several of the freehand annotation features to see how they work. To draw, you select the pen style and then drag the pen pointer in the direction you want to draw.

Choose Felt Tip Pen.

Additional Information
The mouse pointer changes shape depending upon the selected annotation tool.

● **Move the dot pointer to near the word "Send" and then drag the dot pointer until a circle is drawn around the word "Send."**

● **Choose Highlighter from the Pointer options menu and highlight the word "Donation."**

● **Choose Ballpoint Pen from the Pointer options menu.**

Another Method
You also can use [Ctrl] + P to display the Ballpoint Pen.

● **Choose Ink Color from the Pointer options menu and select Light Blue from the Standard Colors bar.**

Additional Information
The Automatic ink color setting determines the default color to use for annotations based upon the slide theme colors.

● **Draw three lines under the word "Help".**

Your screen should be similar to Figure 2.61

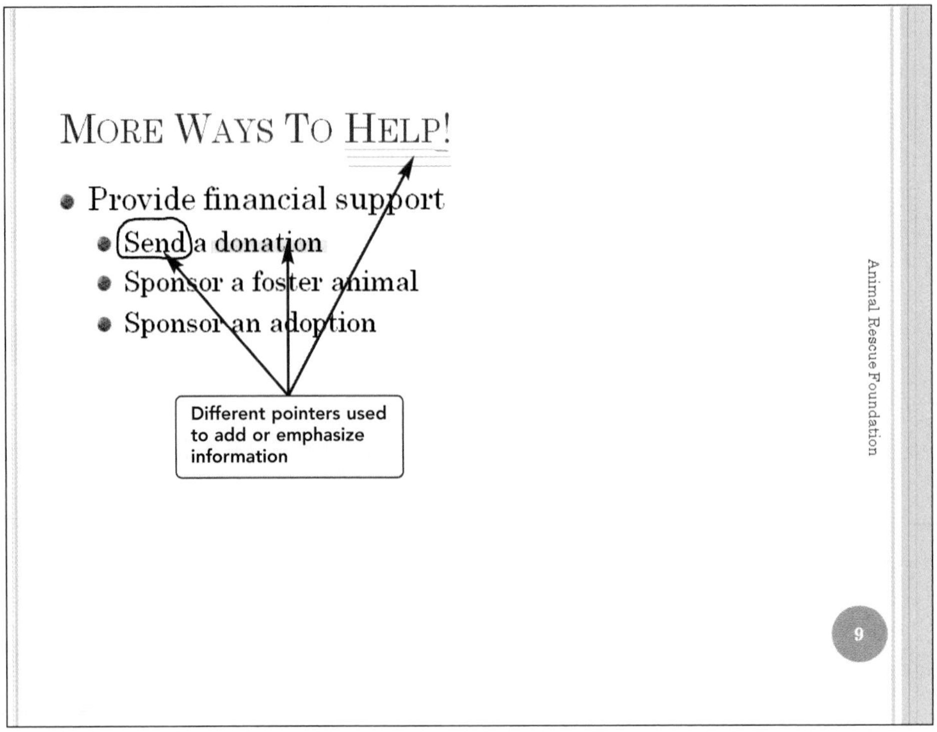

MORE WAYS TO HELP!

● Provide financial support
  ● Send a donation
  ● Sponsor a foster animal
  ● Sponsor an adoption

Different pointers used to add or emphasize information

Animal Rescue Foundation

9

Figure 2.61

The freehand annotation feature allows you to point out and emphasize important information on a slide during the presentation.

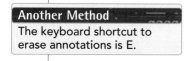

3 • Practice using the freehand annotator to draw any shapes you want on the slide.

• To erase the annotations, select Erase All Ink on Slide from the Pointer options menu.

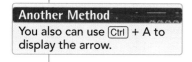

Another Method
The keyboard shortcut to erase annotations is E.

• To turn off freehand annotation, select Arrow from the Pointer options menu.

Another Method
You also can use Ctrl + A to display the arrow.

• Press Esc to end the slide show.

If you do not erase annotations before ending the presentation, you are prompted to keep or discard the annotations when you end the slide show. If you keep the annotations, they are saved to the slides and will appear as part of the slide during a presentation.

Hiding Slides

As you reconsider the presentation, you decide to show the Success Rate slide only if someone asks about this information. To do this, you will hide the slide.

1 • Select slide 6.

• Open the Slide Show tab.

• Click [Hide Slide].

Your screen should be similar to Figure 2.62

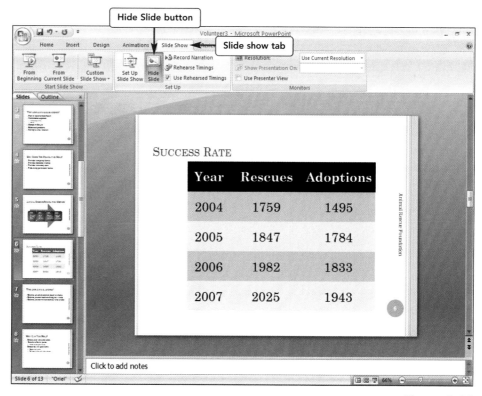

Figure 2.62

Notice that the slide number for slide 6 is surrounded by a box with a slash drawn through it, which indicates that the slide is hidden. Next, you will run the slide show to see how hidden slides work. You will begin the show at the slide before the hidden slide.

2 • Select slide 5.

• Run the slide show from the current slide.

• Click six times to display the slide animation and move to the next slide, which should be Who Are Animal Angels?

Your screen should be similar to Figure 2.63

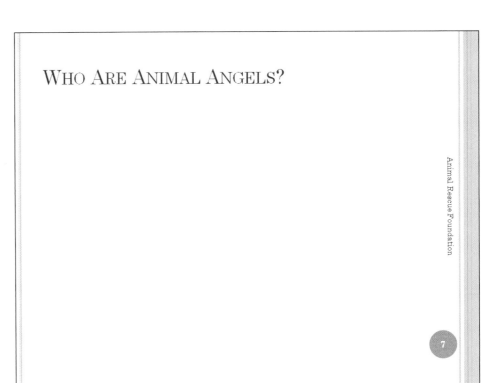

WHO ARE ANIMAL ANGELS?

Animal Rescue Foundation

7

Figure 2.63

Slide 6 was not displayed because it is hidden. To show how to display a hidden slide, you will return to slide 5 and then display slide 6.

3 • Press (Page Up) to display slide 5 again.

• Press H to see slide 6.

Your screen should be similar to Figure 2.64

Another Method .
You also can use Go to Slide on the shortcut menu to display a hidden slide.

SUCCESS RATE

Year	Rescues	Adoptions
2004	1759	1495
2005	1847	1784
2006	1982	1833
2007	2025	1943

Animal Rescue Foundation

6

Figure 2.64

Adding Speaker Notes

When making your presentation, there are some critical points you want to be sure to discuss. To help you remember the important points, you can add notes to a slide and then print the **notes pages.** These pages display the notes below a small version of the slide they accompany. You can create notes pages for some or all of the slides in a presentation. You decide to add speaker notes on slide 5 to remind you about the hidden slide.

1 • Press Esc to end the slide show.

• Display slide 5 in Normal view.

• Click in the notes pane.

• Type **Show the next hidden slide if someone asks about adoption rates.**

Your screen should be similar to Figure 2.65

> **Additional Information**
> You can enlarge the notes area by dragging the pane divider line.

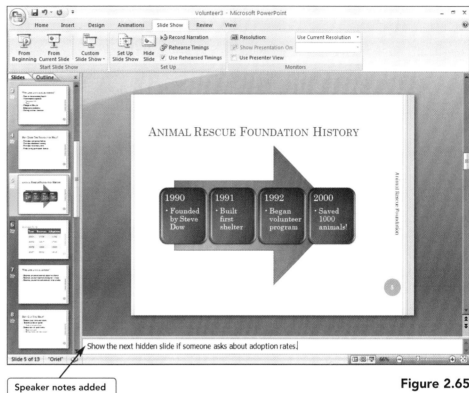

Speaker notes added

Figure 2.65

You will preview the notes page to check its appearance before it is printed.

2 ● Open the View tab.

● Click [Notes Page] in the Presentation Views group.

Your screen should be similar to Figure 2.66

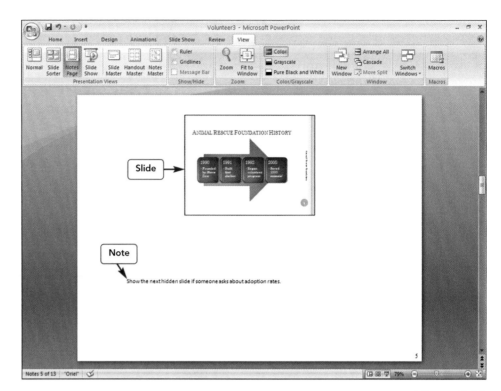

Figure 2.66

The notes pages display the note you added below the slide that the note accompanies.

To make the speaker notes easy to read in a dimly lit room while you are making the presentation, you will increase the font size of the note text.

3 ● Click on the note text to select the placeholder.

● Select the note text.

● Use the Mini Toolbar to increase the font size to 20.

● Click outside the note text border.

Your screen should be similar to Figure 2.67

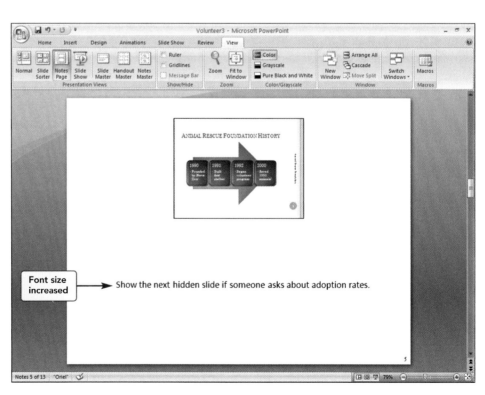

Figure 2.67

Adding Headers and Footers to Notes and Handouts

Currently, the only information that appears in the footer of the notes page is the page number. You want to include the date and your name in the header of the notes and handouts.

1. ● **Open the Insert tab.**

● **Click** [Header & Footer] **in the Text group.**

● **If necessary, open the Notes and Handouts tab.**

Your screen should be similar to Figure 2.68

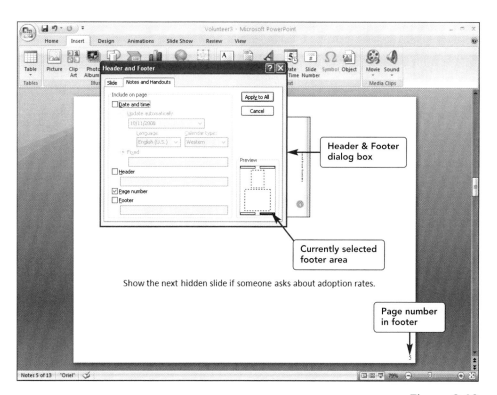

Figure 2.68

As in slides, you can display date and time information and footer text. In addition, on notes and handouts, you can include header text and a page number. The preview area identifies the four areas where this information will appear and identifies the currently selected areas, in this case page number, in bold.

2 ● **Click Date and time to turn on this option and, if necessary, select Update automatically.**

● **Select Header and enter your name in the Header text box.**

● **Click** Apply to All .

Your screen should be similar to Figure 2.69

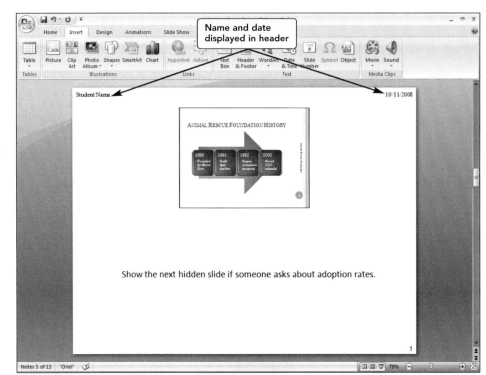

Figure 2.69

The information is displayed in the header as specified.

Documenting a File

Along with the content of the presentation, each file can include additional document properties or settings that are associated with the file. Some of these properties are automatically generated. These include statistics such as the number of words in the file and general information such as the date the document was created and last modified. Others such as the author of the file are properties that you can add to the file.

You will look at the file properties and add documentation as needed.

1 ● **Return to Normal view.**

● **Display slide 1.**

● **Click** 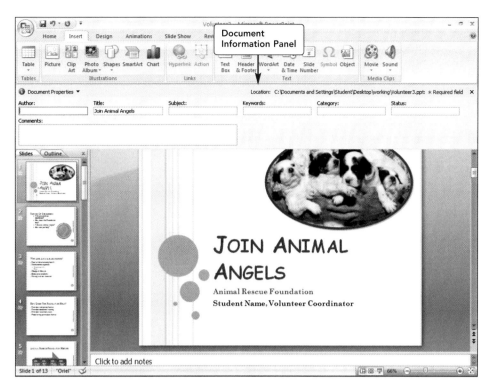 **Office Button and select Prepare.**

● **Choose Properties.**

Your screen should be similar to Figure 2.70

Figure 2.70

The Document Information Panel opens and displays the standard information about the file. The first few words in the first line of a document are used as the default title.

The Standard property fields are used for the following:

Option	Action
Author	Enter the name of the presentation's author. By default this is the name entered when PowerPoint was installed.
Title	Enter the presentation title. This title can be longer and more descriptive than the presentation file name.
Subject	Enter a description of the presentation's content.
Keywords	Enter words that you associate with the presentation so the Find File command can be used.
Category	Enter the name of a higher-level category under which you can group similar types of presentations.
Status	Enter the degree of completion; for example, first draft or final presentation.
Comments	Enter any comments you feel are appropriate for the presentation.

You will modify the information to include your name and a subject description. The default title does not need to be changed. You also will quickly look at the additional information that is stored with the file properties.

2
- In the Author text box, enter your name.

- In the Subject text box, enter **Volunteer recruitment.**

- Click **Document Properties ▼** and choose Advanced Properties.

Your screen should be similar to Figure 2.71

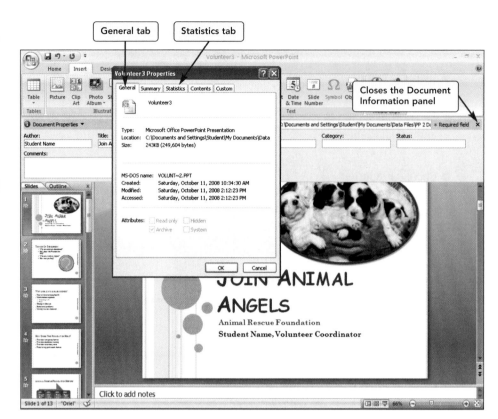

General tab   Statistics tab

Closes the Document Information panel

Figure 2.71

The General tab displays information about the type, location, and size of the document as well as about when the document was created and modified. Next, you will look at the document statistics. This tab identifies who last saved the document, the revision number, and the total editing time in minutes. The table identifies the number of slides, words, paragraphs, and so forth that are included in the presentation. Then you will close the Document Information panel.

3
- Open the Statistics tab.

- Click OK to close the Properties dialog box.

- Click ☒ to close the Document Information panel.

Customizing Print Settings

You have created both slides and a notes page for the presentation. Now you want to print the notes page and some of the slides. Customizing the print settings by selecting specific slides to print and scaling the size of the slides to fill the page are a few of the ways to make your printed output look more professional.

Printing Notes Pages

First you will print the notes page for the slide on which you entered note text.

1 ● Select slide 5.

● Click 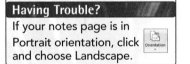 Office Button and choose Print.

● If necessary, select the printer.

● From the Print Range section, select Current Slide.

● From the Print What drop-down list box, select Notes Pages.

● If necessary, select Grayscale from the Color/Grayscale drop-down list box.

● Click [Preview].

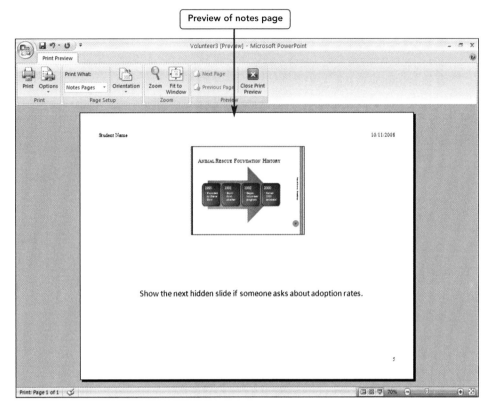

Preview of notes page

Figure 2.72

The notes page is displayed in landscape orientation as it will appear when printed.

Having Trouble?
If your notes page is in Portrait orientation, click 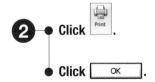 and choose Landscape.

Your screen should be similar to Figure 2.72

2 ● Click [Print].

● Click [OK].

Printing Selected Slides

Next you will print a few selected slides to be used as handouts. You will change the orientation to landscape and scale the slides to fit the paper size.

1 ● Click .

● Click **Slides** in the **Print Range** section.

● In the **Slides** text box, type **1, 2, 6, 13.**

● Specify **Handouts** as the component to print and **4 slides per page.**

● Click .

● Click [Orientation] and change to **Portrait** orientation.

● Click [Options] and select **Scale to Fit Paper.**

Your screen should be similar to Figure 2.73

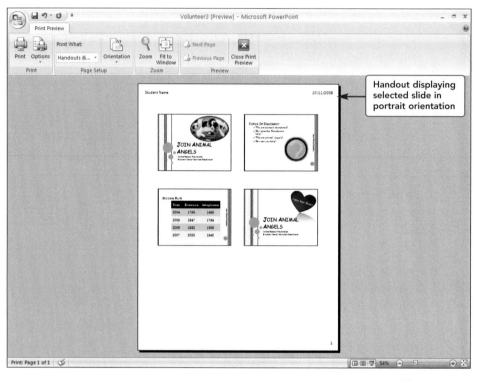

Figure 2.73

The four selected slides are displayed in portrait orientation and the slide images were sized as large as possible to fill the page.

2 ● Print the handout.

● Close the Print Preview window.

● Save the completed presentation.

● Exit PowerPoint.

The view you are in when you save the file is the view that will be displayed when the file is opened. The document properties and print settings are also saved with the file.

Focus on Careers

EXPLORE YOUR CAREER OPTIONS

Communications Specialist

Are you interested in technology? Could you explain it in words and pictures? Communications Specialists, also known as public relations specialists, assist sales and marketing management with communications media and advertising materials that represent the company's products and services to customers. In high-tech industries, you will take information from scientists and engineers and use PowerPoint to transform the data into eye-catching presentations that communicate effectively. You also may create brochures, develop Web sites, create videos, and write speeches. If you thrive in a fast-paced and high-energy environment and work well under the pressure of deadlines, then this job may be for you. Typically a bachelor's degree in journalism, advertising, or communications is desirable. Typical salaries range from $26,000 to $85,000, depending on the industry. To learn more about this career, visit the Web site for the Bureau of Labor Statistics of the U.S. Department of Labor.

Find and Replace (PP2.5)

To make editing easier, you can use the Find and Replace feature to find text in a presentation and replace it with other text as directed.

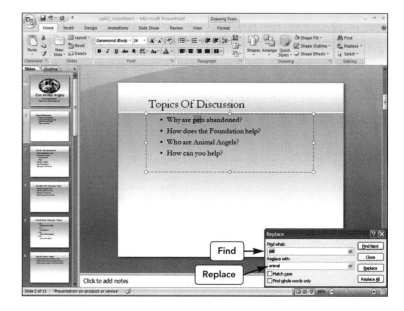

Table (PP2.8)

A table is used to organize information into an easy-to-read format of horizontal rows and vertical columns.

Alignment (PP2.16)

Alignment controls how text entries are positioned within a space.

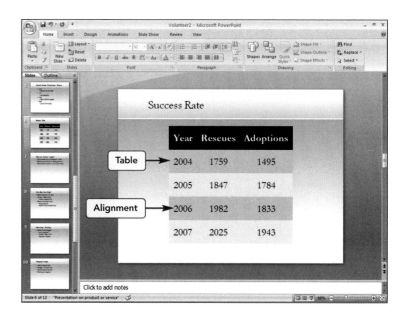

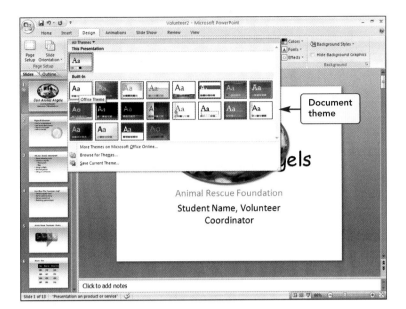

Document Theme (PP2.34)

A document theme is a professionally created slide design that is stored as a file and can be applied to a presentation.

Master (PP2.41)

A master is a special slide or page that stores information about the formatting for all slides in a presentation.

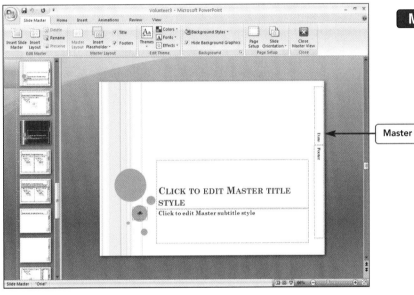

Animations (PP2.47)

Special effects such as animation, sound, and slide transitions are used to enhance the onscreen presentation.

Modifying and Refining a Presentation

command summary

Command	Shortcut	Action
Office Button		
Prepare/Properties		View and edit presentation properties such as Title, Author, and keywords
Home tab		
Font group		
A˄ Increase Font Size	Ctrl + Shift + >.	Increases font size of selected text
Paragraph group		
Align Left	Ctrl + F	Aligns text to the left
Align Center	Ctrl + E	Centers text
Align Right	Ctrl + R	Aligns text to the right
Justify	Ctrl + F	Aligns text to both the left and right margins
Align Text		Sets vertical alignment of text
Editing group		
Find	Ctrl + F	Finds specified text
Replace	Ctrl + H	Replaces located text with replacement text
Insert tab		
Illustrations group		
Shapes		Inserts a shape
SmartArt		Inserts SmartArt shape
Text group		
Text Box		Inserts text box or adds text to selected shape
Header & Footer		Inserts a header and footer
Design tab		
Themes group		
More		Opens gallery of document themes
Colors		Changes the color for the current theme

command summary

Command	Shortcut	Action
Animations tab		
Animations group		
Custom Animation		Creates custom animation for individual objects
Transition to This Slide group		
Apply To All		Applies transitions in current slide to all slides
Slide Show tab		
Set Up group		
Hide Slide		Hides current slide so that it does not appear during the presentation
View tab		
Presentation Views group		
Notes Page		Displays current slide in Notes view to edit the speaker notes
Slide Master		Opens Slide Master view to change the design and layout of the master slides
Drawing Tools Format tab		
Shapes Styles group		
More		Opens the Shape Styles gallery to select a visual style to apply to a shape
Shape Effects		Applies a visual effect to a shape
Arrange group		
Rotate		Rotates or flips the selected object
Picture Tools Format tab		
Adjust group		
Recolor		Recolors picture
Picture Styles		
More		Opens Picture Styles gallery to select an overall visual style for picture
Picture Effects		Applies a visual effect to picture

command summary

Command	Shortcut	Action
SmartArt Tools Design tab		
Layouts group		
More		Opens the Layouts gallery to change the layout for the selected SmartArt shape
SmartArt Styles group		
Change Colors		Change the color variation of a SmartArt graphic
More		Opens the SmartArt Styles gallery to choose an overall visual style for the SmartArt graphic
Table Tools Design tab		
Table Styles group		
More		Opens the table styles gallery to choose a visual style for a table
Shading		Colors background behind selected text or paragraph
Border		Applies a border style
Effects		Applies a visual effect to the table such as shadows and reflections

matching

Match the item on the left with the correct description on the right.

1. animation	_____	**a.**	predefined set of formatting choices that can be applied to an entire document
2. cell	_____	**b.**	slide that stores information about the formatting for all slides or pages in a presentation
3. color theme	_____	**c.**	organizes information into an easy-to-read format of horizontal rows and vertical columns
4. document theme	_____	**d.**	special effects that add action to text and graphics
5. master	_____	**e.**	quickly creates a visual representation of textual information
6. object animation	_____	**f.**	controls the way the display changes as you move from one slide to the next
7. rotate handle	_____	**g.**	consists of 12 colors that are applied to specific elements in a document
8. SmartArt	_____	**h.**	the intersection of a row and column
9. table	_____	**i.**	allows you to spin an object to any degree in any direction
10. transition	_____	**j.**	motion such as clip art that flies in from the left

multiple choice

Circle the letter of the correct response to the questions below.

1. If you wanted to add a company logo on each slide in your presentation, you would place it on the _____.
   a. handout
   b. notes page
   c. outline slide
   d. master

2. To substitute one word for another in a presentation, you would use the _____ feature.
   a. Find and Replace
   b. Locate and Move
   c. Copy
   d. Duplicate

3. The _____ defines the format and placement of the slide image, note text, headers, footers, and other elements that will appear on all speaker notes.
   a. Slide master
   b. Notes master
   c. Handouts master
   d. Title master

4. A _____ theme is a predefined set of formatting choices that can be applied to an entire document in one simple step.
   a. slide layout
   b. document
   c. animation
   d. master

5. _____ add action to text and graphics so they move around on the screen.
   a. Transitions
   b. Masters
   c. Animations
   d. Slides

6. Each _____ theme consists of eight coordinated colors that are applied to different slide elements.
   a. document
   b. slide layout
   c. color
   d. master

7. _____ control the way that the display changes as you move from one slide to the next during a presentation.
   a. Animations
   b. Slide masters
   c. Graphics
   d. Transitions

8. If you want to display information in columns and rows, you would create a _____.
   a. table
   b. text box
   c. slide layout
   d. shape

9. You can change the horizontal placement of an entry in a placeholder or a table cell by using one of the four horizontal alignment settings: left, center, right, and _____.
   a. highlighted
   b. located
   c. marginalized
   d. justified

10. To help you remember the important points during a presentation, you can add comments to slides and print _____.
    a. notes pages
    b. slide handouts
    c. preview handouts
    d. handouts

true/false

Circle the correct answer to the following questions.

1.	A master is a special slide or page on which the formatting for all slides or pages in your presentation is defined.	True	False
2.	A document theme can be applied to selected slides in a presentation	True	False
3.	Tables contain rows and columns.	True	False
4.	Alignment controls the position of text entries in a placeholder.	True	False
5.	SmartArt Style provides ready-made shapes such as rectangles and circles, a variety of lines, block arrows, flowchart symbols, stars and banners, and callouts.	True	False
6.	You can print 12 slides per page using notes page.	True	False
7.	Masters are professionally created slide designs that can be applied to your presentation.	True	False
8.	Find and Replace makes it difficult to locate specific words or phrases.	True	False
9.	Style checking looks for consistency in punctuation and capitalization.	True	False
10.	Columns in a table are identified by letters.	True	False

fill-in

Complete the following statements by filling in the blanks with the correct terms.

1. _____ add action to text and graphics so they move on the screen.

2. Cells in a table are identified by a letter and number, called a _____.

3. _____ provides access to a combination of different formatting options such as edges, gradients, line styles, shadows, and three-dimensional effects.

4. You also can align text _____ in a table cell with the top, middle, or bottom of the cell space.

5. A _____ is a container for text or graphics.

6. A _____ is part of a template that stores information about the formatting for the three key components of a presentation—slides, speaker notes, and handouts.

7. _____ controls the position of text entries within a space.

8. _____ are used to display each bullet point, text, paragraph, or graphic independently of the other text or objects on the slide.

9. The _____ slide is a special slide that stores information about the formatting for all slides or pages in a presentation.

10. Object _____ are used to display each bullet point, text, paragraph, or graphic independently of the other text or objects on the slide.

Hands-On Exercises

step-by-step

Explaining Fad Diets ★

1. You have been asked to give a lunchbox presentation at the Lifestyle Fitness Club on fad diets. You plan to first describe all fad diets and then end with a summary of the benefits of eating according to the USDA's Food Pyramid and proper exercise. The summary of the food pyramid research is complete; now you will need to add information about common fad diets. You want to make the new slides look and feel like a part of the existing presentation, so you will add appropriate graphics and formatting. Three slides from your completed presentation will be similar to those shown here.

a. Open the file pp02_Fad Diets.

b. Run the slide show to see the progress so far.

c. Spell check the presentation, making the appropriate corrections.

d. Find and replace the occurrences of "children" with the word **everyone**.

e. In slide 1:

Insert a new text box.

Type **Presented by**.

Press ⬅Enter and type **Your Name and Lifestyle Fitness**.

Replace "Your Name" with your name.

Set font size 12 and center the text for each line in the text box.

Position the text box just below the existing subtitle.

f. Insert a new slide with Two Content layout after slide 2 in the presentation. In this slide:

Add the title **Fad Diets**.

Insert the picture from the file pp02_Grape Fruit into the right pane.

Add the following bullets to the left content holder:

Cabbage soup

Negative calories

3 day diet

Apple cider vinegar

Beverly Hills diet

AutoFit Text to Placeholder.

Size and position the graphic appropriately.

g. In slide 13:

Change the layout of slide 13 to Title and Content.

Select and right-Click the graphic.

Animate the graphic's entrance to fly in from the bottom left at slow speed.

h. Run the slide show to view the entire presentation.

i. Save the file as Fad Diets.

Enhancing a Staff Training Presentation ★

2. You have continued your work on the staff training presentation for the Sleepy Time Inn. You have already created the introductory portion of the presentation and need to reorganize the topics and make the presentation more visually appealing. Three slides from your modified presentation will be similar to those shown here.

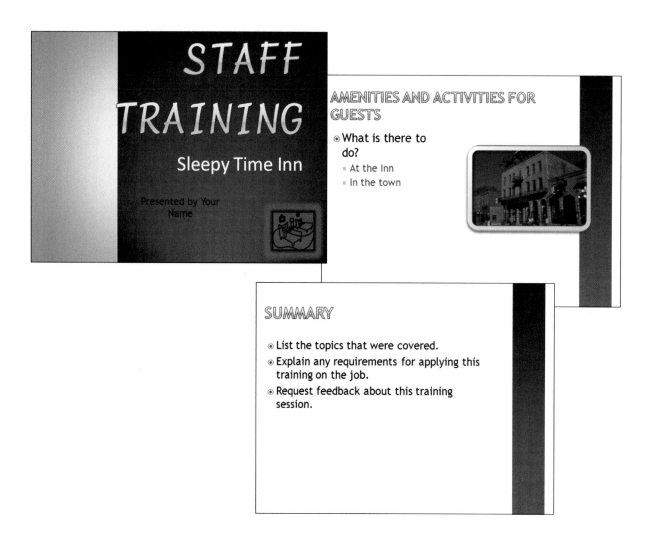

   a. Open the file pp02_Sleepy Time Staff Training.

   b. Run the slide show to see the progress so far.

   c. Spell check the presentation, making the appropriate corrections.

   d. Find and replace any occurrence of "city" with the word **town**.

e. In slide 1:

> Insert a textbox below the subtitle.
>
> Type **Presented by Your Name**.
>
> Replace "Your Name" with your name.
>
> Set font size 24 and center the text box.
>
> Add the following speaker note: **Be sure to introduce yourself and play the name game**.

f. In slide 4:

> Add a shape of your choice.
>
> Enter the text **Terms to Know**.
>
> Position and center the shape appropriately.

g. In slide 5:

> Select the image.
>
> Set the Picture Style to Metal Rounded Rectangle.
>
> Set the Picture Effect to glow Accent color 6, 5 pt glow.

h. Hide slide 13.

i. Change the design of the slides to one of your choice from the Themes gallery.

j. If necessary, resize the title textbox so that the title fits onto the slide. Duplicate slide 1 and move it to the end of the presentation.

k. Add your name to the File properties.

l. Save the file as Sleepy Time Training.

m. Print slides 1, 4, 5 and 14 as handouts (three per page).

Enhancing the Interviewing Tips Presentation ★★

3. To complete this problem, you must have completed Step-by-Step Exercise 5 in Lab 1. Jane has completed the first draft of the presentation for her talk, but she still has some information she wants to add to the presentation. Additionally, she wants to make the presentation look better using many of the PowerPoint design and slide show presentation features. Three slides from your modified presentation will be similar to those shown here.

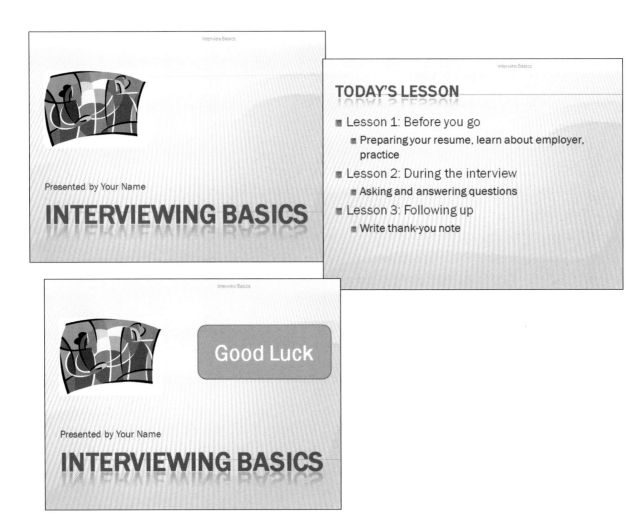

   a. Open the presentation Interviewing Basics. If necessary, switch to Normal view.

   b. Change the document theme to one of your choice. Change the color theme to a color of your choice. If necessary, reposition graphics and change font sizes.

   c. On the master slides:

      Set the bullet style to artsy, bullets, square.

      Set the title and subtitle style to a different font color and size of your choice.

   d. Review the slides in Slide Sorter view and fix the placement and size of the placeholders and pictures as needed.

e. Set the footer **Interview Basics** to display on all slides.

f. Apply a custom animation to the clip art in slide 1 so that the image entrance is fly in from the bottom at a slow speed.

g. Duplicate the title slide and move it to the end of the presentation. Add a shape to this slide that includes the text **Good Luck!**. Format the object and text appropriately.

h. Select an animation scheme of your choice to add transition effects to all the slides. Run the slide show.

i. Add the following note to slide 4 in a point size of 18: **You must be able to give a short biography when asked "Tell me about yourself." Practice until you can tell the story smoothly**.

j. Add file documentation and save the completed presentation as **Interviewing Basics2**.

k. Print the notes page for slide 3. Print slides 1, 2, 6, and 8 as handouts with four slides per page.

Enhancing the Triple Crown Presentation ★★★

4. To complete this problem, you must have completed Step-by-Step Exercise 1 in Lab 1. Logan's work on the Triple Crown Presentation was well received by his supervisor. She would like to see some additional information included in the presentation, including a table of upcoming qualifying hikes. Three slides from your updated presentation will be similar to those shown here.

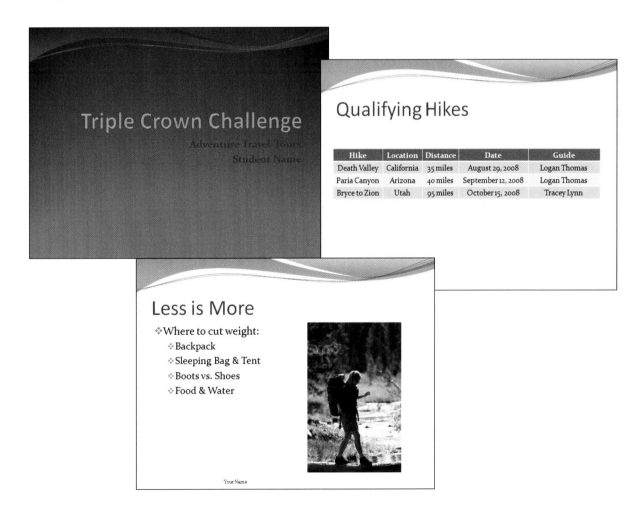

a. Open the file Triple Crown Presentation.

b. Change the document theme to one of your choice. Change the color theme to a color of your choice. If necessary, reposition graphics and change font sizes.

c. Using the master slides, change the text color of the titles and subtitles. Change the bullet styles.

d. Use the Find and Replace command to replace any occurrence of "Apria Canyon" with **Emerald Pools**.

e. Replace slide 3 with a new Title and content slide. In this slide:

Create a table with five columns and four rows.

Enter the title **Qualifying Hikes**.

Enter the following information in the table:

Hike	Location	Distance	Date	Guide
Death Valley	California	35 miles	August 29, 2008	Logan Thomas
Paria Canyon	Page, AZ	40 miles	September 12, 2008	Logan Thomas
Bryce to Zion	Utah	95 miles	October 15, 2008	Tracey Lynn

Change the column and row size as needed.

Center the cell entries both horizontally and vertically in their cell spaces.

Change the table style to one of your choice.

Position the table appropriately.

f. Duplicate slide 1 and place the copy at the end of the presentation. In this slide:

Change the title to **Adventure is Waiting!**.

Add a footer that does not display the date and time but does display your name and the slide number on all slides except the title slide.

Add a shape of your choice to the final slide with the text: **Call us Today!**.

g. Add the following information to the file properties:

Author: **Your Name**

Title: **Triple Crown Presentation**

h. Save the file as Triple Crown Presentation2.

i. Print slides 1, 3, 5, and 6 as a handout with all four slides on one page.

Enhancing the Coffee Presentation ★★★

5. Evan, the owner of the Downtown Internet Café, commissioned a presentation on coffee basics. You have created the presentation and added some formatting enhancements. Evan previewed your work and was so impressed with your presentation on coffee that he has decided to run it periodically throughout the day on a large screen in the cafe so customers can see it as well. To "spiff it up," he wants you to convert it to an onscreen presentation with more graphics as well as other design and animation effects. Three slides from your modified presentation will be similar to those shown here.

a. Open the file pp02_Coffee Talk.

b. Change the document theme to a design of your choice. Select a new color theme of your choice. Check the presentation to see how the new design has affected all slides, and move and size bulleted lists as needed.

c. Use the slide master to change the font color of all first-level bullet text to a different color. Replace "Student Name" with your name in the footer text of all slides.

d. Use the Find and Replace feature to change all occurrences of "Regular Roasts" to **Coffee Categories**. Do the same to replace "Other Offerings" with **Coffee Types**.

e. Apply a custom animation and sound of your choice to the coffee cup clip art on slide 2.

f. On slide 3:

> Change the title to **What's Brewing**.
>
> Delete the clip art.
>
> Copy the clip art from slide 2 to slide 3 and size and position it appropriately.
>
> Add a third bullet with the text: **Coffee Terms**.

g. Delete slide 2.

h. On slide 3, insert, resize, and position the graphic from the file pp02_Coffee Pot.

i. On slide 4, change the title to **Coffees from the World**.

j. Insert a new slide with a Title and Content layout after slide 7. In this slide:

> Enter the title **Coffee Terms**.
>
> Create a table with two columns and five rows.
>
> Enter **What You Say** as the first column heading and **What It Means** as the second column heading.

Copy the terms and definitions from slide 9 into the table.

Change the font size of the text as needed.

Center-align the What You Say column.

Size the columns and table appropriately.

Select a table style of your choice.

k. Duplicate slide 1 and place the copy at the end of the presentation. In this slide:

Change the title to **Come have coffee with us . . . .** .

Delete the subtitle text.

Delete the subtitle placeholder.

Insert a shape of your choice with the text **Open Late!**.

l. Select a slide transition of your choice and apply to all slides the slide transition to automatically advance after 10 seconds. Run the slide show.

m. Add file documentation information.

n. Save the completed presentation as Coffee Talk.

o. Print slides 1, 2, 8, and 9 as handouts, four per page.

Clutter Control ★

1. You work for a business that designs and builds custom closet solutions. You have been asked to prepare a presentation for new clients that will help them prepare for the construction phase. Clients need to organize and categorize their items before the crews arrive on site; your presentation will serve as a "declutter" guide. When construction ceases, the business puts everything into the closet as a service. Research ideas on reducing clutter on the Web. Add transitions, animations, and a document theme that will catch the viewer's attention. When you are done, save the presentation as Custom Closets, and print the presentation as handouts, nine per page.

Enhancing the Car Maintenance Presentation ★

2. To finalize your Car Maintenance presentation that you began in Lab 1 On Your Own Exercise 3, use a document theme and color theme of your choice. Add clip art, sound, and transitions to help hold your audience's interest. Create speaker notes and rehearse the presentation. When you are done, save the presentation as Car Maintenance2; print the presentation as handouts, six per page; and print the notes pages for slides containing notes only.

Enhancing the Careers with Animals ★ ★ ★

3. To add interest to your Careers with Animals presentation that you created in Lab 1 On Your Own Exercise 5, select a document theme and color theme of your choice. Add clip art, sound, and transitions that will hold your audience's interest. Add speaker notes and rehearse the presentation. When you are done, save the presentation as Careers with Animals2, print the presentation as handouts, and print the notes pages for slides containing notes only.

Enhancing the Internet Policy Presentation ★ ★ ★

4. After completing the Internet Policy presentation you created in Lab 1 On Your Own Exercise 1, you decide it could use a bit more sprucing up. You want to add some information about personal computing security. Do some research on the Web to find some helpful tips on protecting personal privacy and safeguarding your computer. Enter this information in one or two slides. Add some animated clip art pictures and transitions to help liven up the presentation. Make these and any other changes that you think would enhance the presentation. Add a table and check the style consistency of the presentation. Add appropriate documentation to the file. When you are done, save it as Internet Policy2; print the presentation as handouts, nine per page; and print the notes pages for slides containing notes only.

Sharing Favorite Vacation Spots ★★★

5. You and your fellow Getaway Travel Club members have decided that each of you should do a presentation on your favorite vacation spot (one you have already been to or one you would like to go to). Pick a location and do some research on the Web and/or visit a local travel agency to get information about your chosen destination. Create a presentation using a document theme and color theme of your choice. Include clip art, animation, sounds, and transitions to make the presentation more interesting. Include your name as a footer or subtitle on at least one slide. Create and enhance a table and speaker notes to remind yourself of additional information you want to relay that is not included in the slides. Add appropriate documentation to the file. Run the slide show and practice your presentation, then save as Travel Favorites and print your presentation and notes pages.

Using Advanced Presentation Features

Objectives

After completing this lab, you will know how to:

Create a new presentation from existing slides.

Insert slides from another presentation.

Create and modify a chart.

Create and modify an organization chart.

Create a numbered list.

Add animated graphics.

Create and modify a WordArt object.

Rehearse timings.

Create custom shows.

Create hyperlinks.

Publish a presentation on the Web.

Animal Rescue Foundation

The volunteer recruitment presentation you created for the Animal Rescue Foundation was a huge success. Now the agency director has asked you to create a new presentation to use during new volunteer orientation programs. To create the orientation presentation, you will modify and expand the recruitment presentation. The director also thinks it would be a good idea to include the completed presentation on the foundation's Web site for volunteers to refer to whenever they want.

As you create the orientation presentation, you will use several specialized PowerPoint 2007 tools to chart numeric data and create an organization chart of the foundation's management structure. You will further enhance the presentation using special text effects and animated graphics. Finally, you will use several features that will make it easier to deliver the presentation.

When the orientation presentation is complete, you will then modify it for use on the Web site and save it as a Web page document file.

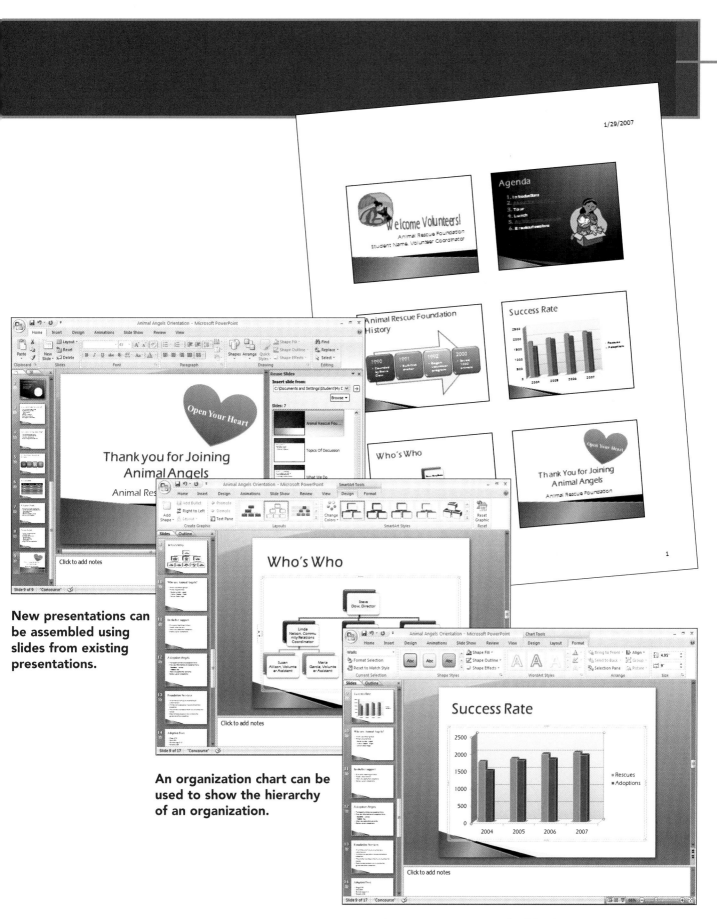

New presentations can be assembled using slides from existing presentations.

An organization chart can be used to show the hierarchy of an organization.

A graphic representation of table data as a chart makes data easier to understand.

Concept Preview

1   **Chart** A chart is a visual representation of numeric data that is used to help an audience grasp the impact of your data more quickly.

2   **Collect and Paste** The collect and paste feature is used to store multiple copied items in the Office Clipboard and then paste one or more of the items into another location or document.

3   **Organization Chart** An organization chart graphically represents the structure of an organization, which usually includes people but can include any items that have a hierarchical relationship.

4   **Animated GIF** An animated GIF file is a type of graphic file that has motion.

5   **WordArt** The WordArt feature is used to enhance slides by changing the shape of text, adding 3-D effects, and changing the alignment of text on a line.

6   **Group** A group is two or more objects that are treated as a single object.

7   **Custom Show** A custom show is a presentation that runs within a presentation.

8   **Hyperlinks** Hyperlinks provide a quick way to jump to other slides, custom shows, presentations, objects, e-mail addresses, or Web pages.

9   **Hypertext Markup Language** The majority of Web pages are written using a language called Hypertext Markup Language (HTML). HTML commands control how the information on a page, such as font colors and size, is displayed.

Creating a Presentation from Multiple Sources

Often, as you are developing a presentation, you will have information from a variety of sources such as slides from other presentations or text from a Word document. You can easily incorporate this information into a presentation without having to recreate it again.

Creating a New Presentation from Existing Slides

To make the task of creating the new presentation easier, you will use an existing presentation, modify it to fit your needs, and save it as a new presentation. Much of the information included in the volunteer recruitment presentation you created will be used again in the volunteer orientation presentation.

You have already started to work on revising the recruitment presentation to fit the needs of the orientation presentation by adding new graphics, removing many slides whose content does not pertain to the orientation program, and changing the theme to Concourse. You will use this file as the basis for the volunteer orientation presentation you will create next.

1
● Start Office
PowerPoint 2007.

● Click 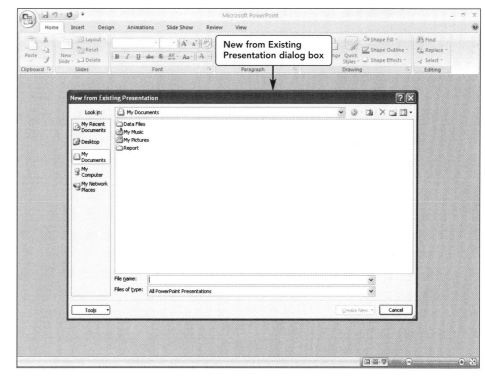 Office Button
and choose New.

● Choose New from
existing.

*Your screen should be
similar to Figure 3.1*

Figure 3.1

From the New from Existing Presentation dialog box, you select the file to
be used to create the new presentation.

2
● Select the location
that contains your
data files.

● Select
pp03_Volunteer3.

*Your screen should be
similar to Figure 3.2*

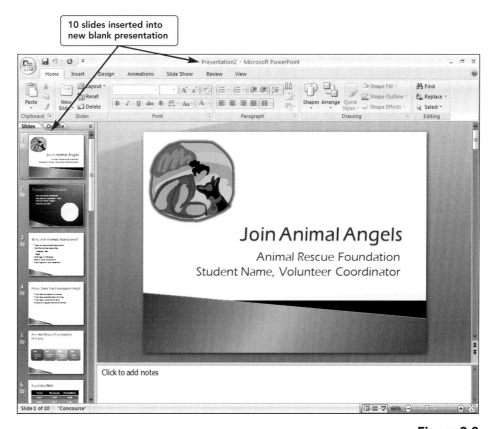

Figure 3.2

The 10 slides from the volunteer presentation are inserted into a new unnamed presentation. In addition to deleting unnecessary slides, you changed the graphic on the opening slide and applied the Concourse theme to the presentation.

The first change you want to make is to change the title of the opening and ending slides. You also will delete a slide that does not contain information relevant to the orientation. Then, before you make any additional changes, you will save the file as a new presentation.

Another Method

You also could copy and rename a presentation to create a new presentation from an existing presentation.

3 ● Modify the title of slide 1 to Welcome Animal Angels.

● Insert Your Name in the subtitle.

● Modify the title of slide 10 to have Thank You for Joining on the first line and Animal Angels on the second line.

● Delete slide 9.

● Save the revised presentation as Animal Angels Orientation.

Your screen should be similar to Figure 3.3

Figure 3.3

The new presentation now consists of nine slides. By modifying an existing presentation and saving it as a new presentation, you have saved a lot of time in the creation of your new presentation.

Inserting Slides from Another Presentation

Next, you want to add a slide to the presentation containing information about the philosophy of the foundation. To save time, you will copy and insert a slide containing this material from another presentation into the new presentation.

1 ● **Open the** [New Slide] **drop-down list in the Slides group on the Home tab.**

● **Choose Reuse slides.**

Your screen should be similar to Figure 3.4

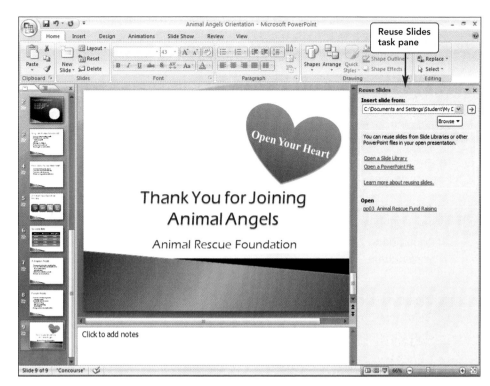

Figure 3.4

The Reuse Slides task pane provides access to presentations stored in the Slide Library or to presentations stored on your computer. The Slide Library is a location on an Office SharePoint Server 2007 that stores and maintains updates to presentation files centrally for use by others in an organization. You will insert a slide from the foundation's fund-raising presentation that is on your computer.

2 ● **Click** [Browse ▼] **and choose Browse File.**

● **Change the Look In location to the location of your data files.**

● **Select** pp03_Animal Rescue Fund Raising.

● **Click** [Open].

Your screen should be similar to Figure 3.5

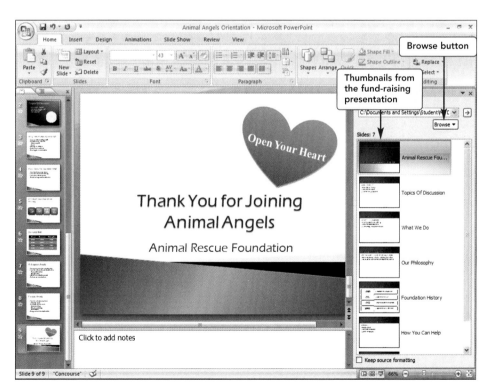

Figure 3.5

Thumbnails of the slides from the Animal Rescue Fund-Raising presentation are displayed in the Reuse Slides task pane. You will insert the "Our Philosophy" slide into the orientation presentation after slide 3.

3
- **Select slide 3 in the Orientation presentation.**

- **Click the "Our Philosophy" thumbnail in the task pane.**

- **Close the Reuse Slides task pane.**

Your screen should be similar to Figure 3.6

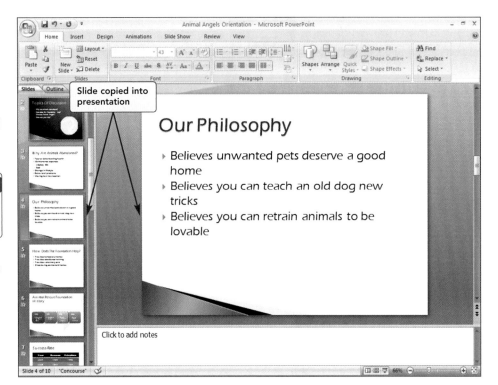

Figure 3.6

The selected slide from the Animal Rescue Fund-Raising presentation file was inserted into the Animal Angels Orientation presentation and the template design used in the presentation is applied to the inserted slide.

Now you would like to add more information about the foundation and about the Animal Angels volunteer group.

Inserting Text from a Word Document

You have already started developing the content for the new orientation presentation by creating an outline in Word. Instead of retyping this information, you will insert slides containing the Word text for the presentation by importing the outline. For best results, the document you want to import should be formatted using heading styles so PowerPoint can easily convert the file content to slides. PowerPoint uses the heading levels to determine the slide title and levels for the slide body text. If heading levels are not available, PowerPoint determines these features from the paragraph indentations.

As you used Outline view in Word to create the materials for the presentation, heading styles were automatically applied. Now all you have to do is import the outline into PowerPoint. You will insert the new content at the end of the presentation and then move the slides to the appropriate location in the presentation.

1 ● Switch to Slide Sorter view to better see the sequence of topics.

● Select slide 10.

● Open the New Slide drop-down list and choose Slides from Outline. . . .

● Change to your data file location.

● Select the Word document pp03_Orientation Outline.

● Click Insert .

● Reduce the zoom to 70%.

Your screen should be similar to Figure 3.7

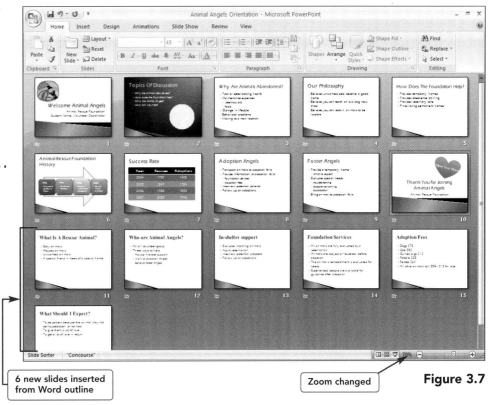

6 new slides inserted from Word outline

Zoom changed

Figure 3.7

The outline text is imported into the presentation and inserted as six separate slides at the end of the presentation. Each level 1 heading in the outline is used as the slide title. Text formatted as a level 2 heading is a main body text point, a level 3 heading is a second-level body text point, and so on. The first slide from the outline is automatically formatted using the Title slide layout.

Now you want change the layout of slide 11 to Title and Content and then you will rearrange the slide order.

2

- Change the layout of slide 11 to Title and Content.

- Move slide 11 to follow slide 2.

- Move slides 12 and 13 to follow slide 8.

- Move slides 14 and 15 to follow slide 11.

- Move slide 16 to follow slide 14.

- Save the changes you have made to the presentation.

- Run the slide show from the beginning.

Your screen should be similar to Figure 3.8

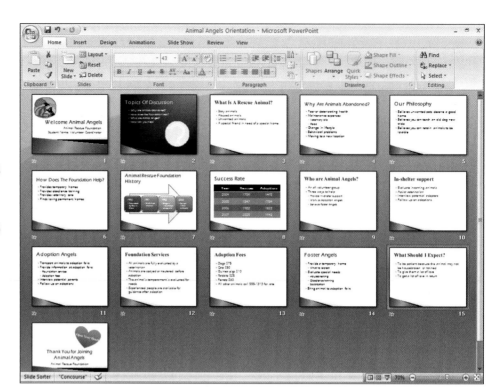

Figure 3.8

Now that the new slides are in the correct order and the majority of the content for the presentation is complete, you are ready to add some more enhancements to the presentation.

Creating a Chart Slide

The first change you want to make is to show the adoption success rate data in slide 8 as a chart rather than a table.

Concept 1

Chart

1 A **chart**, also called a **graph**, is a visual representation of numeric data. When you are presenting data to an audience, they will grasp the impact of your data more quickly if you present it as a chart. PowerPoint 2007 includes a separate program, Microsoft Graph, designed to help you create 14 types of charts with many different formats for each type.

Each type of chart represents the data differently and has a different purpose. It is important to select the type of chart that will provide the right emphasis to support your presentations. The basic chart types are described below.

Type of Chart	Description
Area	Shows the relative importance of a value over time by emphasizing the area under the curve created by each data series.
Bar	Displays categories vertically and values horizontally, placing more emphasis on comparisons and less on time. Stacked-bar charts show the relationship of individual items to a whole by stacking bars on top of one another.
Column	Similar to a bar chart, except categories are organized horizontally and values vertically. Shows data changes over time or comparison among items.
Line	Shows changes in data over time, emphasizing time and rate of change rather than the amount of change.
Pie	Shows the relationship of each value in a data series to the series as a whole. Each slice of the pie represents a single value in a data series.

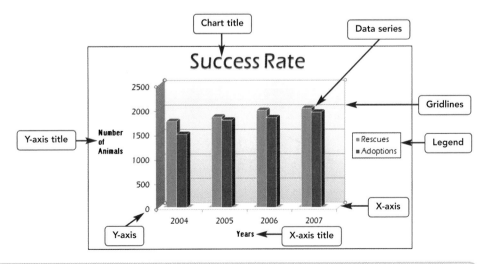

Most charts are made up of several basic parts as identified on the previous page and described below.

Part	Description
X axis	The bottom boundary of the chart, also called the category axis, is used to label the data being charted; the label may be, for example, a point in time or a category.
Y axis	The left boundary of the chart, also called the value axis, is a numbered scale whose numbers are determined by the data used in the chart. Each line or bar in a chart represents a data value. In pie charts, there are no axes. Instead, the data that are charted are displayed as slices in a circle or pie.
Data Series	Each group of related data that are plotted in a chart.
Legend	A box containing a brief description identifying the patterns or colors assigned to the data series in a chart.
Titles	Descriptive text used to explain the contents of the chart.

You will create the chart in a new slide following the slide containing the table of data on success rates.

1 ● Insert a new slide using the Title and Content slide layout after slide 8.

● Double-click on slide 9.

● Click ▦ in the center icons.

Another Method

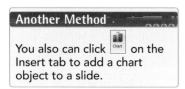

You also can click Chart on the Insert tab to add a chart object to a slide.

Your screen should be similar to Figure 3.9

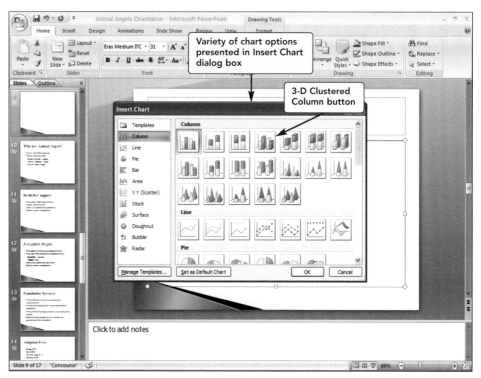

Figure 3.9

From the Insert Chart dialog box, you select the type of chart you want to create.

- Select 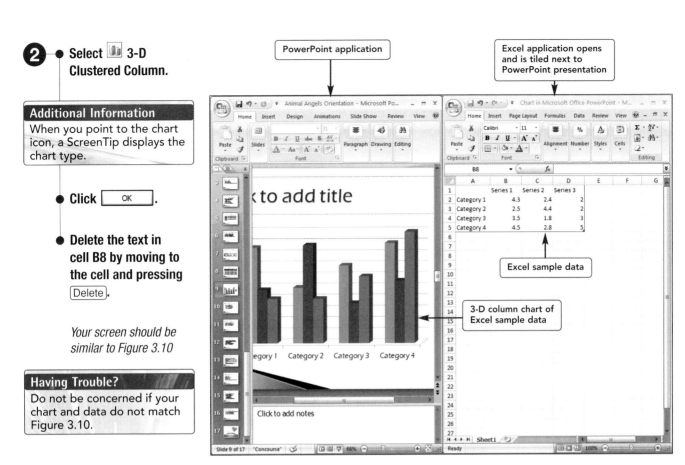 3-D Clustered Column.

Additional Information

When you point to the chart icon, a ScreenTip displays the chart type.

- Click [OK].

- Delete the text in cell B8 by moving to the cell and pressing [Delete].

Your screen should be similar to Figure 3.10

Having Trouble?

Do not be concerned if your chart and data do not match Figure 3.10.

PowerPoint application

Excel application opens and is tiled next to PowerPoint presentation

Excel sample data

3-D column chart of Excel sample data

Figure 3.10

The Microsoft Office Excel 2007 application opens and is tiled on the screen next to the PowerPoint window so you can see both the Excel and PowerPoint applications at the same time. The Excel worksheet contains sample data and the PowerPoint slide displays a 3-D column chart of the sample data. You need to replace the sample data in the worksheet with the success rate data.

Copying Data to the Office Clipboard

Because the data are already contained in the table in slide 8, you will copy the data from the table into the chart. You also will copy the title text from slide 8 into the chart slide. You could copy and paste the selections one after the other, or you can use the Office Clipboard to collect multiple items and paste them as needed.

Concept 2

Collect and Paste

2 The **collect and paste** feature is used to store multiple copied items in the Office Clipboard and then paste one or more of the items into another location or document. For example, you could copy a chart from Excel and a paragraph from Word, then switch to PowerPoint and copy the two stored items into a slide in one easy step. This saves you from having to switch back and forth between documents and applications multiple times.

The Office Clipboard and the system Clipboard are similar, but separate, features. The major difference is that the Office Clipboard can hold up to 24 items, whereas the system Clipboard holds only a single item. The last item you copy to the Office Clipboard is always copied to the system Clipboard. When you use the Office Clipboard, you can select from the stored items to paste in any order.

The Office Clipboard is available in all Office 2007 applications and is accessed through the Clipboard task pane. Once the Clipboard task pane is opened, it is available for use in any program, including non-Office programs. In some programs where the Cut, Copy, and Paste commands are not available, or in non-Office programs, the Clipboard task pane is not visible, but it is still operational. You can copy from any program that provides copy and cut capabilities, but you can only paste into Word, Excel, Access, PowerPoint, and Outlook.

First you will copy the slide title text from slide 8 to the Office Clipboard.

1 ● Open the PowerPoint Home tab.

● Click 🔲 to open the Clipboard group.

● If necessary, click **Clear All** to empty the Office Clipboard contents.

● Select slide 8 and triple-click on the title text to select it.

● Click 📋 Copy.

Your screen should be similar to Figure 3.11

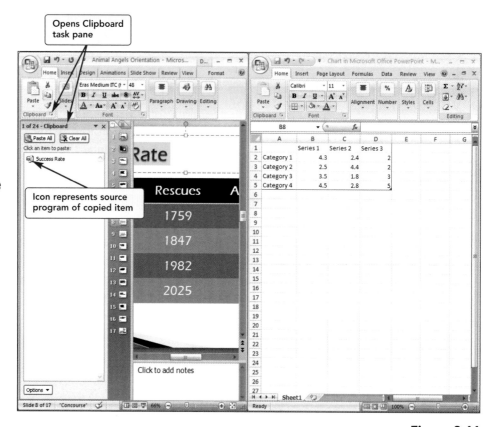

Figure 3.11

The Clipboard task pane displays a PowerPoint icon identifying PowerPoint as the application source of the copied item and a preview of the copied selection. Next, you will copy the contents of the table into the Office Clipboard. As items are copied, they are added sequentially to the Office Clipboard with the last-copied item at the top of the list.

2 ● Click on the table in slide 8 to select the object.

● Press Ctrl + A to select the entire contents of the table.

● Click 🗐 Copy.

Your screen should be similar to Figure 3.12

Additional Information

The **Office Clipboard** is automatically activated if you copy or cut two different items consecutively in the same program; if you copy one item, paste the item, and then copy another item in the same program; or if you copy one item twice in succession.

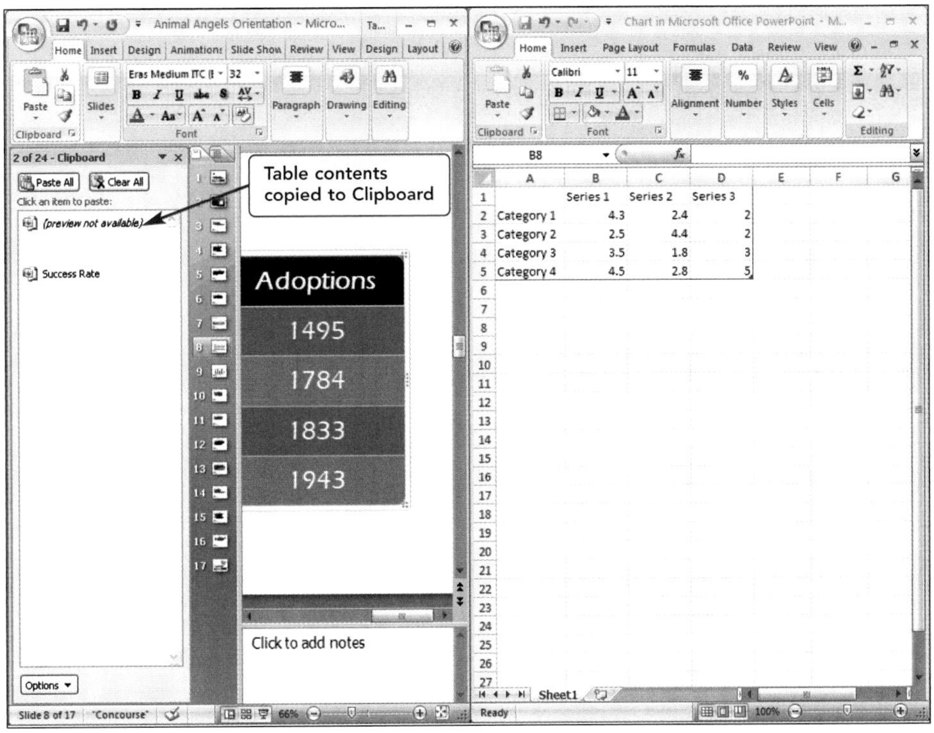

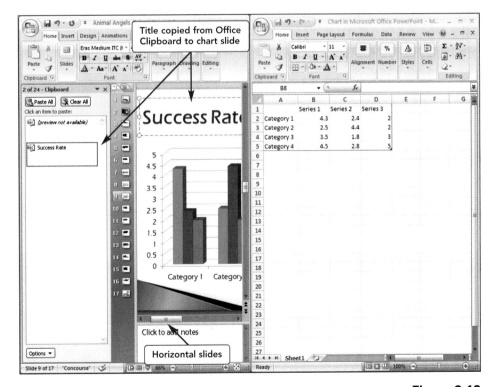

Figure 3.12

The Office Clipboard now contains two PowerPoint document icons, one for each copied item. A preview for the copied table is not available. Next, you will paste the title into slide 9.

3 ● Select slide 9.

● Click in the slide title placeholder.

● Click on the "Success Rate" item in the Clipboard task pane.

● Move the horizontal slider to the left to make the title more visible.

Your screen should be similar to Figure 3.13

Figure 3.13

The contents of the first-copied item are pasted from the Office Clipboard into the title of the slide.

Specifying the Chart Data

Now you are ready to replace the sample data in Excel with the data from the table.

1
- Select all the worksheet data (A1:D5) and press ⌊Delete⌋.

- Move to cell A1.

- In Excel, open the Clipboard.

- Click on the table data item in the Clipboard.

- Best fit the Excel columns to fully display the data.

Having Trouble?
Double-click on the column header border line to best fit a column.

Your screen should be similar to Figure 3.14

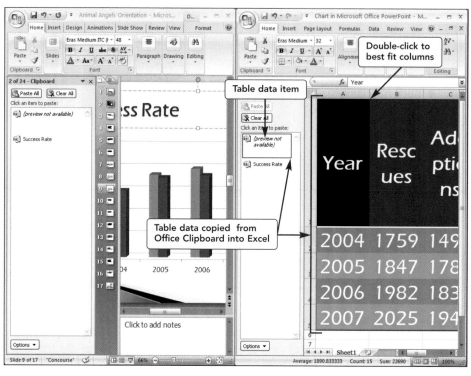

Figure 3.14

The worksheet displays the data and the chart in the slide represents the new worksheet data.

2
- Click ⌊Clear All⌋ to clear the contents of the Office Clipboard.

- Close the Excel Clipboard task pane and exit Excel.

- Close the PowerPoint Clipboard task pane.

Your screen should be similar to Figure 3.15

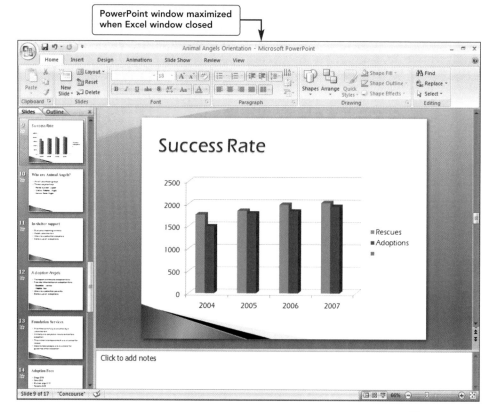

Figure 3.15

Excel is closed and the PowerPoint application is active and maximized in the window. The column chart is a visual representation of the data in slide 8. Each data series has a unique color or pattern assigned to it to identify the different series. The legend identifies the color or pattern associated with each data series.

Changing Chart Style

Next, you want to change the color and appearance of the data series to make it easier to differentiate the two data series. To do this, you will change the chart style.

- **If necessary, select the chart object.**

- **Open the Chart Tools Design tab.**

- **Click ▾ More in the Chart Styles group.**

- **Choose Style 10.**

Your screen should be similar to Figure 3.16

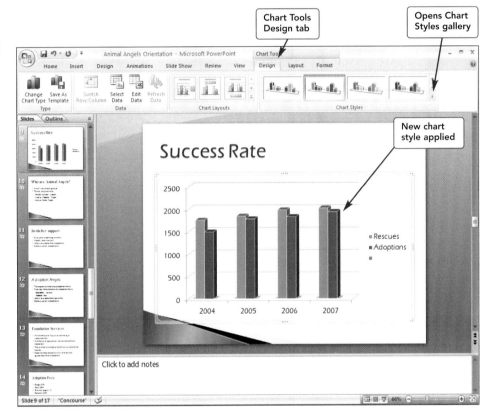

Figure 3.16

You like the change to the column style and the three-dimensional effect. You also would like to add color to the chart background by applying a shape style to the back wall of the chart only. Finally, you want to remove the extra bullet from the legend.

2 ● **Open the Chart Tools Format tab.**

● **Click on the back wall of the chart.**

● **Choose Subtle Effect – Accent 1 (second column of the fourth row) from the Shape Styles gallery.**

● **Click on the legend and then click on the bottom bullet to select it.**

● **Press** Delete **to remove it.**

Your screen should be similar to Figure 3.17

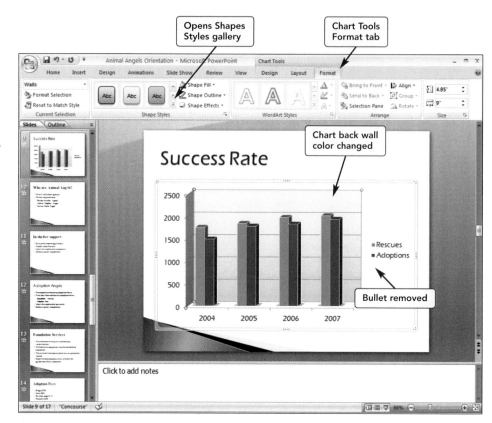

Figure 3.17

The chart is now more attractive and more meaningful. Now that the success rate data are represented in a chart, you will delete slide 8 containing the same information in a table.

3 ● **Switch to Slide Sorter view.**

● **Delete slide 8.**

● **Save the presentation.**

Your screen should be similar to Figure 3.18

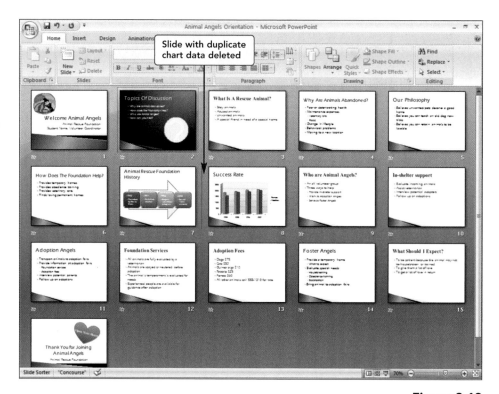

Figure 3.18

Creating an Organization Chart

To provide the volunteers with an overview of the structure of the Animal Rescue Foundation organization, you want to include an organization chart in the presentation.

Concept 3

Organization Chart

3 An **organization chart** graphically represents the structure of an organization. Traditionally, it includes names and job titles, but also can include any items that have a hierarchical relationship. A **hierarchy** shows ranking, such as reporting structures within a department in a business.

There are several different styles of organization charts from which you can choose, depending on how you would like to display the hierarchy and how much room you have on your slide. A basic organization chart is shown below. All organization charts consist of different levels that represent the hierarchy. A level is all the boxes at the same hierarchical position regardless of the boxes each reports to. The topmost box in the organization chart is at level 1. All boxes that report directly to it are at level 2. Those boxes reporting to a level 2 box are at level 3, and so forth. An organization chart can have up to 50 levels.

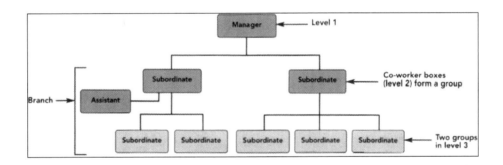

The **manager box** is the top-level box of a group. Subordinate boxes report to the manager box. Co-worker boxes are boxes that have the same manager. Co-workers form a group. A group consists of all the boxes reporting to the same manager, excluding assistant boxes. **Assistant boxes** represent administrative or managerial assistants to a manager. A **branch** is a box and all the boxes that report to it. A level is all the boxes at the same level regardless of the boxes each reports to.

You will add a new slide following slide 8 to display the organization chart. To create the chart, you will use a SmartArt graphic.

1 ● Insert a new Title and Content slide after slide 8.

● Display slide 9 in Normal view.

● Click ⬛ Insert SmartArt Graphic from the slide placeholder icon.

● Choose Hierarchy as the category.

● Select ⬛ Organization Chart.

● Click ⬛ OK ⬛.

Your screen should be similar to Figure 3.19

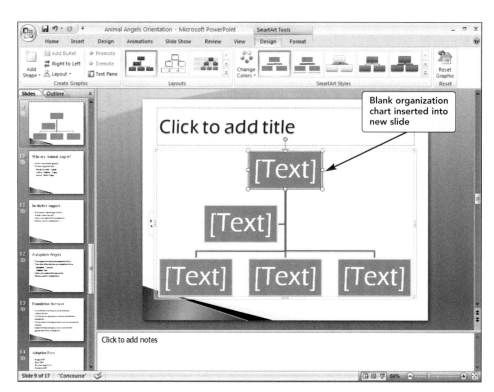

Figure 3.19

A blank organization chart, consisting of five shapes, is displayed.

Adding Text to the Organization Chart

To enter information into the organization chart, you can type or copy the information directly in the shapes. Alternatively, you can use the text pane. Using the Text pane, you will enter the name of the director of the Animal Rescue Foundation in the top-level shape. Each bullet in the Text pane represents one of the shapes in the graphic.

1 ● Click [⬚ Text Pane] from the Create Graphic group.

Another Method:

You also can click ⦙ on the left edge of the SmartArt graphic object to open and close the Text Pane.

● Click in the top text box and type **Steve Dow, Director.**

● Click on the next bullet in the Text pane.

● Type **Linda Nelson, Community Relations Coordinator.**

Having Trouble?
Do not be concerned if your screen displays "Community" split between two lines. As you proceed, the end will be rejoined on a single line.

Your screen should be similar to Figure 3.20

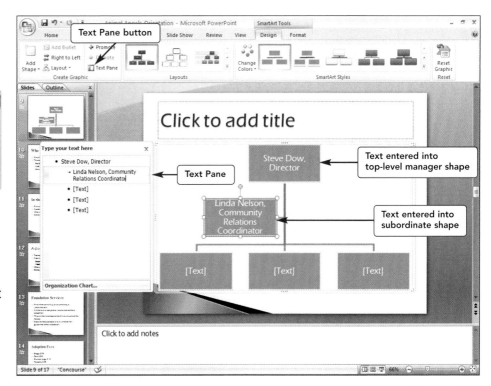

Figure 3.20

The text appears in the existing graphic shapes as you type in the Text pane. The text for the director appears in the top-level manager shape and the text for the community relations coordinator appears in the subordinate shape below it. Occasionally, a word gets split between two lines. As you proceed to another text placeholder, these split words are typically recombined automatically.

The next position you want to add is also at the subordinate level in the organization. Since there are no other shapes at this level, you will need to add a shape at the same level. In the Text pane, this is accomplished simply by pressing ⏎Enter to complete the current entry and to create a new shape at the same level.

2 Press ⏎Enter.

Type Ronnie Carey, Fund Raising Coordinator.

Your screen should be similar to Figure 3.21

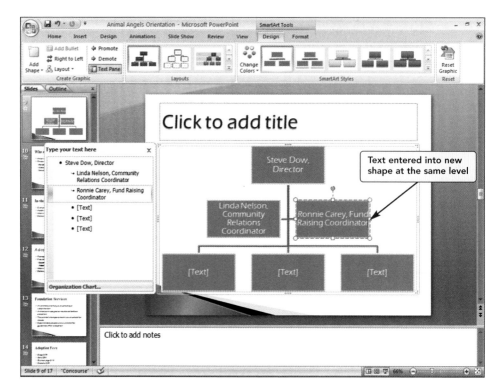

Figure 3.21

Each time you press ⏎Enter, a new shape is added at the same level. Notice, the font size of the text decreases in all the shapes to the size needed to display the largest entry in the shapes. You have two more names and positions to add. You will enter the text for the last positions directly in the shape, remove the last empty shape, and enter a title for the slide.

3

- Close the Text pane.

- Click on the placeholder in the next empty shape to activate it.

- Type **Your Name, Volunteer Coordinator.**

- Click on the placeholder of the next empty shape to activate it.

- Type **Carlos Rodriguez, Foster Angel Recruiter.**

- Select the next empty shape and press [Delete] to eliminate the shape.

- Type **Who's Who** as the slide title.

Your screen should be similar to Figure 3.22

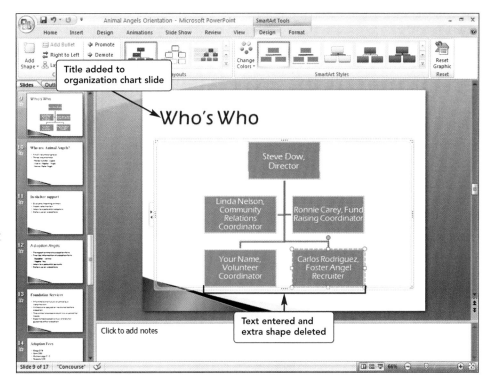

Figure 3.22

The new positions have been added and the extra shape deleted. Although the layout of the organization chart is close, it still does not reflect the hierarchy within the organization.

Changing the Organization Chart Layout

You will change the layout to better illustrate the foundation's staffing.

1 ● Select the Organization Chart object.

● Open the SmartArt Tools Design tab.

● Click ▥ Hierarchy in the Layouts gallery.

Your screen should be similar to Figure 3.23

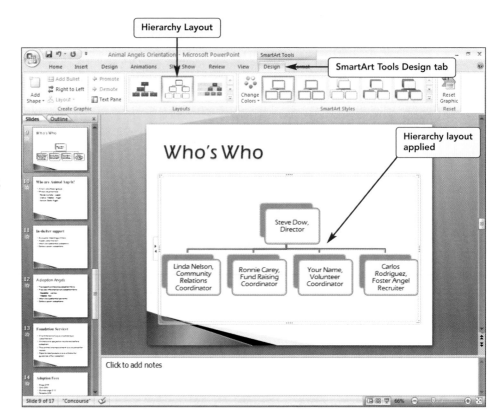

Figure 3.23

This new layout better reflects the organization structure. You, Ronnie, and Linda report directly to the director. However, Carlos Rodriguez works in your department and reports directly to you. You will change the layout to reflect this.

2 ● Select the shape for Carlos Rodriguez.

● Click ⇨ Demote in the Create Graphic group.

Your screen should be similar to Figure 3.24

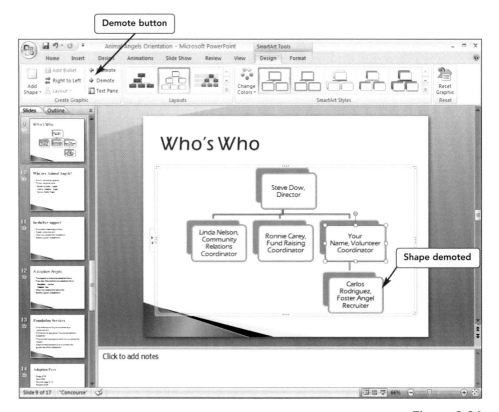

Figure 3.24

The organization chart now correctly identifies the relationships of the people in the organization. Now, you realize you have forgotten to include the name of the Animal Angel recruiter in the organization. This person also reports to the Volunteer Coordinator.

Adding Shapes to the Organization Chart

You will need to add an additional shape to accommodate the missing position. To add a shape, you first select an existing shape that is located closest to where you want to add the new shape. Then you add the new shape relative to the location of the selected shape. In this case, you want to add a shape at the same level as the Carlos Rodriguez shape.

1 ● Open the **[Add Shape]** drop-down list in the Create Graphic group of the SmartArt Tools Design tab.

● Choose **Add Shape After.**

● Type **Serina Johnson, Animal Angel Recruiter.**

Your screen should be similar to Figure 3.25

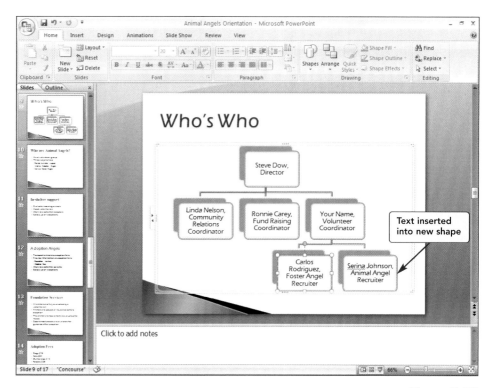

Figure 3.25

The new shape takes the same position as the selected shape, but after it. You also decide to add to the chart the names of the volunteer assistants who work for the coordinators.

2

- Select the shape with Linda Nelson's name.

- From the [Add Shape] drop-down list, choose Add Shape Below.

- Click [Add Shape] and choose Add Shape After to add a second shape at the same level.

- Enter Susan Allison, Volunteer Assistant and Maria Garcia, Volunteer Assistant into the shapes.

- In a similar manner, under Ronnie Carey's shape, add a subordinate shape and enter George Matthews, Volunteer Assistant.

Your screen should be similar to Figure 3.26

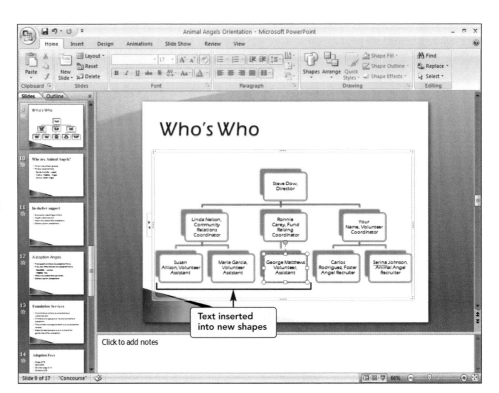

Figure 3.26

Enhancing the Organization Chart

To make the organization chart more interesting, you want to enhance its appearance. You could select each element individually and make changes, but PowerPoint includes a variety of prepackaged styles in the SmartArt Styles group. You will change both the colors and the design characteristics.

1 • Click  in the SmartArt Styles group.

• Choose Colorful Range Accent Colors 5 to 6.

• Click ⬇ More in the SmartArt Styles group.

• Choose 3-D Polished.

Your screen should be similar to Figure 3.27

Additional Information

If you do not like the changes you have made to a shape, you can quickly restore the default settings using Reset Graphic.

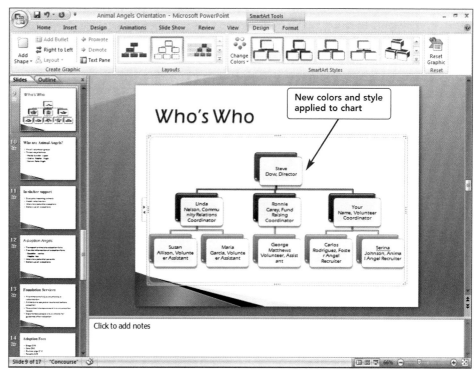

Figure 3.27

The changes to the organization chart are complete. You can click on the chart to further modify the chart at any time.

2 • Save the presentation.

• To see how all the changes you have made to the presentation look, run the presentation beginning with slide 1.

Additional Information

Press F5 to quickly start the presentation from the beginning.

Adding Interest to the Presentation

The presentation has been updated with new content from a variety of sources and contains information that will help new volunteers understand the foundation. After viewing the presentation again, you decide some of the slides need additional changes to add visual interest.

Creating a Numbered List

First, you want to change the second slide, which shows the topics of discussion, to a slide showing the agenda for the orientation. Since the agenda shows a sequential order of events, you want to use a numbered list rather than bullets.

1

- Display slide 2.

- Change the title to **Agenda**.

- Select the four bulleted items.

- Type the following text to replace the bulleted items:

  Introductions
  About the Foundation
  Tour
  Lunch
  Animal Angels overview
  Breakout sessions

- Select the six bulleted items on the slide.

- Click ▤▾ **Numbering** in the Paragraph group of the Home tab.

Your screen should be similar to Figure 3.28

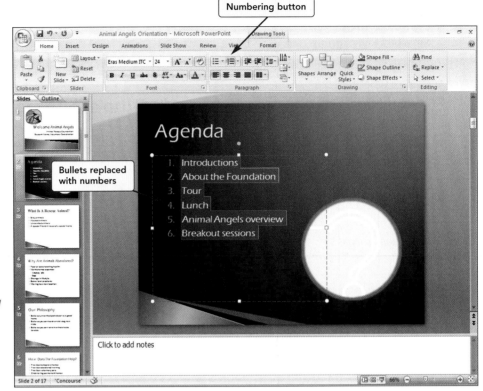

Figure 3.28

The bullets have been replaced with numbers, indicating a sequential order of events.

You would like to change the size of the numbers so they will stand out more on the slide.

Another Method

You also can change a bulleted list to a numbered list by typing. To do this, press [←Backspace] to remove the bullet at the beginning of the line, type 1, A, a, I, or i followed by a period or closing parenthesis, type the text, and then press [←Enter] to start a new line. The next line is automatically numbered using the same style.

2 ● Open the [≡▾] Numbering drop-down list and choose Bullets and Numbering.

● Increase the Size percentage to 125%.

● Click [OK].

● Click [B] Bold.

● Deselect the text.

Your screen should be similar to Figure 3.29

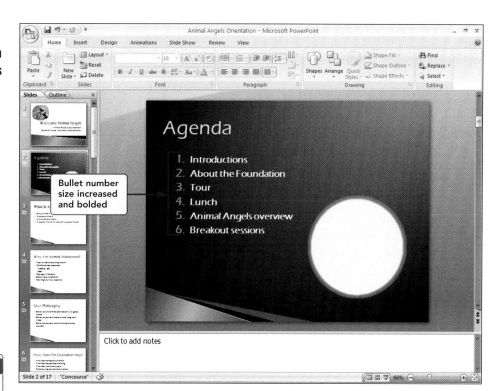

Figure 3.29

The numbers have changed to the size you selected and the entire list is bold.

Adding Animated Graphics

Next, you want to enhance the Agenda slide by adding an animated graphic from an animated GIF file.

Concept 4

Animated GIF

4 An **animated GIF** file is a type of graphic file that has motion. It consists of a series of GIF (Graphic Interchange Format) images that are displayed in rapid succession to produce an animated effect. They are commonly used on Web pages and also can be incorporated into PowerPoint presentations.

When an animated GIF file is inserted into a PowerPoint slide, it does not display action until you run the presentation. If you save the presentation as a Web page and view it in a browser, the animated GIF files run as soon as you view the page containing the graphic.

You cannot modify an animated graphic image using the features in PowerPoint. If you want to make changes to the graphic, such as changing the fill color or border, you need to use an animated GIF editing program.

You want to add an animated graphic to slide 2 that will really capture the attention of viewers. To make space for the new graphic, you will first move the question mark graphic to slide 3.

1 • Select the question mark graphic.

• Click 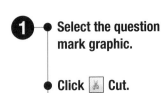 Cut.

• Display slide 3.

• Click **Paste**.

• Reposition and resize the text placeholder and position the graphic as in Figure 3.30.

Your screen should be similar to Figure 3.30

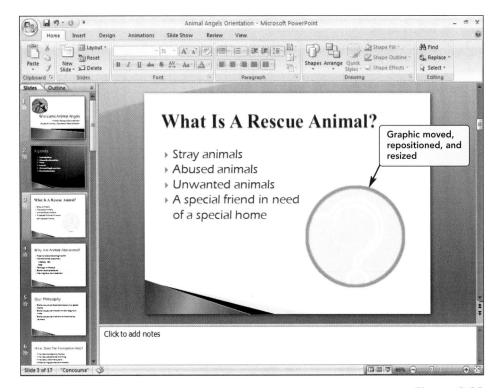

Figure 3.30

Now you will add an animated graphic to slide 2. The graphic will not exhibit motion until you run the slide show.

2 • Display slide 2.

• Click **Picture** from the Illustrations group on the Insert tab.

• Specify your data file location and select pp03_Adoptions.

• Click **Insert**.

Additional Information

The Microsoft Clips Online Web site includes many animated graphics in the Motion category.

Your screen should be similar to Figure 3.31

Figure 3.31

Next you will size and position the graphic appropriately then you display the slide in slide show view to see the animation.

3 • Size and position the graphic as shown in Figure 3.32.

• Display the slide in Slide Show view to see the animation.

• Press [Esc] to stop the slide show.

Your screen should be similar to Figure 3.32

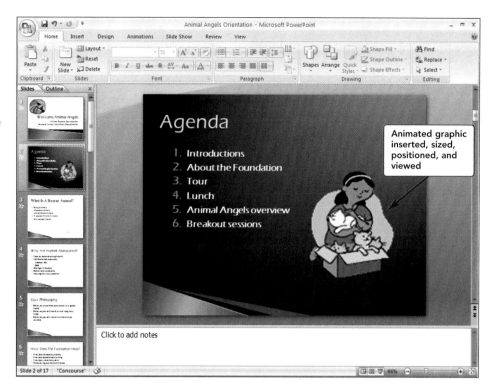

Animated graphic inserted, sized, positioned, and viewed

Figure 3.32

Creating a WordArt Object

The next change you want to make is to change the title on slide 1 to make it more interesting. To make the title unique and more interesting, you will enter it using the WordArt feature.

Concept 5

WordArt

5 The **WordArt** feature is used to enhance slides by changing the shape of text, adding 3-D effects, and changing the alignment of text on a line. You also can rotate, flip, and skew WordArt text. The text that is added to a slide using WordArt is a graphic object that can be edited, sized, or moved to any location on the slide.

Use WordArt to add a special touch to your presentations, but limit its use to a single element on a slide. You want the WordArt to capture the viewer's attention. Here are some examples of WordArt.

You will create a WordArt object for the slide title to appear next to the graphic on slide 1. It will replace the title text that is currently on the slide.

1
• Display slide 1.

• Delete the Title text and placeholder.

• Open the Insert tab.

• Click 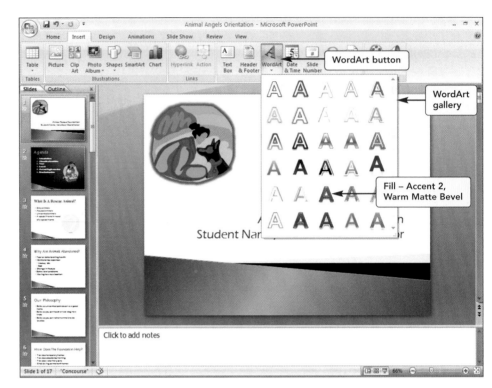 in the Text group.

Your screen should be similar to Figure 3.33

Figure 3.33

The first step is to select one of the 30 styles or designs of WordArt from the WordArt gallery. These styles are just a starting point. As you will see, you can alter the appearance of the style by selecting a different color, shape, and special effect.

2
• Select Fill – Accent 2, Warm Matte Bevel.

• Move the WordArt placeholder to the blank area as shown in Figure 3.34.

Having Trouble?
Drag the selected object just like any other graphic object to move it.

Your screen should be similar to Figure 3.34

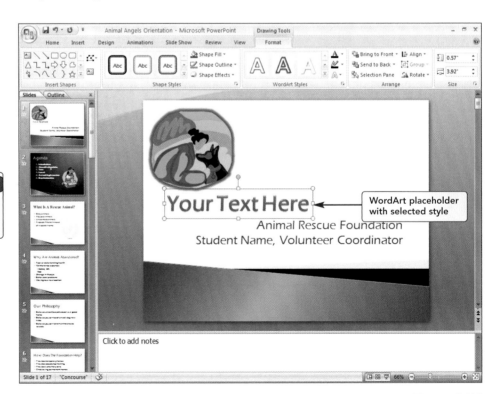

Figure 3.34

A WordArt object placeholder with the selected style is inserted. You need to enter the text you want displayed using the selected WordArt design. The handles surrounding the WordArt object indicate that it is selected. Notice the object is surrounded with a solid border that indicates you can format, size, or move the entire object. Clicking on the object will change the border to a dashed border and display an insertion point. This indicates you can enter or edit the text.

3 ● **Click in the WordArt object and select the placeholder text.**

● **Type Welcome Volunteers!.**

Your screen should be similar to Figure 3.35

Additional Information
You can easily edit the WordArt text at any point by selecting the object.

Figure 3.35

Now the text you entered is displayed in the selected WordArt style on the slide. Whenever a WordArt object is selected, the Drawing Tools Format tab is available for use with the shape.

Enhancing a WordArt Object

Now you want to change the appearance of the WordArt object to make it more interesting. First you will change the shape of the object.

1 Click **A** Text Effects in the WordArt Styles group and select Transform.

Your screen should be similar to Figure 3.36

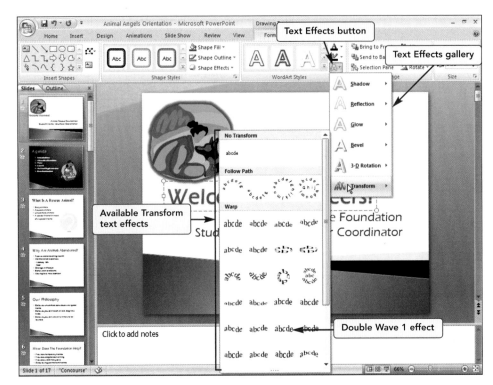

Figure 3.36

A variety of text effects are available that will change the shape of your WordArt object. You will preview several and apply a style.

2 Point to several effects to see how they look in Live Preview.

● Choose the Double Wave 1 effect.

● Move and size the WordArt object as shown in Figure 3.37.

Your screen should be similar to Figure 3.37

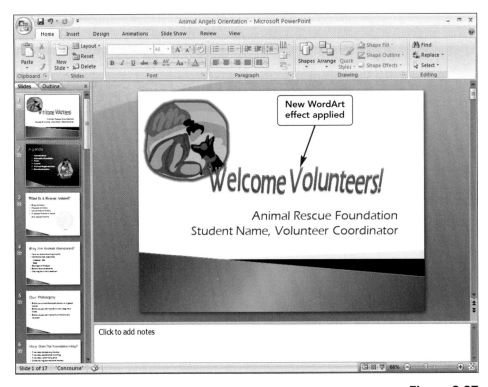

Figure 3.37

The shape of the WordArt has changed to the selected wave effect.

Grouping Objects

You like how the two graphic pieces are positioned on the slide and want to keep this placement. To do this, you will group the objects.

Concept 6

Group

6 A **group** is two or more objects that are treated as a single object. Many clip art pictures are composed of several different elements that are grouped together. This allows you to easily move, resize, flip, or rotate all pieces of the group as a single unit. Features or **attributes** such as line or fill color associated with all objects in the group also can be changed at one time.

Grouped

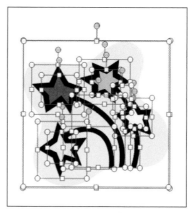

Ungrouped

Sometimes you may want to ungroup the parts of an object so that the individual parts can be manipulated independently. Other times you may want to combine several objects to create your own graphic object that better suits your needs.

You will combine the two graphics into one by grouping them, and then you will size them appropriately on the slide.

1 ● **Select both graphics.**

Having Trouble?
Select two or more graphic objects by holding down ⇧Shift while clicking on each object.

● **Right-click on one of the selected graphics and choose Group/Group from the shortcut menu.**

● **Size and position the grouped graphic and subtitle objects as in Figure 3.38.**

Your screen should be similar to Figure 3.38

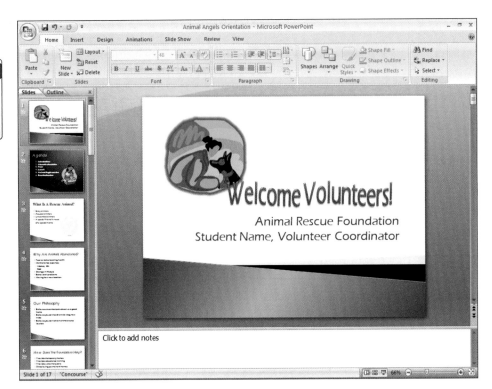

Figure 3.38

Additional Information
To select an object within a grouped object, select the group first, then click on the object you want to select.

Because the objects are grouped, they size and move as a single object. You also could change features associated with all objects in the group at once, such as changing the fill or line color of all objects. Even when objects are grouped, you can still select an object within a group and modify it individually without ungrouping the object.

Delivering Presentations

Typically, presentations are delivered by connecting a computer to a projector to display the slides on a large screen. Before delivering a presentation, it is important to rehearse it so that you are well prepared and at ease with both the equipment and the materials. It is best to rehearse in a setting as close as possible to the real situation with a small audience who will give you honest feedback. Since most presentations are allotted a set amount of time, as part of the rehearsal, you also may want to keep track of the time spent on each slide and the total time of the presentation.

Rehearsing Timing

Additional Information
If your computer has a microphone, you could even record your narration using ⏺ Record Narration in the Set Up group of the Slide Show tab.

To help with this aspect of the presentation, PowerPoint includes a timing feature that records the length of time spent on each slide and the total presentation time while you are rehearsing. If the presentation runs either too long or too short, you can quickly see which slides you are spending too much or too little time on and adjust the presentation accordingly.

1 ● **Open the Slide Show tab.**

● **Click** [Rehearse Timings] **in the Set Up group.**

Your screen should be similar to Figure 3.39

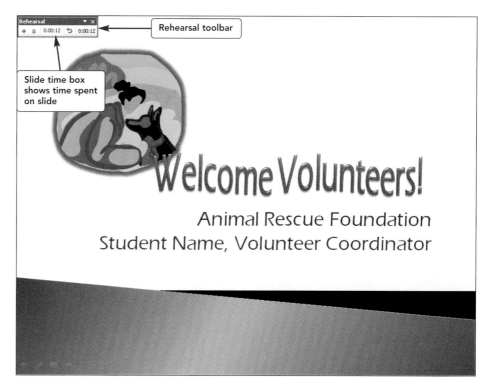

Figure 3.39

The Rehearsal toolbar appears and starts a clock to time your delivery. The [→] button advances to the next step in the show and the [II] will pause the timing. You also can return to the previous slide to repeat the rehearsal and apply new timings to the slide using the [↺] button on the toolbar.

Normally you would read your narration aloud while you rehearse the timing. For this exercise, think about what you would say for each slide. The toolbar will record the time for each slide. When you reach the end of the presentation, a message box displays the total time for the presentation.

2 ● Advance through the slide show as you would during the actual presentation.

● When finished, click [Yes] to keep the slide timings.

Your screen should be similar to Figure 3.40

Slide timing

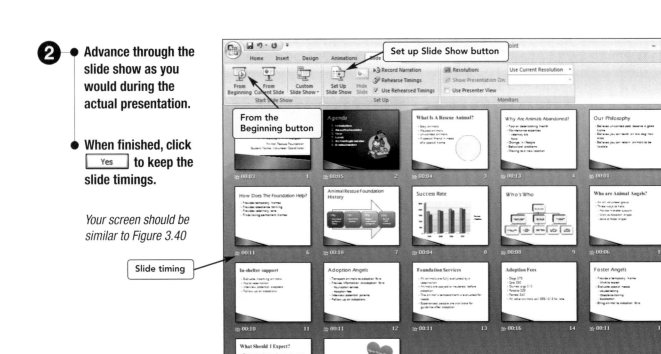

Figure 3.40

Slide Sorter view is displayed and the timings for each slide are displayed below each slide. Now that you can see the individual timings, you can easily see where you are spending too little or too much time. You may have noticed on slide 9 that some of the shapes contained words that were separated and displayed on two lines. If this is the case, resize the shapes to avoid the splitting of words before you proceed.

Using Timings

Once the slide show includes preset timings for each slide, you can use the timings to advance the slides automatically for you during the presentation.

1 ● Click [Set Up Slide Show] in the Set Up group on the Slide Show tab.

● Choose Using timings, if present in the Advance slides category.

Another Method
You also can turn this feature on or off using [✓ Use Rehearsed Timings] in the Set Up group.

● Click [OK].

● Click [From Beginning] from the Start Slide Show group and watch the slide show advance automatically.

● Press [Esc] to end the slide show.

Using this feature is ideal for creating a presentation that is self-running, such as in a kiosk, or if you are very sure of your timings. Generally, when presenting a slide show personally, it is just as easy to advance the slides manually; this allows you to pace the show to the audience.

Creating Custom Shows

After rehearsing the presentation, you have decided to divide the presentation into two parts based upon the materials you plan to present in the morning and afternoon sessions. To do this, you will create two custom shows.

Concept 7
Custom Show

7 A **custom show** is a presentation that runs within a presentation. For example, you may have one presentation that you need to give to two different groups. The overview slides are the same for both groups, but there are a few slides that are specific to each group. Rather than create two separate presentations, you can include all the slides in your main presentation and then group the specific slides into two custom shows that run after the overview slides. While you are running the slide show, you can jump to the specific custom show that you created for that audience.

The morning session will cover the materials about the foundation and the afternoon session will cover the materials about the Animal Angels volunteer group. You will create two custom shows that will display only those slides for each session.

You will create the custom show for the afternoon session first.

1 ● If necessary, open the Slide Show tab.

● Click ⟦Custom Slide Show⟧ and choose Custom Shows from the Start Slide Show group.

● Click ⟦ New... ⟧.

Your screen should be similar to Figure 3.41

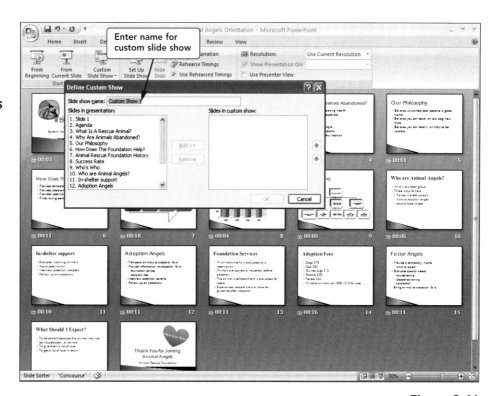

Figure 3.41

In the Define Custom Show dialog box, you name the custom show and select the slides that will run within the show. All the slides in a custom show also must be in the main presentation.

2
- In the Slide Show Name text box, type **Animal Angels**.

- In the Slides in presentation list box, select slides 10 through 17.

- Click [Add >>].

Your screen should be similar to Figure 3.42

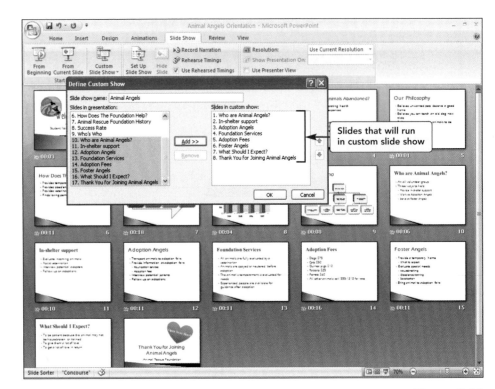

<figure>Figure 3.42</figure>

The selected slides are listed in the Slides in custom show area.

Next you want to create the custom slide show for the morning session about the foundation in general. When the custom show ends, you want the Agenda slide to display again, so you are ready to begin the afternoon session. To do this, you will include the Agenda slide as the last slide in the custom show. After adding the slides for the custom show, you will change the slide order so that the Agenda slide will be last. To change the order of the slides in the custom show, select a slide in the Slides in custom show list box and then click 🔼 to move the slide up in the list or 🔽 to move the slide down.

3 ● **Click** [OK] **to complete the Animal Angels show.**

● **Create another custom show titled** Foundation**.**

● **In the Slides in presentation list box, select slides 2 through 9.**

● **Click** [Add >>]**.**

● **Select slide 1 from the Slides in custom show list box.**

● **Click**  **seven times.**

Your screen should be similar to Figure 3.43

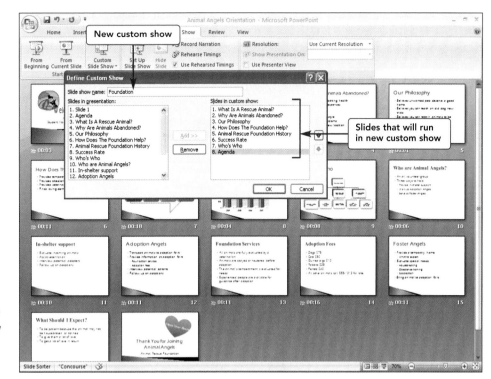

Figure 3.43

Changing the slide order in a custom show does not change the order of the slides in the main presentation. Now you will see how the Foundation custom show runs.

4 ● **Click** [OK]**.**

● **Click** [Show] **to run the Foundation custom show.**

● **View the slides and press** [Esc] **to end the custom show when the Agenda slide is displayed.**

The Foundation custom show displays the slides in the order they were listed in the custom show list. The timings associated with the slides also are used.

Adding Hyperlinks

Next, you need to create a method to start the custom shows from the Animal Angels orientation presentation. To do this, you will add hyperlinks from the bulleted item on the Agenda slide to its corresponding custom show.

Concept 8

Hyperlinks

8 **Hyperlinks** provide a quick way to jump to other slides, custom shows, presentations, objects, e-mail addresses, or Web pages. You can assign the hyperlink to text or to any object, including pictures, tables, clip art, and graphs. You can jump to sites on your own system or network as well as to sites on the Internet and the Web. The user jumps to the referenced location by clicking on the hyperlink.

First, you will add the hyperlink to the Foundation custom show.

1 ● Display slide 2 in Normal view.

● Select the second bulleted item.

● Open the Insert tab.

● Click [Hyperlink] from the Links group.

Your screen should be similar to Figure 3.44

Figure 3.44

You need to specify the location of the document to link to and the specific slide.

2 • Choose Place in This
      Document from the
      Link to list.

  • Select Foundation
    under Custom Shows.

  • Click [OK].

  *Your screen should be
  similar to Figure 3.45*

Having Trouble?
Use the vertical scroll bar
to display the Foundation
Custom Show name.

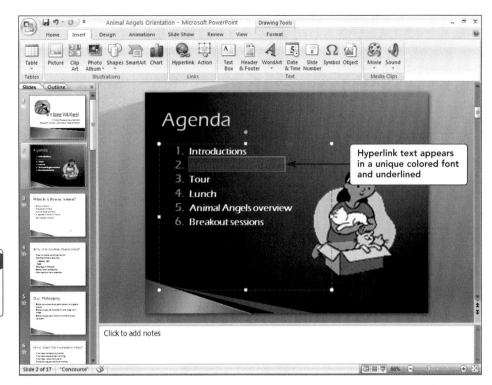

Figure 3.45

The hyperlink text appears underlined and in color. The color of the hyperlink text is determined by the presentation's color scheme. When the second bulleted item is selected, it will start the Foundation custom show.

Next, you need to add the hyperlink to the Animal Angels custom show.

3 • Create another hyperlink from agenda item 5 to the Animal Angels custom show.

The fifth bulleted agenda item is now a hyperlink to the custom slide show.

Using Hyperlinks

Now you want to try out one of the hyperlinks to see how they work. To activate the hyperlinks, you need to run the slide show.

1 ● Run the slide show from the beginning.

Having Trouble?
Pressing F5 starts the slide show at slide 1.

● Click on the Animal Angels overview hyperlink when slide 2 is displayed.

Additional Information
The mouse pointer shape changes to a ⁀ when pointing to a hyperlink.

● Press Esc to end the show when the last slide is displayed.

Your screen should be similar to Figure 3.46

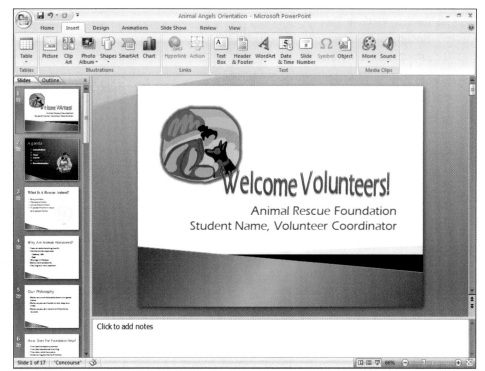

Figure 3.46

The slide show jumps to the first slide in the Animal Angels custom show and runs the custom show slides. Now you are ready for the presentation!

2 ● Add appropriate file documentation.

● Save the presentation.

● Print a handout with four slides per page showing slides 1, 2, 8, and 9 in landscape orientation.

Publishing a Presentation

The Director wants you to **publish** or save a copy of the presentation file for use on the foundation's Web site for volunteers to review whenever they want. You want viewers to be able to easily control the slide show so that they can go back to review a slide immediately or go forward more quickly to see other slides.

Before you publish the presentation, you want to make several changes to the Agenda slide. First, you will change the slide content to display a list of the major topics from the presentation. Then you will edit one of the slides.

1 ● Display slide 2 in Normal view.

● Change the slide title to Learn About Us.

● Delete the Introductions, Tour, and Lunch bullets.

● Change "Breakout Sessions" to Adoption Angels.

● Add a fourth bullet, Adoption Fees.

● Add a fifth bullet, Foster Angels.

● Edit the second bullet by capitalizing the first letter of Overview.

Your screen should be similar to Figure 3.47

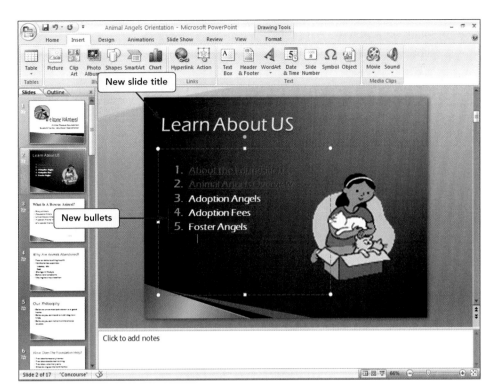

Figure 3.47

Unfortunately, custom shows will not run from a Web browser. Therefore, in order for the presentation to run from the foundation's Web site, you need to change the hyperlinks to the custom shows to links to the appropriate slides in the presentation. Fortunately, most other features in the presentation, including transitions and sound, will run in most new versions of Web browser programs.

You will edit the existing hyperlinks and then add new hyperlinks for the other bulleted items on slide 2. This will allow viewers to make a selection from the bulleted list, and the presentation will jump directly to the slide containing the relevant information.

2 ● Right-click on the About the Foundation hyperlink and choose Edit Hyperlink.

● Change the link to slide 3.

● Change the Animals Angels Overview hyperlink to link to slide 10.

● To create a hyperlink for the Adoption Angels bullet, select the bullet, right-click on the selection, and choose Hyperlink.

● Select slide 12 and click [OK] to complete the hyperlink.

● Create a hyperlink for Adoption Fees to slide 14.

● Create a hyperlink for Foster Angels to slide 15.

Your screen should be similar to Figure 3.48

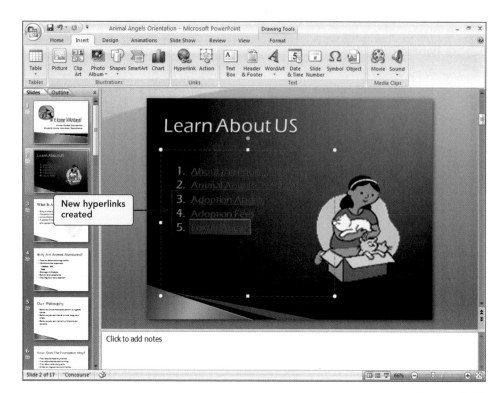

Figure 3.48

Saving the Presentation as a Web Page

Now that the presentation is ready for Web delivery, you will save it as a Web page. Publishing a file saves the file in Hypertext Markup Language (HTML) format.

9 All Web pages are written using a programming language called **Hypertext Markup Language** (HTML). HTML commands control how the information on a page such as font colors and size is displayed. HTML also allows users to click on highlighted text or images and jump to other locations on the same page, to other pages in the same site, or to other sites and locations on the Web altogether.

HTML commands are interpreted by the browser software program you are using to access the WWW. A browser is a program that connects you to remote computers and displays the Web pages you request. The computer that stores the Web pages and sends them to a browser when requested is called the server.

You can save a presentation in two ways:

- Web Page—Saves the presentation as a Web page and creates an associated folder that contains supporting files such as bullets, background textures, and graphics.

- Single File Web Page—Saves the presentation as a Web page that integrates all supporting information, including graphics and other files, into a single file.

You will save it to a single file Web page, which is the default file type.

1 ● **Click**  **Office Button and choose Save as.**

● **Specify the location to save the file.**

● **Enter the file name** Volunteer Orientation Web.

● **Choose Single File Web Page as the file type.**

Your screen should be similar to Figure 3.49

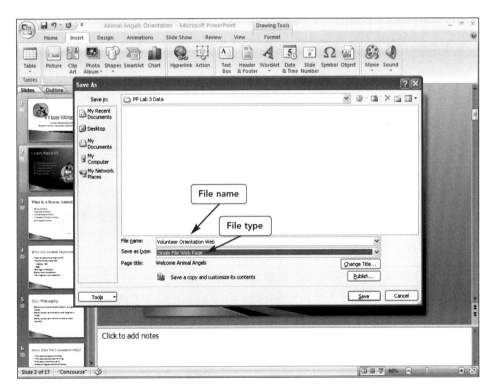

Figure 3.49

Additional Information

Clicking Change Title... allows you to specify a different page title.

Notice that the page title, the name that will appear in the title bar of the browser when the page is displayed, is the same as the title in the first slide. This is an appropriate page title and does not need to be changed. Next, you will set several additional Web page formatting and display options.

2 ● Click Publish... .

Your screen should be similar to Figure 3.50

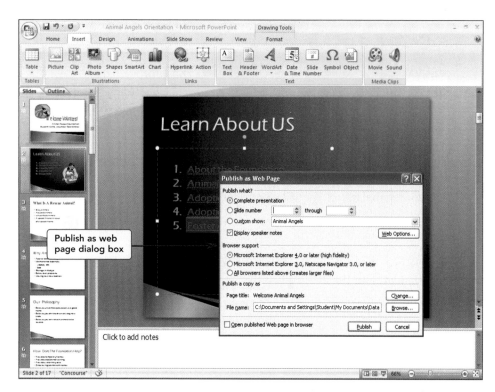

Figure 3.50

In the Publish as Web Page dialog box, you can specify the slides you want to publish under Publish what? and optimize the Web page for a particular browser or browser version, under Browser support. The default settings, Complete Presentation and Microsoft Internet Explorer 4.0 or later, in both areas are appropriate for your needs. You do want to specify some additional Web options.

3 ● Click Web Options... .

● **In the General tab, select Show slide animation while browsing.**

● **If necessary, select the other two appearance option.**

Your screen should be similar to Figure 3.51

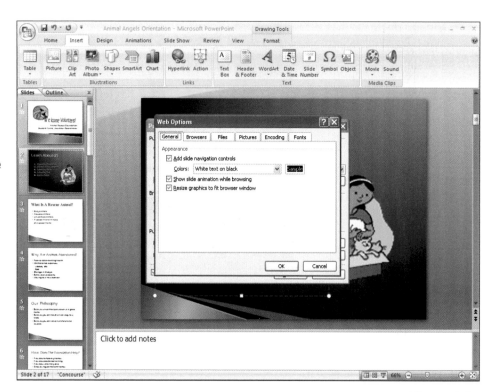

Figure 3.51

The Add slide navigation controls option will display a table of contents listing that can be used to navigate the presentation. The Show slide animation while browsing will display transition effects and other animations as long as the browser supports those features. The Resize graphics to fit browser window automatically sizes the slides to fit the browser window.

4 ● Click [OK].

● To immediately see how your published Web presentation looks in your browser after you publish it, select the Open published Web page in browser.

● Click [Publish...].

● If necessary, respond appropriately to allow blocked content.

● Maximize the browser window.

Having Trouble?
Your browser may not allow the presentation to be displayed. If this is the case, skip to the end of this lab.

Your screen should be similar to Figure 3.52

Additional Information
A Single File Web Page file type has a file extension of .mht or .mhtml.

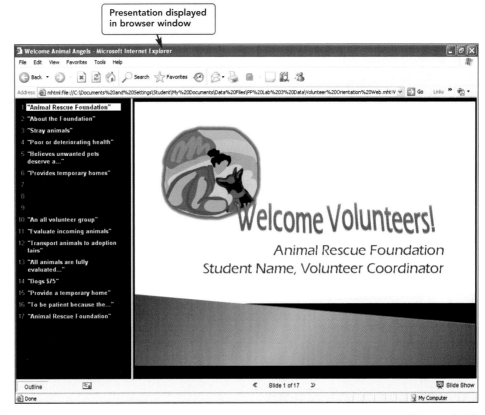

Figure 3.52

The file is converted to an HTML document and saved as a Single File Web Page file type. This file contains all the elements on the page such as images and hyperlinks and all supporting files such as those for bullets, graphics, and background. Any graphics that were added to the page that were not already JPEG or GIF files are converted to that format.

The browser on your system is loaded offline, and the page you created is displayed in the browser window. The left side of the window displays a table of contents relating to the slides of the presentation. Clicking on an item will display the associated slide on the right side. To navigate through the presentation, you can use the table of contents list, the hyperlinks on slide 2, or the navigation buttons located below the slide.

5 ● Click on slide 2 in the Navigation pane to display the contents list.

● Click on item 2 in slide 2 to see the first slide in the Animal Angels Overview.

● Try out the various methods of navigation in the presentation.

● When you are finished, click ⊠ Close to exit the browser.

● Close PowerPoint (do *not* save these changes to the Animal Angels orientation presentation if prompted).

Additional Information
Slide timings are not saved with the Web page.

Now that you can see how easy it is to convert a presentation to a Web page, you will use this feature often to make information available to more people.

You have two copies of the orientation presentation: the copy you will use to present the program personally to the new volunteers and the other that will be used on the foundation's Web site.

Focus on Careers

EXPLORE YOUR CAREER OPTIONS

Training Specialist

In today's job market, learning new skills is the only way to keep current with ever-changing technology. A training specialist in a corporate environment is responsible for teaching employees how to do their jobs, which usually involves computer training. Training specialists use PowerPoint to create materials for their lectures and can automate the presentations and package to a CD to send to employees at remote locations. The position of training specialist usually requires a college degree. Typical salaries range from $36,500 to $120,000 depending an experience and skill. To learn more about this career, visit the Web site for the Bureau of Labor Statistics of the U.S. Department of Labor.

Using Advanced Presentation Features

Chart (PP3.11)

A chart is a visual representation of numeric data that is used to help an audience grasp the impact of your data more quickly.

Collect and Paste (PP3.14)

The collect and paste feature is used to store multiple copied items in the Office Clipboard and then paste one or more of the items into another location or document.

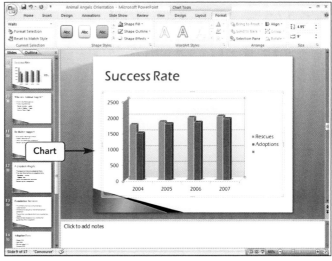

Organization Chart (PP3.19)

An organization chart is a map of a group, which usually includes people but can include any items that have a hierarchical relationship.

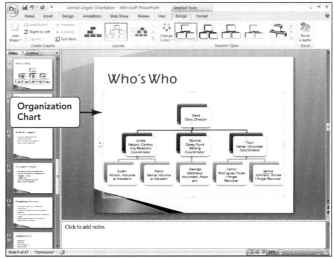

Animated GIF (PP3.29)

An animated GIF file is a type of graphic file that has motion.

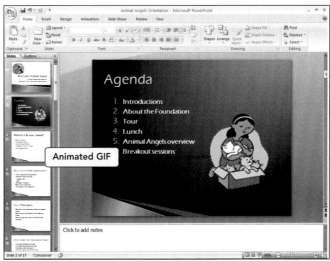

WordArt (PP3.31)

WordArt enhances slides by changing the shape of text, adding 3-D effects, and changing the alignment of text on a line.

Group (PP3.35)

A group is two or more objects that are treated as a single object.

Custom Show (PP3.39)

A custom show is a presentation that runs within a presentation.

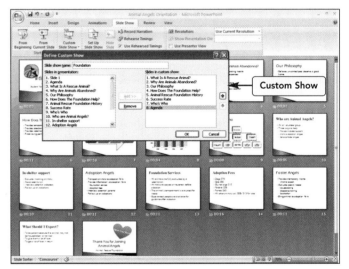

Hyperlinks (PP3.42)

Hyperlinks provide a quick way to jump to other slides, custom shows, presentations, objects, e-mail addresses, or Web pages.

Hypertext Markup Language (PP3.47)

All Web pages are written using a programming language called Hypertext Markup Language (HTML). HTML commands control how the information on a page such as font colors and size is displayed.

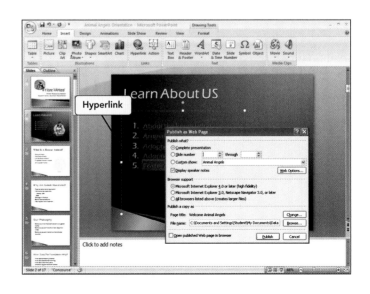

key terms

animated GIF PP3.29

assistant box PP3.19

attribute PP3.35

branch PP3.19

chart PP3.11

collect and paste PP3.14

co-worker box PP3.19

custom show PP3.39

graph PP3.11

group PP3.35

hierarchical relationship PP3.19

hierarchy PP3.19

hyperlink PP3.42

Hypertext Markup Language (HTML) PP3.47

manager box PP3.19

organization chart PP3.19

publish PP3.44

WordArt PP3.31

command summary

Command	Shortcut	Action
Office Button		
New/New from existing		Inserts an existing presentation as a new unnamed presentation
Home tab		
Clipboard group		
		Opens Clipboard task pane
Slides group		
/Slides from Outline		Inserts new slides using a Word outline
/Reuse Slides		Inserts new slides from another presentation
Paragraph group		
Numbering		Creates a numbered list
Insert tab		
Illustrations group		
Picture		Inserts a picture from a file
Chart		Inserts a chart
Text group		
WordArt		Inserts a WordArt graphic object
Links group		
Hyperlink	Ctrl + K	Creates a link to a Web page, a picture, an e-mail, or a program
Slide Show tab		
Start Slide Show group		
From Beginning	F5	Starts the slide show from the first slide of the presentation
Custom Slide Show		Creates or plays a custom slide show
Set Up group		
Set Up Slide Show		Specifies advanced options for a slide show

command summary

Command	Shortcut	Action
🕑 Rehearse Timings		Practices timing or pace of a presentation
Chart Tools Design tab		
Chart Styles group ⊟ More		Displays Chart Styles gallery, presenting alternative chart styles including chart color and appearance
Chart Tools Format tab		
Shape Styles group ⊟ More		Opens the Shape Style gallery to choose a visual style for the shape or line
Drawing Tools Format tab		
WordArt Styles group ⊟ More		Opens the WordArt Style gallery to choose a visual style for the WordArt text.
SmartArt Tools Design tab		
SmartArt graphic *Create Graphic group* Add Shape ▾		Adds a shape to SmartArt graphic
⇨ Demote		Demotes selected element of SmartArt graphic
Layouts group ⊟ More		Opens the Layouts gallery to choose the layout for the SmartArt shape
SmartArt Styles group Change Colors ▾		Changes the color variation of a SmartArt graphic
⊟ More		Opens the SmartArt Styles gallery to choose an overall visual style for the SmartArt graphic

matching

Match the item on the left with the correct description on the right.

1. attribute   _____   **a.** Hypertext Markup Language

2. collect and paste   _____   **b.** Feature such as line or fill color associated with an object

3. custom show   _____   **c.** Consists of all the boxes reporting to the same manager, excluding assistant boxes

4. group   _____   **d.** Used to show the hierarchy of an organization

5. hierarchy   _____   **e.** Used to enhance slides by changing the shape of text, adding 3-D effects, and changing the alignment of text on a line

6. hyperlink   _____   **f.** Save a copy of a presentation file for use on a Web site

7. HTML   _____   **g.** Store multiple copied items in the Office Clipboard and then paste one or more of the items into another location

8. organization chart   _____   **h.** Provides a quick way to jump to other slides, custom shows, presentations, objects, e-mail addresses, or Web pages

9. publish   _____   **i.** Shows ranking such as reporting structures within a department in a business

10. WordArt   _____   **j.** Presentation that runs within a presentation

multiple choice

Circle the letter of the correct answer to the following questions.

1. An animated _____ file is a type of graphic file that has motion.
   a. AVI
   b. MOV
   c. MPEG
   d. GIF

2. Features or _____ such as line or fill color associated with all objects in the group also can be changed at one time.
   a. characteristics
   b. themes
   c. groups
   d. attributes

3. If you needed to create a chart that shows the relationship of each value in the data series to the series as a whole, you would select the _____ chart.
   a. line
   b. pie
   c. column
   d. bar

4. A _____ is a presentation that runs within a presentation.
   a. build
   b. transition
   c. custom show
   d. related show

5. _____ is the capability of a program to store multiple copied items in the Office Clipboard and then paste one or more of the items into another location or document.
   a. Collecting and pasting
   b. Copying and pasting
   c. Collecting and storing
   d. Duplicating and inserting

6. A(n) _____ chart can include any items that have a hierarchical relationship.
   a. pie
   b. organization
   c. bar
   d. area

7. _____ commands control how the information on a page such as font colors and size is displayed.
   a. HTML
   b. Master
   c. Presentation
   d. Alignment

8. Hyperlinks provide a quick way to _____ other slides, custom shows, presentations, objects, e-mail addresses, or Web pages.
   a. copy from
   b. align
   c. jump to
   d. paste to

9. The _____ is the top-level box of a group.
   a. co-worker box
   b. manager box
   c. subordinate box
   d. branch

10. A _____ is two or more objects that are treated as a single object.
   a. property
   b. quality
   c. group
   d. characteristic

true/false

Circle the correct answer to the following questions.

1.	An animated GIF is a map of a group, which usually includes people, but can include any items that have a hierarchical relationship.	True	False
2.	Many branches are composed of several different elements that are grouped together.	True	False
3.	Co-workers represent administrative or managerial assistants to a manager.	True	False
4.	A custom show is a presentation that runs within a presentation.	True	False
5.	A bar chart shows the relative importance of a value over time by emphasizing the area under the curve created by each data series.	True	False
6.	In a pie chart, each slice of the pie represents a single value in a data series.	True	False
7.	The WordArt feature is used to enhance slides by changing the shape of text, adding 3-D effects, and changing the alignment of text on a line.	True	False
8.	To make changes throughout a presentation, you must make changes to all pairs of masters.	True	False
9.	The Y axis is also known as the category axis.	True	False
10.	A group is three or more objects that are treated as a single object.	True	False

Complete the following statements by filling in the blanks with the correct terms.

1. _____ boxes have the same manager.

2. A _____ is a visual representation of numeric data that is used to help an audience grasp the impact of the data.

3. A(n) _____ chart emphasizes the area under the curve.

4. A(n) _____ is a box and all the boxes that report to it.

5. A(n) _____ presentation can be opened and viewed from an e-mail.

6. The _____ feature is used to enhance slides by changing the shape of text, adding 3-D effects, and changing the alignment of text on a line.

7. The _____ contains a brief description identifying the patterns or colors assigned to the data series in a chart.

8. All organization charts consist of different levels that represent the _____.

9. When a(n) _____ GIF file is inserted into a PowerPoint slide, it does not display action until you run the presentation.

10. Line color and fill color are features or _____ associated with an object.

Hands-On Exercises

step-by-step

Future Job Statistics ★

1. The presentation **Interviewing Basics2** created in Lab 2 Step-by-Step Exercise 3 was very well received. You did some additional research on the Department of Labor's Web site and found the projected number of college-level jobs in 2008. You think these new data will fit nicely into the presentation as a chart. Several slides of your completed presentation will be similar to those shown here.

   a. Open the PowerPoint file Interviewing Basics2.

   b. On slide 7, change the bullets to numbers. Change the color of the numbers to red.

   c. Insert a new Title and Content slide after slide 1. Title the slide **College-Level Jobs**. Insert a Stacked Bar in 3-D chart using the following data:

	2007	2008
Professional	14,860	19,250
Executive	9,200	11,320
Marketing and Sales	2,640	3,400
Technician	1,250	1,690

   d. Insert, resize, and position the clip art from file pp03_Interview into slide 6.

   e. Replace the three bulleted items in slide 8 by inserting the SmartArt Basic Chevron, entering the bulleted text items into the appropriate location in the SmartArt graphic, and deleting the bulleted items. Set the SmartArt Style to White Outline.

   f. Save your completed presentation as Interviewing Basics3. Print the presentation as handouts with six slides per page.

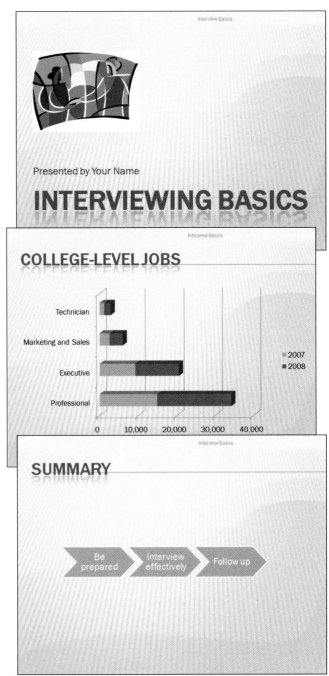

Nutrition and Exercise Presentation ★★

2. Annette Ramirez is the new Lifestyle Fitness Club nutritionist. She would like to use a presentation on exercise currently in use by the club to discuss the benefits of a nutrition plan. She has asked you to modify the current presentation to include some nutrition information. Several slides of your completed presentation will be similar to those shown here.

   a. Start PowerPoint and open the file pp03_Exercise.
   b. Change the Slide Design to one of your choice. Check all slides and adjust the text and graphics as needed throughout.
   c. On slide 1:
      Change the title to **Fitness and Nutrition**.
      Select and group the three images and move the group to the center of the slide.
      Reposition the title as needed.
   d. Change the title on slide 2 to **What Exercise and Nutrition Can Do for You**.
   e. Change the bulleted list on slides 3 and 4 to a numbered list. Change the color of the numbered list to blue.
   f. Change the layout of slide 6 to Title and Content. Resize the content placeholder box and reposition the image to fit the slide.

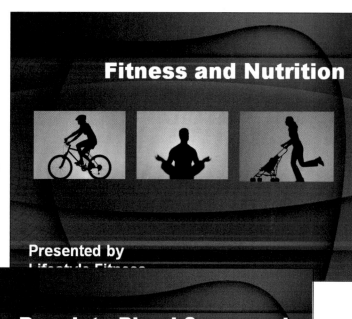

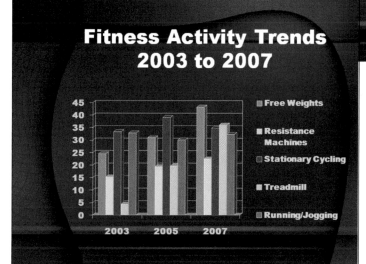

g. On slide 9:

Change the appearance of the table by applying a table style of your choice.

Circuit Training has been changed to Advanced Step. Adjust the entries accordingly and resize the table as needed.

h. Insert a new Title and Content slide after slide 10. On this slide:

Add the title **Fitness Activity Trends**.

Insert a 3-D Column chart using the data below:

	2003	2004	2005	2006	2007
Free Weights	24.5	31.7	43.2	53.8	59.3
Resistance Machines	15.3	19.4	22.5	28.4	35.6
Stationary Cycling	33.4	39.1	34.8	33.8	32.3
Treadmill	4.4	19.7	36.1	42.1	45.2
Running/Jogging	32.9	30.1	32.3	34.2	35.1

Change the color and appearance of the chart by selecting a chart style and shape style of your choice.

i. On the last slide, delete the text box and the subtitle placeholder. Create WordArt in a shape of your choice and add the text **Make it part of your life!** Set a WordArt style and shape style of your choice. Size and position the WordArt appropriately.

j. Insert the logo in file pp03_LFC Logo into slides 1 and 12. Position and resize the logo as needed.

k. Run the presentation and make any changes necessary. Save the presentation as Fitness and Nutrition. Print the outline. Print the presentation as handouts with six slides per page.

Employee Morale Presentation ★★

3. Chirag Shah works in the personnel department of a manufacturing company. Chirag has recently been studying the ways that employee morale can affect production levels and employee job satisfaction. Chirag has been asked to hold a meeting with department managers to suggest methods that can be used to improve employee morale. He has already started a PowerPoint presentation to accompany his talk but still needs to make several changes and enhancements to the presentation. Several slides of your completed presentation will be similar to those shown here.

a. Open the presentation pp03_Employee Motivation. Replace the Student Name placeholder with your name.

b. Change the design layout on slide 5 to Two Content. Insert the graphic picture from the file pp03_Motivation into the right pane of slide 5.

c. Reuse slides from pp03_Motivation Techniques. Insert the slides into the presentation as follows:
   "Vision Statement" after slide 2.
   "Available Options" after slide 4.
   "Recommendation" after slide 8.

d. Convert the five demoted bullets on slide 4 to a numbered list. Change the color of the numbers.

e. Demote the last three bullets on slide 5.

f. Create WordArt using a style of your choice with the text **You are doing a good job, Thanks!** to slide 7. Size and position the shape appropriately on the slide.

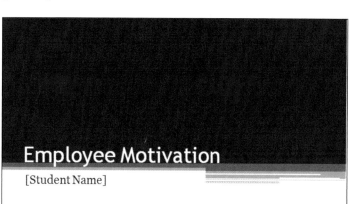

g. Change the theme of the presentation to one of your choice. Adjust the text and graphics on the slides as needed.

h. Add the following hyperlinks to slide 4:
    From Flexibility to slide 6.
    From Positive feedback to slide 7.
    From Expert input to slide 8.
    From Sharing the wealth to slide 10.
    From Creating a team to slide 11.

i. Run the presentation to review the slides and test the hyperlinks. Make any changes necessary.

j. Save the presentation as Employee Motivation2. Print the presentation as handouts, six slides per page.

k. Save the presentation as a single file Web page as Employee Motivation2 Web.

Traveling with Your Dog ★★

4. The Animal Rescue Foundation has asked you to help them create a presentation to inform the community about traveling with dogs. The presentation is partially completed, and you have been asked to enhance it so that it can be used at an upcoming meeting. You also will reuse some of the slides from another presentation you are working on. Several slides of your completed presentation will be similar to those shown here.

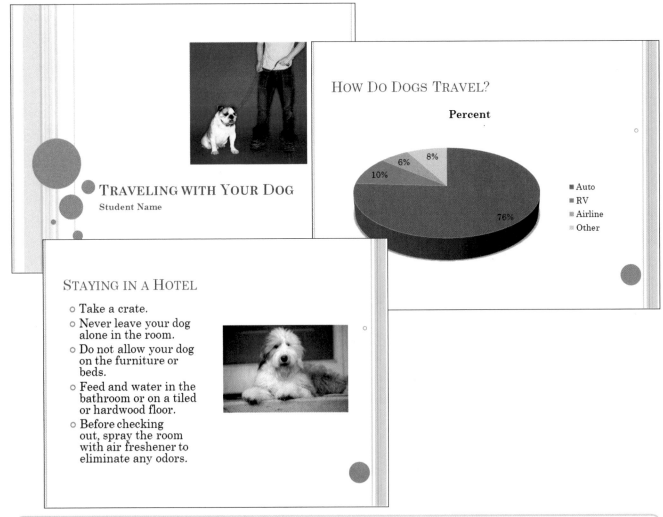

a. Open the pp03_Doggie Travel presentation. Enter your name on the first slide in place of Student Name.

b. Reuse slides from pp03_Car Trip Tips. Insert the slides into the presentation as follows:

"Introduction" after slide 1.

"Lesson 1: Before You Go" after slide 6.

"Lesson 1: Wrap-up" after slide 7.

c. Change the title of slide 7 to **Before You Go**. Change the title of slide 8 to **Car Trip: In Summary**.

d. Insert a Title and Content slide after slide 3. On this new slide:

Insert a Pie 3-D chart.

Copy the data from slide 3 into the chart.

Display the chart with Chart Style 11 and Chart Layout 6.

Resize and reposition the chart as needed.

Copy the slide title from slide 3.

e. Delete slide 3.

f. Slides 10, 11, and 12 are all titled "Trip Tips" and have similar content. Delete slides 10 and 12.

g. On slide 10, change from a bulleted list to a numbered list. Increase the size of the numbers to 110%.

h. Insert a copy of the first slide at the end of the presentation. On this new slide, insert WordArt displaying **Have a great time!**. Set a WordArt style and shape style of your choice. Size and position the WordArt appropriately.

i. Save the presentation as Doggie Travel Tips. Print the presentation as handouts with six slides per page.

Flu Prevention Presentation ★★★

5. You work in the student health services of a local university. You have been asked to create a presentation that will help students stay healthy during flu season. You have already started to compile the information you will present, but you still need to make several changes to the presentation. Your final presentation will include a chart on infection rates and a graphic that describes the life cycle of the virus. Several slides of your completed presentation will be similar to those shown here.

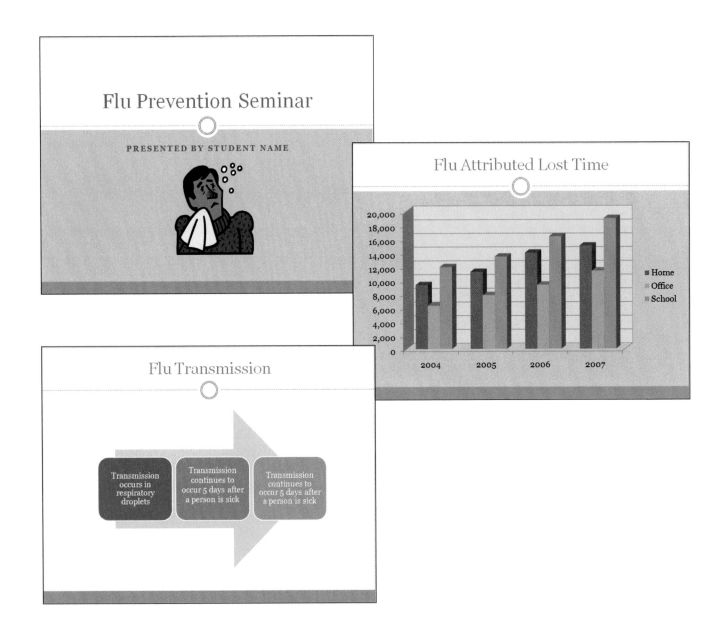

a. Open the file pp03_Flu Prevention.
b. Replace the placeholder with your name in the subtitle on slide 1.
c. Reuse slides from pp03_Flu Prevention Techniques. Insert all the slides, except slide 1, into the presentation after slide 3.
d. Insert the outline pp03_Flu Symptoms as slides before the last slide.
e. Create a numbered list with the bulleted text on slide 9.
f. Insert a new slide using the Title and Content slide layout after slide 5. In this new slide, enter the title **Flu Attributed Lost Time** and create a chart using the following table:

	Home	Office	School
2004	9,314	6,309	11,913
2005	11,211	7,833	13,418
2006	13,981	9,323	16,391
2007	15,002	11,354	19,010

g. Change the color and appearance of the chart by selecting a chart style and shape style of your choice.
h. Add WordArt on the last slide with the text **Flu Prevention Starts with You!** Set a WordArt style and shape style of your choice. Size and position the WordArt appropriately.
i. Using the text in the bulleted items in the "Flu Transmission" slide, create a Continuous Block Process SmartArt graphic for this slide. Remove the bulleted items. Change the colors and design of the SmartArt graphic by selecting a SmartArt style of your choice.
j. Insert and position the following graphics:
   File pp03_Flu into slide 1.
   File pp03_Objectives into slide 3.
   File pp03_Hands into slide 8.
   File pp03_Vaccine into slide 12.
k. Run the presentation and make any necessary changes.
l. Save the presentation as Flu Prevention Seminar. Print the presentation with six slides per page. Rehearse the timing of the presentation.

Digital Darkroom ★

1. You have recently bought a digital camera and are interested in utilizing all of its features and improving your skills as a photographer in general. Use the Web to research basic digital photography techniques. Then, using the skills you have learned so far, create a presentation that includes an organization chart composing shots and other graphic features to add interest to the presentation. Save your presentation as Digital Darkroom and print it with six slides per page.

Lifeguard Orientation ★

2. As part of your job as Head Lifeguard at the local pool, you have been asked to create a presentation for the new lifeguard training seminar. Use the data provided in pp03_Lifeguard to create a presentation on pool safety. Use the skills you have learned in the lab to include a numbered list of steps on water safety. Create an organization chart to explain the chain of command. Format the slides as you like. Include your name as a footer on the first slide. Save your presentation as Lifeguard Presentation. Print the slides.

Updating the Travel Presentation ★★

3. Your fellow Getaway Travel Club members are really excited about choosing the club's upcoming summer trip. Your presentation Travel Favorites created in Lab 2 On Your Own Exercise 5 was a hit and your locale was chosen to be among the finalists to present to the club officers. If chosen, your presentation will be placed on the club's Web site. You need to do more research on your locale to include the costs associated with the trip. You decide that the data would be easier to understand and more convincing if they were presented in chart form. Using your file Travel Favorites, modify the presentation. Create charts for the costs you researched. Update your information on the key tourist attractions with better graphics. Save your updated presentation as Travel Favorites2. Print the handouts nine per page.

Mountain Flyer Presentation ★★★

4. You work in a mountain bike shop called Mountain Flyer. The owner has asked you to put together a new employee orientation presentation. Your completed presentation should include a chart that tracks sales, a numbered list that includes sales tips, animated graphics, and an organization chart. Include your name as a subtitle on the first slide. Save your presentation as Mountain Flyer Orientation and e-mail your presentation to your instructor.

Preventing Network Infection Presentation ★★★

5. Your computer survey class requires you to do a research project on computer viruses and worms. Do some research on the Web to learn more about viruses and worms and how companies and schools are protecting their networks from infection. Create a PowerPoint presentation that includes the features, products, and methodologies you have learned about. Search the Web for appropriate clip art images that you can group or ungroup as necessary to enhance your slides. If appropriate data are available, create a chart that displays the increase in viruses reported over the last five years. Include your name and the current date as a footer on all the slides. Save your presentation as Preventing Network Infection. Print the outline and six-slides-per-page handouts.

Working Together 1: Copying, Embedding, and Linking between Applications

Case Study

Animal Rescue Foundation

Now that the presentation for the Animal Angels volunteer orientation program is well underway, you want the director to review the presentation. To do this, you send a copy of the presentation to the agency director and request that he add comments and make changes directly in the presentation and return it to you.

One of the comments you receive back from the director suggests that you include information about the steps to becoming a volunteer. These steps are detailed in a Word document. As you will see, you can easily share information between applications, saving you both time and effort by eliminating the need to recreate information that is available in another application. You will learn how to share information between applications while you create the new slides.

Then you will send a revised copy of the presentation back to the director. You will embed it in a letter that you plan to send volunteers thanking them for attending the presentation. The letter containing the embedded presentation is shown here.

Note: The Working Together section assumes that you already know how to use Office Word 2007 and that you have completed Lab 3 of PowerPoint.

Developer notes and reviewer comments can be inserted directly onto presentation slides.

A PowerPoint presentation can run within a Word document.

Text and graphics can be copied from one program's application and pasted into another program's application.

Reviewing a Presentation

You want several people in the Animal Rescue Foundation organization to review the presentation and provide you with feedback about how it can be improved. You will do this by sending a copy of the presentation by e-mail to each person. You will ask them to run the presentation, insert their comments directly in the presentation, and then return it to you.

Adding a Comment

Before you send the presentation for review, you want to add a comment to the reviewers. A **comment** is a remark that is displayed in a separate box and attached to a file. Comments about specific items such as text or an object on a slide can be associated directly with the item by selecting the text or object and then adding the comment. General comments are added to a slide simply by clicking on the slide. First you will add a general comment to the reviewers.

1 ● **Start Office PowerPoint 2007.**

● **Open the file** ppwt_Volunteer Orientation.

● **Display slide 1 in Normal view.**

● **Open the Review tab.**

● **Click** [New Comment] **in the Comments group**

Your screen should be similar to Figure 1

Having Trouble?
Do not be concerned if the name and date in your comment are not the same as in Figure 1.

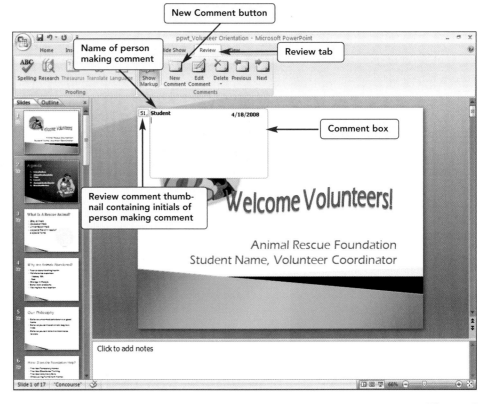

Figure 1

A large **comment box** is displayed in which you type the text of the comment. The name of the person inserting the comment appears on the first line followed by the system date. A **review comment thumbnail** containing the initials of the person who created the comment also appears in the upper-left corner of the slide. It is followed by a comment number, in this case 1, because this is the first comment that has been entered by this person.

2 ● Type the following comment text: Please add your comments directly in the presentation and return it to me. Thank you for your help.

Your screen should be similar to Figure 2

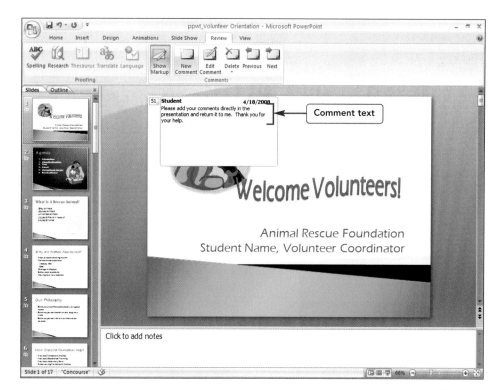

Figure 2

Additional Information
Double-click on the review comment thumbnail to reopen the comment box.

After entering comment text, clicking outside the comment closes the comment box. The review comment thumbnail is still displayed to show that a comment has been added to the slide. To see the comment text again, simply point to the comment thumbnail.

3 ● Click outside the comment.

● Point to the comment marker.

Your screen should be similar to Figure 3

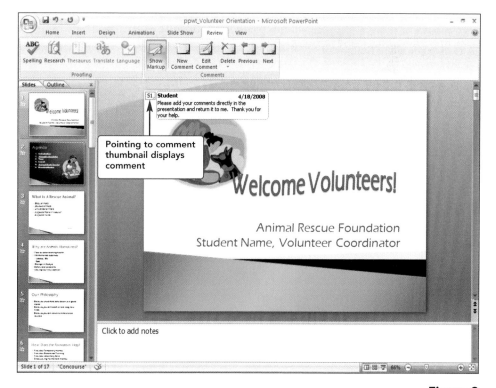

Figure 3

The comment is displayed in a balloon that is sized to fit the contents. The comment thumbnail of a general comment is always displayed in the upper-left corner of the slide.

You will add a second comment on slide 2 to advise the reviewers about the two custom shows.

4 ● **Display slide 2.**

● **Click**  .

● **Type Click on items 2 and 5 to start a custom slide show about these topics.**

● **Click outside the comment box.**

● **Save the presentation as** Volunteer Orientation **to your solution file location.**

Your screen should be similar to Figure 4

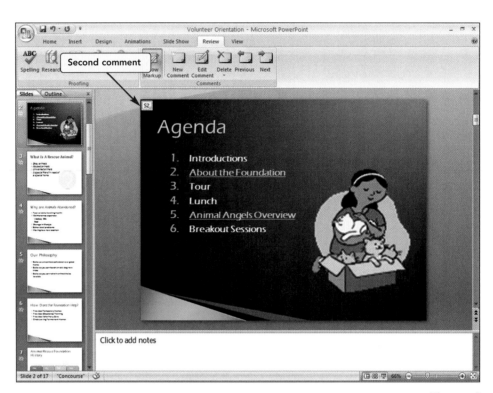

Figure 4

The review comment thumbnail indicates this is the second comment entered by the same person in the presentation. It is positioned close to the text object to show the comment is associated with the object.

Sending the Presentation for Review

Now you will send the presentation to the director, Steve Dow, and to several foundation coordinators, via e-mail for them to review.

1 • Click 🔲 Office Button, select Send, and choose E-mail.

• In the To field, enter your e-mail address.

Your screen should be similar to Figure 5

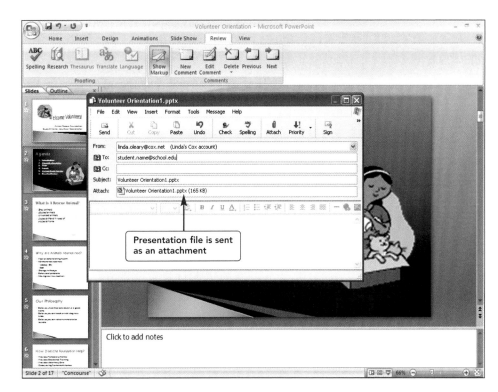

Presentation file is sent as an attachment

Figure 5

The presentation is automatically included as an attachment to the e-mail message. You will change the subject text and add a brief note.

2 • Replace the information in the subject line with Volunteer Orientation Presentation.

• In the body of the e-mail, type the following message: Please review the attached volunteer orientation presentation and return it to me with your comments by Friday. Thanks!.

• Press [Enter] twice and type your name.

Your screen should be similar to Figure 6

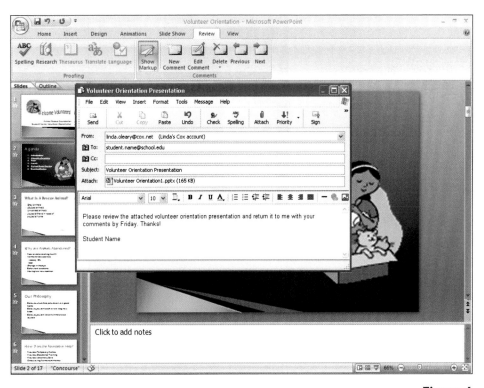

Figure 6

If you were connected to the Internet, you would send the message next. Instead, you will save the message as a text file.

3 ● **Choose File/Save As (from the e-mail window) and save the message as a Word Document or Text file type using the file name** Volunteer Orientation Email **to your solution file location.**

● **Close the e-mail window.**

● **Close the** Volunteer Orientation **presentation.**

Checking a Reviewed Presentation

The next day while checking your e-mail for new messages, you see that the agency director has returned the presentation with comments. You have downloaded the attachment and saved it on your computer system. Now you want to look at the suggested changes.

1 ● **Open the file** ppwt_Volunteer Orientation Review**.**

Your screen should be similar to Figure 7

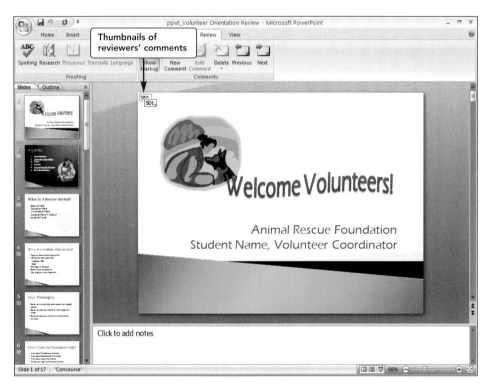

Figure 7

The comments from the reviewed presentation are included in the original presentation that was sent for review. The first slide has two review comment thumbnails in the upper-left corner with the reviewers' initials and the number of the comment. Each reviewer's comments appear in a different color and are numbered independently.

To quickly navigate through a presentation to locate and display comments, you can use the and buttons.

 **Click** Next **repeatedly until you reach the end of the presentation.**

● **Click** Continue **to continue at the beginning.**

Your screen should be similar to Figure 8.

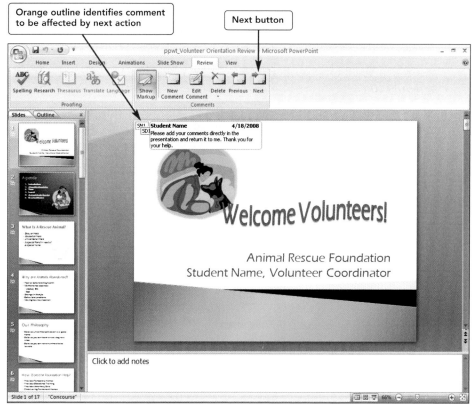

Figure 8

There are five comments in the presentation, including your original comments.

Deleting a Comment

Notice the selected comment placeholder is surrounded in an orange outline. This identifies the comment that will be affected by your next actions. Since this is just a general comment, you will delete it. You also will delete another comment you originally entered.

1 If necessary, select your comment on slide 1.

Click 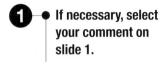.

Your screen should be similar to Figure 9

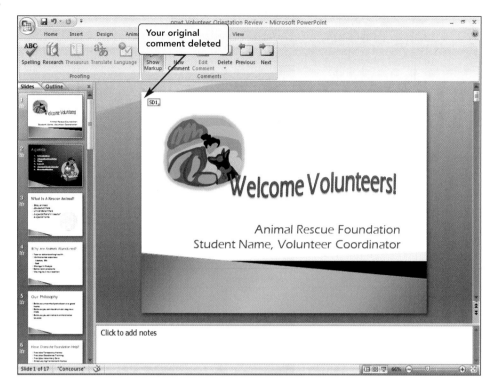

Figure 9

The first comment is now from Steve Dow. Before proceeding to read his other comments, you will delete your other comment on slide 2.

2 Move to slide 2.

Select and delete your comment on this slide.

Click [Next].

Your screen should be similar to Figure 10

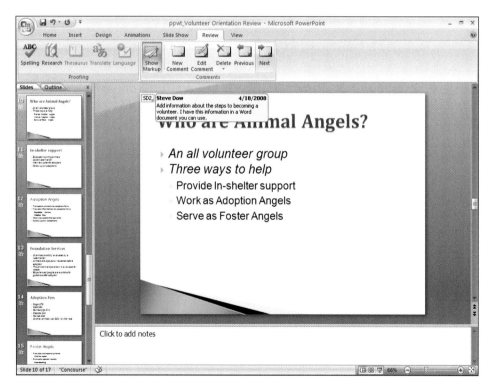

Figure 10

Editing a comment

On this slide, the director has suggested adding the steps to becoming a volunteer. You like this idea but will make the change later when you have the Word document. You will edit the comment to include a reminder to add the new content and add a second bulleted item to the current slide in preparation.

1 • **Click** [Edit Comment icon]

• **Press** Enter **2 times.**

• **Type** Create new slide showing suggested content after this slide.

• **Add a new bulleted item,** Steps to volunteering, **as the second item on slide 10.**

Your screen should be similar to Figure 11

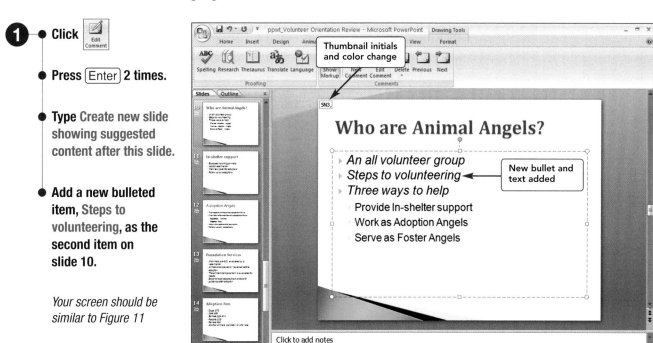

Figure 11

The review comment thumbnail initials and color have changed to the color and initials of the current reviewer.

Copying between Applications

You contacted the director about the steps-to-volunteering materials and he sent you the file via e-mail. The document contains a graphic that was created using SmartArt in Word. You will use this graphic as the basis for the new slide you need to create.

All the 2007 Microsoft Office System applications have a common user interface such as similar ribbons and features. In addition to these obvious features, they have been designed to work together, making it easy to share and exchange information between applications.

You will copy the graphic from the Word document into a new slide in the presentation. You also can use the same procedures to copy information from PowerPoint or other Office applications into Word.

Copying from Word to a PowerPoint Slide

First, you will insert a new slide after slide 10. Then you will copy the information from the Word document file into the PowerPoint presentation.

1 ● **Insert a new slide with the Title and Content layout after slide 10.**

● **Start Office Word 2007.**

● **Open the document** ppwt_Volunteer Steps.

Your screen should be similar to Figure 12

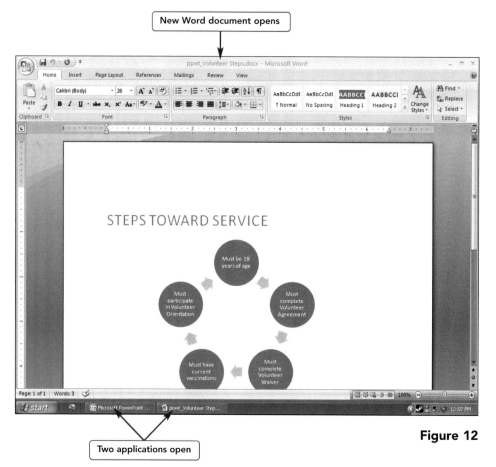

New Word document opens

Two applications open

Figure 12

There are now two open applications, Word and PowerPoint. PowerPoint is open in a window behind the Word application window. Both application buttons are displayed in the taskbar. There are also two open files, Volunteer Steps in Word and Volunteer Orientation Review in PowerPoint. To make it easier to work with two applications, you will tile the windows to view both on the screen at the same time.

2 ● **Right-click on a blank area of the taskbar to open the shortcut menu.**

● **Choose Tile Windows Vertically.**

● **Click on the Word document window to make it active.**

Your screen should be similar to Figure 13

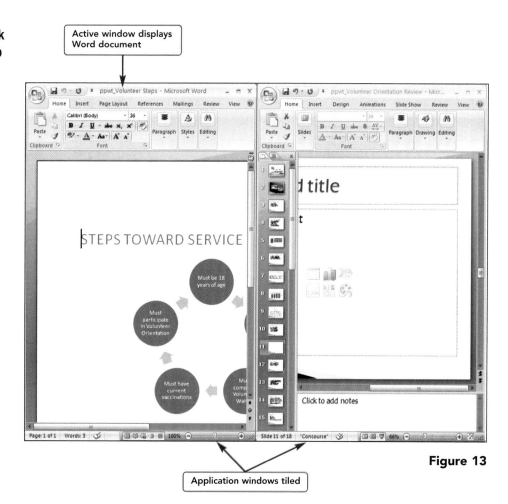

Active window displays Word document

Application windows tiled

Figure 13

First, you will copy the title from the Word document into the title placeholder of the slide. While using the Office Word and PowerPoint applications, you have learned how to use cut, copy, and paste to move or copy information within the same document. You also can perform these same operations between documents in the same application and between documents in different applications. The information is pasted in a format that the application can edit, if possible.

3 • Select the title "Steps Toward Service." in the Word document window.

• Drag the selection to the title placeholder on the slide in the PowerPoint presentation window.

Another Method
You also could use Copy and Paste to copy the title to the slide.

Your screen should be similar to Figure 14

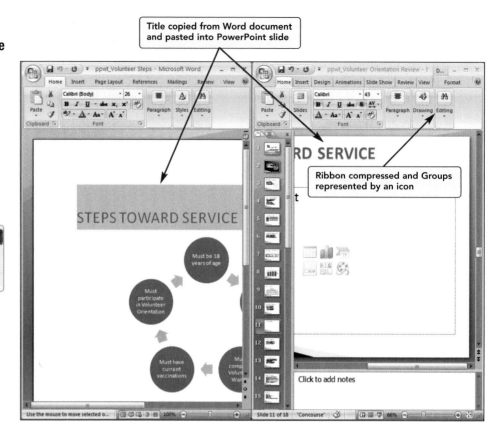

Title copied from Word document and pasted into PowerPoint slide

Ribbon compressed and Groups represented by an icon

Figure 14

The title has been copied into the slide and can be edited and manipulated within PowerPoint. The formats associated with the slide master are applied to the copied text. However, when the copied text included formatting such as color, it overrides the slide master settings, just as if you formatted a slide individually to make it unique. You will reset the slide to the master slide settings using the Reset command in the Slides group so that all the titles in the presentation are the same.

Because the window is tiled, the Ribbon is smaller and there is not enough space to display all the commands. Depending on how small the ribbon is, the groups on the open tab shrink horizontally and show a single icon that displays the group name. The most commonly used commands or features are left open. Clicking the icon opens the group and displays the commands.

Your screen should be similar to Figure 15

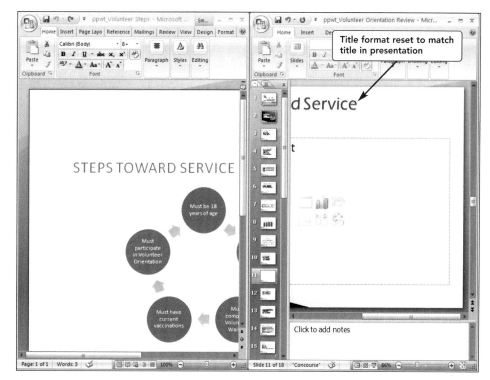

Figure 15

The title text is reset so the title matches the format of other slides in the presentation.

Next you want to copy the graphic of the volunteer steps to the slide.

⑤ ● Select the graphic in the Word document window.

● Click 📋 Copy.

● Select the content area in the PowerPoint window.

● Open the Paste drop-down menu and choose Paste Special.

Your screen should be similar to Figure 16

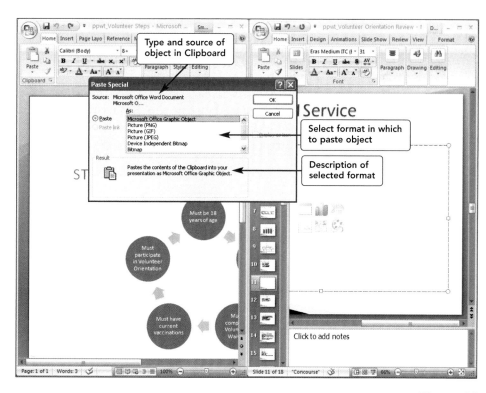

Figure 16

The Paste Special dialog box displays the type of object contained in the Clipboard and its location in the Source area. From the As list box, you select the type of format in which you want the object inserted into the destination file. The default option inserts the copy in HTML (Hypertext Markup Language) format. The Result area describes the effect of your selections. In this case, you want the object inserted as a Microsoft Office Graphic Object.

6 ● If necessary, select Microsoft Office Graphic Object from the As list box.

● Click [OK].

Your screen should be similar to Figure 17

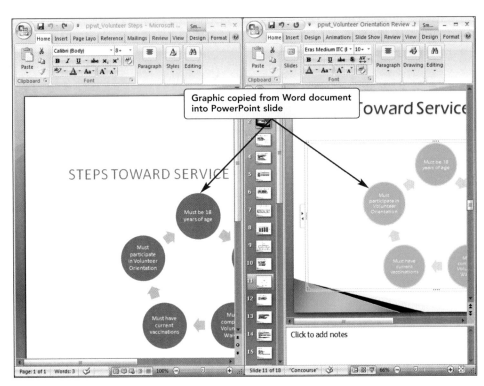

Figure 17

The graphic is copied into the slide as a graphic object that can be manipulated using the SmartArt graphics features of PowerPoint. The graphic's colors are reset to the slide theme colors. However, you want to further change the SmartArt graphic colors.

7 • Right-click on the taskbar and choose Undo Tile from the taskbar shortcut menu.

• If necessary, click on the graphic in the slide to select it.

• Click [Change Colors] in the SmartArt Tools Design tab.

• Choose [⠿] Colorful – Accent Colors.

• Save the presentation as Volunteer Orientation2.

Your screen should be similar to Figure 18

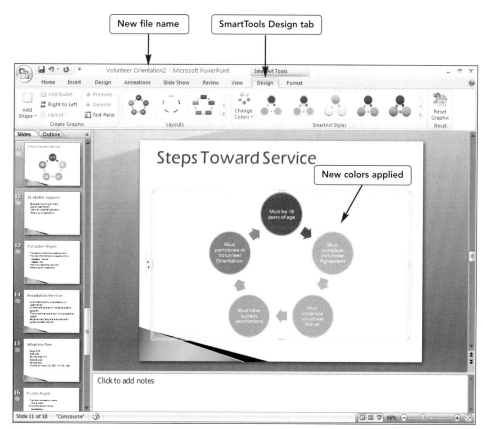

Figure 18

Embedding a Presentation

The agency director has asked you to send a letter to all the new volunteers thanking them for volunteering. You thought it would be a good idea to include a copy of the presentation with the letter for future reference. You have already written the letter and are now ready to insert the presentation.

To insert the presentation in the letter, you will open the letter in Word and embed the PowerPoint presentation file in the document. An **embedded object** is stored in the file that it is inserted into, called the **destination file,** and becomes part of that file. The embedded object can then be edited using features from the **source program,** the program in which it was created. Since the embedded object is part of the destination file, modifying it does not affect the original file, called the **source file.**

1 ● **Display the Word 2007 application window.**

Having Trouble?
Click on the application icon in the taskbar to switch application windows.

● **Close the** ppwt_Volunteer Steps **document file.**

● **Open the file** ppwt_Volunteer Letter.

Your screen should be similar to Figure 19

Additional Information
Always remove your personal information from the file's properties before distributing a presentation to avoid the distribution of this information to others. Use Office Button/Prepare/Inspect Document to check for hidden metadata or personal information.

Destination file is a Word document

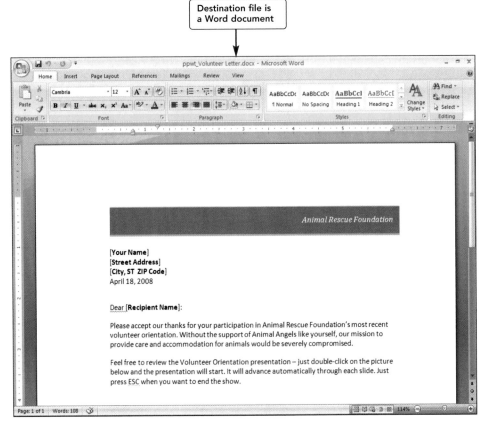

Figure 19

Now you want to embed the presentation. When you embed a PowerPoint presentation, the first slide of the presentation is displayed in the document. You want the embedded presentation to appear below the first paragraph of the letter.

2

- Move to the blank line below the second paragraph.

- Switch to the Volunteer Orientation2 presentation.

- Switch to Slide Sorter view and select all of the slides.

Having Trouble?

Use Ctrl + A to quickly select all the slides.

- Click 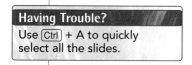 Copy.

- Switch to the open Word file.

- Open the Paste drop-down menu and choose Paste Special.

- Choose Microsoft Office PowerPoint Presentation Object.

- Click [OK].

Your screen should be similar to Figure 20

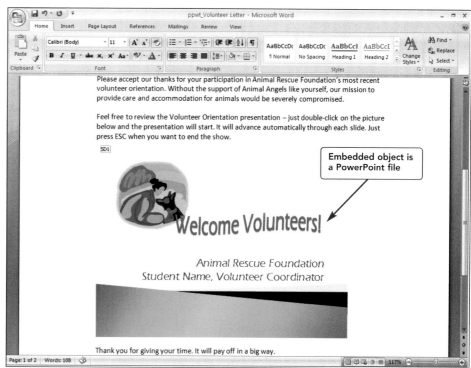

Figure 20

The opening slide of the presentation is displayed in the document. The entire presentation has been inserted as an embedded object in the letter. Before you send the letter, you want to run the slide show to make sure that it looks good and runs correctly. The directions to run the presentation from within the Word document file are included in the second paragraph of the letter.

3 • Select the PowerPoint object.

• Resize the object so that the entire letter fits on one page. Reposition the object as needed.

• Double-click on the embedded object to start the presentation.

Another Method
You also can choose Presentation Object/Show from the object's shortcut menu.

• View the entire presentation and press Esc to end the show.

Your screen should be similar to Figure 21

below and the presentation will start. It will advance automatically through each slide. Just press ESC when you want to end the show.

SD1

Welcome Volunteers!

Animal Rescue Foundation
Student Name, Volunteer Coordinator

Thank you for giving your time. It will pay off in a big way.

Sincerely,

[Your Name]
Volunteer Coordinator

Resized and repositioned object

Figure 21

Editing an Embedded Object

As you view the presentation, you think that the last slide would look better if it included an animation. You decide to add an animated graphic of a dog wagging its tail to the slide. You also realize you forget to remove all the reviewer comments.

Rather than editing the PowerPoint presentation file and then reinserting it into the letter, you will make the changes directly to the object that is embedded in the letter. The source program, the program used to create the embedded object, is used to edit data in an embedded object.

1 • Choose Presentation Object/Edit from the object's shortcut menu.

PowerPoint Ribbon open in Word document

Having Trouble?
Right-clicking on the object opens the shortcut menu.

Your screen should be similar to Figure 22

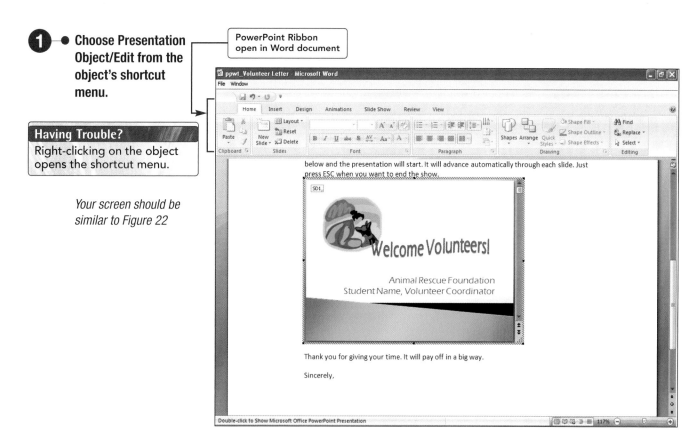

Figure 22

The presentation is open in an editing window, and the PowerPoint Ribbon replaces the Word application Ribbon. Now you can use the PowerPoint commands to edit the object.

- Use the editing window scroll bar to display the last slide.

- Delete the Heart graphic.

- Insert the graphic ppwt_Dog Wagging from your data file location.

- Position and size the graphic as in Figure 23.

- Use the rotate handle to change the angle of the graphic as in Figure 23.

Your screen should be similar to Figure 23

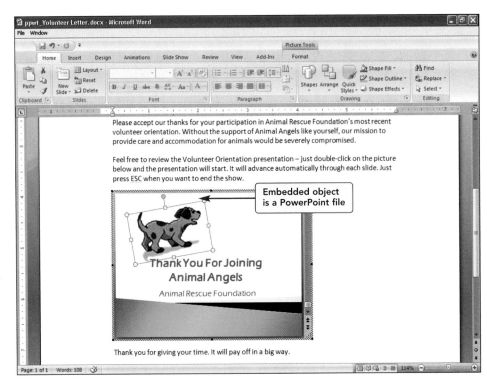

Figure 23

Finally, you will remove all the review comments and view the slide show again to see the animated graphic .

- Open the Review tab.

- Open the ⌧ Delete drop down menu and choose Delete all Markup in the Presentation.

- Click [Yes] in response to the confirm message box.

- Run the slide show from the current slide.

- Press [Esc] to end the show after seeing the animated graphic.

- Click outside the embedded presentation object to close the source program.

Your screen should be similar to Figure 24

Figure 24

The reviewer comments are no longer displayed in the embedded object.

4 ● Replace [Your Name] in the closing with your name.

● Save the letter as Volunteer Presentation Letter to your solution file location.

● Preview and print the letter.

● Exit Word.

Now that the letter is complete, you plan to send it as an attachment via e-mail to the director so he can see how embedding the presentation works. You also want him to see the changes you have made to the presentation.

Next you will update the presentation in PowerPoint with the same changes you made in the presentation in the Word document.

5 ● Display slide 18 in Normal view.

● Delete the Heart graphic.

● Insert the graphic ppwt_Dog Wagging from your data file location.

● Position and size the graphic as you did in the embedded presentation in the letter.

● Remove all reviewer comments.

● Save the revised presentation.

● Exit PowerPoint 2007.

The presentation still needs some additional work, but you feel you have made good progress. The comments from the director were very helpful and you think you have made good progress toward completing the presentation in time for the orientation meeting.

Copying, Embedding, and Linking between Applications

key terms

comment PPWT1.2	**embedded object** PPWT1.15	**source file** PPWT1.15
comment box PPWT1.2	**review comment**	**source program** PPWT1.15
destination file PPWT1.15	**thumbnail** PPWT1.2	

command summary

Command	Shortcut	Action
 **Office Button**		
Prepare/Inspect Document		Checks the presentation file for hidden metadata or personal information
Send/E-mail		Sends e-mail with a copy of a presentation as an attachment
Home tab		
Clipboard group		
[Paste] /Paste Special	Ctrl + Alt + V	Pastes contents of Clipboard into presentation
Drawing group		
[Arrange] /Rotate/Flip Horizontal		Rotates selected object
Review tab		
Comments group		
[New Comment]		Adds a comment about the selection
[Edit Comment]		Edits the selected comment
[Delete]		Deletes selected comment
[Previous]		Moves to previous comment
[Next]		Moves to next comment

Step-by-Step

Copying from a Word document ★

1. At the Lifestyle Fitness Club, you have been working on a presentation on Massage Therapy. Your manager has reviewed the presentation and has made a few suggestions including the request to include a slide presenting the new massage therapy costs. He has provided these costs to you in a Word document. You are to revise the presentation and return it to him for his approval.

   a. Start Word and open the file ppwt_Massage Prices.

   b. Start PowerPoint and open the file ppwt_Massage Therapy.

   c. In the presentation, replace the current footer with your name.

   d. Add a new slide after slide 9 using the Title Only layout.

   e. Copy the title from the Word document into the slide title placeholder and reset the formatting of the slide.

   f. Copy the table into the open area below the slide title and then exit Word.

   g. Resize, apply a new design of your choice, and reformat the table as needed.

   h. Add the comment **This is a new slide. Do you like the format and content?**.

   i. Run the presentation and make any changes necessary.

   j. Save the presentation as Massage Therapy.

   k. Print the new slide.

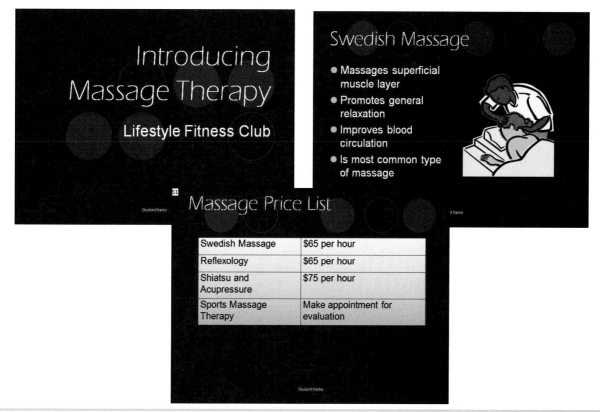

2. The Fitness and Nutrition presentation you created in Lab 3 On-Your-Own Exercise 3 has received positive feedback from several members of the Lifestyle Fitness club. You have decided to provide the presentation to affiliated clubs in other states. You will do this by embedding the presentation in a Word document.

a. Start Word and open the file ppwt_Fitness Presentation Letter.

b. Start PowerPoint and open the file ppwt_Fitness and Nutrition Presentation.

c. Embed the ppwt_Fitness and Nutrition Presentation in the letter and then exit PowerPoint.

d. Edit the embedded presentation to include at least two comments about how the recipients can customize the presentation for their own use.

e. Resize and reposition the embedded object in the Word document.

f. Run the presentation and make any necessary changes.

g. Add at least three comments to the presentation offering suggestions to improve the presentation.

h. Replace "Student Name" in the memo with your name.

i. Save the document as Fitness Presentation Letter.

j. Print the letter.

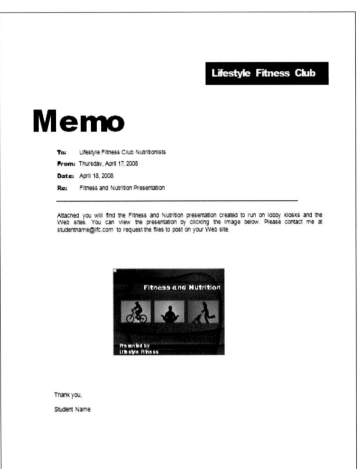

Sending an Embedded Presentation in a Word Document ★★

3. The Sports Company has a kiosk at the company store that continuously runs a Power Point presentation designed to promote the company. You have been asked to send this presentation to store managers of other stores in the state and to encourage them to use the presentation in their stores. You have decided to send the presentation in a Word document attached to an e-mail message.

a. Start Word and open the file ppwt_Sports Company Letter.

b. Embed the ppwt_Sports Company Kiosk Presentation in the letter and exit Power Point.

c. Edit the first slide by replacing "Student Name" with your name. Then add at least five comments recommending changes to the presentation.

d. Run the presentation and make any changes necessary.

e. Reduce the size of the embedded object and positon it appropriately.

f. Insert your name in the closing of the letter.

g. Save the document as Sports Company Letter.

h. E-mail the document as an attachment to your instructor for review.

i. Print the letter.

PowerPoint 2007 Command Summary

Command	Shortcut	Action
⊕ Office Button		**Opens File menu**
New		Opens a new presentation
New/New from existing		Inserts an existing presentation as a new unnamed presentation
Open	Ctrl + O	Opens an existing presentation
Save	Ctrl + S	Saves presentation
Save As	F12	Saves presentation using new file name and/or location
Print/Print	Ctrl + P	Prints presentation
Print/Print Preview		Displays preview of presentation
Print/Print Preview/Print Preview/Print What		Specifies what is to be printed
Print/Print Preview/ Print Preview/ Orientation		Sets either Portrait or Landscape layout
Prepare/Properties		Specifies presentation properties such as Title, Author, and keywords
Prepare/Inspect Document		Checks presentation file for hidden metadata or personal information
Send/E-mail		Sends e-mail with a copy of a presentation as an attachment
Close		Closes presentation
✕ Exit PowerPoint		Closes PowerPoint
Quick Access Toolbar		
💾 Save	Ctrl + S	Saves presentation
↩ Undo	Ctrl + Z	Reverses last action
Home tab		
Clipboard group		
Paste	Ctrl + V	Pastes item from Clipboard
Paste /Paste Special	Ctrl + Alt + V	Pastes contents of Clipboard into presentation

Command	Shortcut	Action
✄ Cut	Ctrl + X	Cuts selection to Clipboard
🗐 Copy	Ctrl + C	Copies selection to Clipboard
🗐		Opens Clipboard
Slides group		
New Slide ▾	Ctrl + M	Inserts new slide with selected layout
New Slide ▾ /Slides from Outline		Inserts new slides using a Word outline
New Slide ▾ /Reuse Slides		Inserts new slides from another presentation
🗐 Layout ▾		Changes layout of a slide
✄ Delete		Deletes slide
Font group		
Eras Medium ITC ▾ Font		Specifies font type
48 ▾ Size		Specifies font size
A˄ Increase Font Size	Ctrl + Shift + >	Increases font size of selected text
Paragraph group		
☰ ▾ Bullets/Bullets and Numbering/Bulleted		Formats bullets and numbers
☰ ▾ Numbering		Creates a numbered list
☰ Align Left	Ctrl + F	Aligns text to the left
☰ Align Center	Ctrl + E	Centers text
☰ Align Right	Ctrl + R	Aligns text to the right
☰ Justify	Ctrl + F	Aligns text to both the left and right margins
☰▾ Align Text		Sets vertical alignment of text
Drawing group		
Arrange ▾ /Rotate/Flip Horizontal		Rotates an object
Editing group		
🔍 Find	Ctrl + F	Finds specified text
ᵃᵇₐc Replace ▾	Ctrl + H	Replaces located text with replacement text
⬚ Select ▾ /Select All	Ctrl + A	Selects everything in the placeholder box

Insert tab

Illustrations group

Picture		Inserts a picture from a file
Clip Art		Inserts clip art

Command	Shortcut	Action
Shapes		Inserts a shape
SmartArt		Inserts SmartArt shape
Chart		Inserts a chart
Text group		
Text Box		Inserts text box or adds text to selected shape
Header & Footer		Inserts a header and/or footer
WordArt		Inserts WordArt
Links group		
Hyperlink	Ctrl + K	Creates a link to a Web page, a picture, an e-mail, or a program

Design tab

Command	Shortcut	Action
Themes group		
More		Opens gallery of document themes
Colors		Changes the color for the current theme

Animations tab

Command	Shortcut	Action
Animations group		
Custom Animation		Creates custom animation for individual objects
Transition to This Slide group		
Apply To All		Applies transitions in current slide to all slides

Slide Show tab

Command	Shortcut	Action
Start Slide Show group		
From Beginning	F5	Displays presentation starting with the first slide
From Current Slide	Shift + F5	Displays presentation starting with the current slide
Custom Slide Show		Creates or plays a custom slide show
Set Up group		
Set Up Slide Show		Specifies advanced options for a slide show
Hide Slide		Hides current slide so that it does not appear during the presentation
Rehearse Timings		Practices timing or pace of a presentation

Command	Shortcut	Action
Review tab		
Proofing group		
ABC ✓ Spelling	F7	Spell-checks presentation
Comments group		
New Comment		Adds a comment about the selection
Edit Comment		Edits the selected comment
Delete		Deletes the selected comment
Previous		Moves to previous comment
Next		Moves to next comment
View tab		
Presentation Views group		
Normal		Switches to Normal view
Slide Sorter		Switches to Slide Sorter view
Notes Page		Displays current slide in Notes view to edit the speaker notes
Slide Show		Runs slide show
Slide Master		Opens Slide Master view to change the design and layout of the master slides
Chart Tools Format tab		
Shape Styles group		
⌄ More		Opens the Shape Styles gallery to choose a visual style for the shape or line
Chart Tools Design tab		
Chart Styles group		
⌄ More		Applies a chart style including chart color and appearance

Command	Shortcut	Action
Drawing Tools Format tab		
Shape Styles group		
⬇ More		Opens the Shape Styles gallery to select a visual style to apply to a shape
Shape Effects ▾		Applies a visual effect to a shape
WordArt Styles group		
⬇ More		Opens the WordArt Styles gallery to choose a visual style for the WordArt text
Arrange group		
Rotate ▾		Rotates or flips a selected object
Picture Tools Format tab		
Adjust group		
Recolor ▾		Recolors picture
Picture Styles group		
⬇ More		Opens Picture Styles gallery to select an overall visual style for picture
Picture Shape ▾		Changes shape of drawing
Picture Border ▾		Applies a border style to picture
Picture Effects ▾		Applies a visual effect to picture
Size group		
Crop		Crops selected picture to remove unwanted parts
SmartArt Tools Design tab		
Create Graphic group		
Add Shape ▾		Adds a shape to SmartArt graphic
➡ Demote		Demotes selected element of SmartArt graphic
Layouts group		
⬇ More		Opens the Layouts gallery to choose the layout for the SmartArt shape
SmartArt Styles group		
Change Colors ▾		Changes the color variation of a SmartArt graphic
⬇ More		Opens the SmartArt Styles gallery to choose an overall visual style for the SmartArt graphic

Command	Shortcut	Action
Table Tools Design tab		
Table Styles group		
⬚ More		Opens the Table Styles gallery to choose a visual style for a table
🪣▾ Shading		Colors background behind selected text or paragraph
⊞▾ Border		Applies a border style
▾ Effects		Applies a visual effect to the table such as shadows and reflections
Print Preview tab		
Page *Setup group*		
Slides ▾ Print What		Specifies what is to be printed
Orientation ▾		Sets either Portrait or Landscape layout

Glossary of Key Terms

alignment   Controls the position of text entries within a space.

animated GIF   A type of graphic that has motion.

animation   Effect that adds action to text and graphics so they move around on the screen.

assistant box   An element in an organization chart that represents administrative or managerial assistants to a manager.

attribute   A feature such as line or fill color associated with all objects in a group.

AutoCorrect   Feature that makes certain types of corrections automatically as you enter text.

AutoRecover   Feature that automatically saves work to a temporary recovery file.

branch   A box and all the boxes that report to it in an organization chart.

cell   The intersection of a row and column in a table.

character formatting   Formatting features that affect the selected characters only.

chart   A visual representation of numeric data.

clip art   Professionally drawn images.

collect and paste   Used to store multiple copied items in the Office Clipboard and then paste one or more of the items into another location or document.

comment   Remark that is displayed in a separate box and attached to a presentation file.

comment box   Rectangular box that displays comments.

co-worker box   Boxes that have the same manager in an organization chart.

current slide   The slide that will be affected by any changes you make.

custom dictionary   A dictionary you can create to hold words you commonly use but that are not included in the dictionary that is supplied with the program.

custom show   A presentation that runs within a presentation.

default setting   The initial program setting.

demote   To move a topic down one level in the outline hierarchy.

destination file   The document receiving the linked or embedded object.

document theme   Predefined set of formatting choices that can be applied to an entire document in one simple step.

drawing object   An object consisting of shapes such as lines and boxes that can be created using the Drawing toolbar.

embedded object   An object that is inserted into another application and becomes part of the document. It can be edited from within the document using the source program.

Find and Replace   A feature that allows you to find text in a presentation and replace it with other text.

font   A set of characters with a specific design. Also called a typeface.

font size   The height and width of a character, commonly measured in points.

formatting   Enhancing the appearance of a slide to make it more readable or attractive.

graph   A visual representation of numeric data.

graphic A nontext element, such as a chart, drawing, picture, or scanned photograph, in a slide.

group Two or more objects that are treated as a single object.

hierarchical relationship Relative positions of elements in a group.

hierarchy Shows ranking, such as reporting structures within a department in a business.

hyperlink A connection to locations in the current document, other documents, or Web pages. Clicking a hyperlink jumps to the specified location.

Hypertext Markup Language (HTML) Language used to create Web pages.

keyword A word or phrase that is descriptive of the type of graphic you want to locate.

landscape Orientation of the printed output across the length of the paper.

layout A predefined slide organization that is used to control the placement of elements on a slide.

Live Preview Feature that automatically displays how a selected item affects a slide.

main dictionary Dictionary that comes with the Office 2007 programs.

manager box The top-level box in an organization chart.

master A special slide on which the formatting of all slides in a presentation is defined.

notes page Printed output that shows a miniature of the slide and provides an area for speaker notes.

Notes pane Working area in Normal view for entering notes to a current slide.

object An item on a slide that can be selected and modified.

object animation Used to display movement of a bullet point, text, paragraph, or graphic independently of the other text or objects on the slide.

organization chart Graphic representation of the structure of an organization.

Outline tab Working area in Normal view that displays the text content of each slide in outline format.

paragraph formatting Formatting features that affect entire paragraphs.

picture An image such as a graphic illustration or a scanned photograph.

picture style A combination of border, shadow, and shape effects applied to all pictures in a presentation.

placeholder Box that is designed to contain objects such as the slide title, bulleted text, charts, tables, and pictures.

placeholder text Sample text suggesting content for a slide.

point A unit of type measurement. One point equals about 1/72 inch.

portrait Orientation of the printed output across the width of the paper.

promote To move a topic up one level in the outline hierarchy.

publish Save a copy of a presentaion file in a format suitable to show the presentation on a Web site.

review comment thumbnail Graphic containing the initials of a person who created a comment.

rotate handle The 🔧 on the selection rectangle of a selected object that allows you to rotate the object in any direction.

sans serif font A font that does not have a flair at the base of each letter, such as Arial or Helvetica.

selection rectangle Hashed border that surrounds a selected placeholder.

serif font A font that has a flair at the base of each letter, such as Roman or Times New Roman.

sizing handles Small boxes surrounding selected objects that are used to change the size of the object.

slide An individual page of the presentation.

Slide panel Working area in Normal view that displays the selected slide.

slide show Used to practice or to present the presentation. It displays each slide in final form.

Slides tab Working area in Normal view that displays each slide as a thumbnail.

SmartArt Graphic that presents a visual representaion of textual information.

source file The file from which a linked or embedded object is obtained.

source program   The program used to create the linked or embedded object.

spelling checker   Locates all misspelled words, duplicate words, and capitalization irregularities as you create and edit a presentation, and proposes possible corrections.

stacking order   The order in which objects are inserted into layers in the slide.

table   An arrangement of horizontal rows and vertical columns.

table reference   The letter and number that identify a table cell.

table style   Combinations of shading, colors, borders, and visual effects such as shadows and reflection that can be applied to a table.

template   A file that includes predefined settings that can be used as a pattern to create many common types of presentations.

text box   A container for text or graphics.

thumbnail   A miniature representation of a slide.

transition   An effect that controls how a slide moves off the screen and the next one appears.

typeface   A set of characters with a specific design. Also called a font.

view   A way of looking at the presentation.

WordArt   Feature to enhance slides by changing the shape of text, adding 3-D effects, and changing the alignment of the text on a line.

workspace   The large area containing the slide where your presentations are displayed as you create and edit them.

Reference 1

$$\boxed{\text{Data File List}}$$

Supplied/Used	Created/Saved As
Lab 1	
Within Lab	
pp01_Product (template)	
	Volunteer
pp01_Volunteer1	Volunteer1
pp01_Puppy (graphic)	
pp01_Dog (graphic)	
Step-by-Step	
1. pp01_Triple Crown	Triple Crown Presentation
pp01_Jump (graphic)	
pp01_Stream (graphic)	
2. pp01_Resume	Resume1
pp01_Success (graphic)	
3. pp01_Distracted Driving	Distracted_Driving
pp01_Cell Phone	
pp01_Car Logo (graphic)	
4. pp01_Claremont Hotel	
pp01_Claremont Hotel Logo (graphic)	Claremont Hotel Orientation
5. pp01_Interviewing	Interviewing Basics
pp01_Interview (graphic)	
On Your Own	
1. pp01_Internet Policy	Internet Policy
2. pp01_Memo	Phone Etiquette
3.	Car Maintenance
4.	School Rules
5. pp01_Animal Careers	Careers with Animals

Supplied/Used	Created/Saved As
Lab 2	
Within Lab	
pp02_Volunteer2	Volunteer2
pp02_Question Mark (graphic)	
Step-by-Step	
1. pp02_Fad Diets	Fad Diets
pp02_Grape Fruit (graphic)	
2. pp02_Sleepy Time Staff Training	Sleepy Time Training
3. Interviewing Basics (from Lab 1)	Interviewing Basics2
4. Triple Crown Presentation (from Lab 1)	Triple Crown Presentation2
5. pp02_Coffee Talk	Coffee Talk
pp02_Coffee Pot (graphic)	
On Your Own	
1.	Custom Closets
2. Car Maintenance (from Lab 1)	Car Maintenance2
3. Careers with Animals (from Lab 1)	Careers with Animals2
4. Internet Policy (from Lab 1)	Internet Policy2
5.	Travel Favorites
Lab 3	
Within Lab	
pp03_Volunteer3	Animal Angels Orientation
pp03_Animal Rescue Fund Raising	Volunteer Orientation Web
pp03_Orientation Outline (Word)	
pp03_Adoptions (graphic)	
Step-by-Step	
1. Interviewing Basics2 (from Lab 2)	Interviewing Basics3
pp03_Interview (graphic)	
2. pp03_Exercise	Fitness and Nutrition
pp03_LFC Logo (graphic)	
3. pp03_Employee Motivation	Employee Motivation2
	Employee Motivation2 Web
pp03_Motivation Techniques	
pp03_Motivation (graphic)	

Supplied/Used	Created/Saved As
4. pp03_Doggie Travel	Doggie Travel Tips
pp03_Car Trip Tips	
5. pp03_Flu Prevention	Flu Prevention Seminar
pp03_Flu Prevention Techniques	
pp03_Flu Symptoms	
pp03_Flu (graphic)	
pp03_Objectives (graphic)	
pp03_Hands (graphic)	
pp03_Vaccine (graphic)	

On Your Own

1.	Digital Darkroom
2. pp03_Lifeguard	Lifeguard Presentation
3. Travel Favorites (from Lab 2)	Travel Favorites2
4.	Mountain Flyer Orientation
5.	Preventing Network Infection

Working Together

Within Lab

ppwt_Volunteer Orientation	Volunteer Orientation
	Volunteer Orientation Email (Word)
ppwt_Volunteer Orientation Review	Volunteer Orientation2
ppwt_Volunteer Steps (Word)	
ppwt_Volunteer Letter (Word)	Volunteer Presentation Letter (Word)
ppwt_Dog Wagging (graphic)	

Step-by-Step

1. ppwt_MassagePrices (Word)	
ppwt_Massage Therapy	Massage Therapy
2. ppwt_Fitness Presentation Letter (Word)	Fitness Presentation Letter (Word)
ppwt_Fitness and Nutrition Presentation	
3. ppwt_Sports Company Letter (Word)	Sports Company Letter (Word)
ppwt_Sports Company Kiosk Presentation	

Index